4th Workshop on Computational Typology and Multilingual NLP (SIGTYP 2022)

Online
14 July 2022

ISBN: 978-1-7138-5639-9

Printed from e-media with permission by:

Curran Associates, Inc.
57 Morehouse Lane
Red Hook, NY 12571

CURRAN ASSOCIATES INC. proceedings.com

Some format issues inherent in the e-media version may also appear in this print version.

Association for Computational Linguistics
209 N. Eighth Street
Stroudsburg, Pennsylvania 18360

Phone: 1-570-476-8006
Fax: 1-570-476-0860

acl@aclweb.org

Additional copies of this publication are available from:

Curran Associates, Inc.
57 Morehouse Lane
Red Hook, NY 12571 USA
Phone: 845-758-0400
Fax: 845-758-2633
Email: curran@proceedings.com
Web: www.proceedings.com

SIGTYP 2022

The 4th Workshop on Computational Typology and Multilingual NLP

Proceedings of the Workshop

July 14, 2022

The SIGTYP organizers gratefully acknowledge the support from the following sponsors.

Supported By

Google

Order copies of this and other ACL proceedings from:

Association for Computational Linguistics (ACL)
209 N. Eighth Street
Stroudsburg, PA 18360
USA
Tel: +1-570-476-8006
Fax: +1-570-476-0860
acl@aclweb.org

Introduction

SIGTYP 2022 is the fourth edition of the workshop for typology-related research and its integration into multilingual Natural Language Processing (NLP). The workshop is co-located with the 2022 Annual Conference of the North American Chapter of the Association for Computational Linguistics (NAACL 2022), which takes place in Seattle, Washington. This year our workshop features a shared task on prediction of cognate reflexes.

The final program of SIGTYP contains 3 keynote talks, 5 shared task papers, 6 archival papers, and 4 extended abstracts. This workshop would not have been possible without the contribution of its program committee, to whom we would like to express our gratitude. We should also thank Kristen Howell, Isabel Papadimitriou, and Graham Neubig for kindly accepting our invitation as invited speakers. The workshop is generously sponsored by Google. Please find more details on the SIGTYP 2022 website: https://sigtyp.github.io/ws2022-sigtyp.html

Organizing Committee

Workshop Organizers

Ekaterina Vylomova, The University of Melbourne
Hila Gonen, University of Washington
Jonas Pfeiffer, New York University
Edoardo Ponti, The University of Edinburgh
Alexey Sorokin, Moscow State University
Andrey Shcherbakov, The University of Melbourne
Sabrina Mielke, Johns Hopkins University
Gabriella Lapesa, University of Stuttgart
Harald Hammarström, Uppsala University
Pranav A, Dayta AI
Ryan Cotterell, ETH Zürich
Ritesh Kumar, Dr. Bhimrao Ambedkar University

Program Committee

Program Chairs

Johannes Bjerva, Aalborg University
Emily Ahn, University of Washington
Miriam Butt, University of Konstanz
John Mansfield, The University of Melbourne
Daan van Esch, Google AI
Elisabetta Ježek, University of Pavia
Paola Merlo, University of Geneva
Joakim Nivre, Uppsala University
Robert Östling, Stockholm University
Ivan Vulić, The University of Cambridge
Richard Sproat, Google Japan
Željko Agić, Corti
Agnieszka Falenska, University of Stuttgart
Edoardo Ponti, The University of Edinburgh
Alexey Sorokin, Moscow State University
Andrey Shcherbakov, The University of Melbourne
Tanja Samardžić, University of Zurich
Kemal Kurniawan, The University of Melbourne
Aryaman Arora, Georgetown University
Samopriya Basu, The University of North Carolina at Chapel Hill
Badr M. Abdullah, Saarland University
Guglielmo Inglese, KU Leuven
Olga Zamaraeva, University of Washington
Nianwen Xue, Brandeis University
Borja Herce, University of Zurich
Chinmay Choudhary, National University of Ireland, Galway
Bradley Hauer, The University of Alberta
Michael Hahn, Stanford University

Keynote Talk: Grammar Inference for Local Languages. Leveraging Typology for Automatic Grammar Generation

Kristen Howell
University of Washington

Abstract: In this talk I will describe the benefit of implemented grammars as well as the challenges involved in creating them. I present an inference system that can be used to automatically generate such grammars on the basis of interlinear glossed text (IGT) corpra. The inference system, called BASIL – Building Analyses from Syntactic Inference in Local Languages, leverages typologically informed heuristics to infer syntactic and morphological information from linguistic corpora to select analyses that model the language. We will engage with the question of whether and to what extent typological features are apparent in IGT data and how effectively grammars generated with these features can model human language.

Bio: Kristen Howell is a data scientist at LivePerson Inc. in Seattle, Washington. Her research interests range from grammar engineering and grammar inference to conversational NLP. Throughout this research, the common thread is multilingual NLP across typologically diverse languages. Kristen received her PhD from the University of Washington in 2020, where she engaged with typological literature to develop technology for automatically generating grammars for local languages. Recent work at LivePerson has focused on multilingual NLP, leveraging deep learning techniques for conversational AI.

Keynote Talk: Graham Neubig's Invited Talk

Graham Neubig
Carnegie Mellon University

Abstract: Will be announced later.

Bio: Graham is an associate professor at the Language Technologies Institute of Carnegie Mellon University. His research focuses on multilingual natural language processing, natural language interfaces to computers, and machine learning methods for NLP, with the final goal of every person in the world being able to communicate with each-other, and with computers in their own language. He also contributes to making NLP research more accessible through open publishing of research papers, advanced NLP course materials and video lectures, and open-source software, all of which are available on his web site.

Keynote Talk: Learning from our Differences. How Typologically Distinct Modalities of Data Help Demystify Language Models

Isabel Papadimitriou
Stanford University

Abstract: Looking beyond a single language, or to non-linguistic forms of data, can yield new insights into linguistic representation and use in language models. This talk will explore this theme in two threads: Firstly, what can we learn from passing non-linguistic data through language models? From natural modalities like music to controlled synthetic parentheses languages, we can use datasets with different underlying structures to explore knowledge in language model transfer learning. Knowing the structures in this data lets us understand if and how different features are acquired and generalized in language model training. Secondly, we will look at how typologically-aware analysis can help us understand joint multilingual representation in language models, with experiments that focus on agenthood and case in different languages in multilingual models. The typological diversity of agenthood gives us a handle into understanding how representations can be shared and also separated between languages. Examining language models at the points where diverse data differs – and systematically knowing the ways in which data differs – offers a useful window into how linguistic knowledge is represented in language models.

Bio: Isabel is a PhD student at Stanford in the Natural Language Processing group, advised by Dan Jurafsky. Her main research focuses on exploring the linguistic basis of computational language methods. She likes to focus on how language is both a discrete symbolic system and a system of continuous gradations, and exploring the limits of how large neural models can emcompass this combination. She is very interested in looking at the behavior of large language models in multilingual settings, and analyizing the ways in which languages and dialects co-occur and interfere in single models.

Table of Contents

Multilingualism Encourages Recursion: a Transfer Study with mBERT
Andrea Gregor De Varda and Roberto Zamparelli 1

Word-order Typology in Multilingual BERT: A Case Study in Subordinate-Clause Detection
Dmitry Nikolaev and Sebastian Pado 11

Typological Word Order Correlations with Logistic Brownian Motion
Kai Hartung, Gerhard Jäger, Sören Gröttrup and Munir Georges 22

Cross-linguistic Comparison of Linguistic Feature Encoding in BERT Models for Typologically Different Languages
Yulia Otmakhova, Karin Verspoor and Jey Han Lau 27

Tweaking UD Annotations to Investigate the Placement of Determiners, Quantifiers and Numerals in the Noun Phrase
Luigi Talamo 36

A Database for Modal Semantic Typology
Qingxia Guo, Nathaniel Imel and Shane Steinert-Threlkeld 42

The SIGTYP 2022 Shared Task on the Prediction of Cognate Reflexes
Johann-Mattis List, Ekaterina Vylomova, Robert Forkel, Nathan Hill and Ryan Cotterell 52

Bayesian Phylogenetic Cognate Prediction
Gerhard Jäger 63

Mockingbird at the SIGTYP 2022 Shared Task: Two Types of Models forthe Prediction of Cognate Reflexes
Christo Kirov, Richard Sproat and Alexander Gutkin 70

A Transformer Architecture for the Prediction of Cognate Reflexes
Giuseppe Celano 80

Approaching Reflex Predictions as a Classification Problem Using Extended Phonological Alignments
Tiago Tresoldi 86

Investigating Information-Theoretic Properties of the Typology of Spatial Demonstratives
Sihan Chen, Richard Futrell and Kyle Mahowald 94

How Universal is Metonymy? Results from a Large-Scale Multilingual Analysis
Temuulen Khishigsuren, Gábor Bella, Thomas Brochhagen, Daariimaa Marav, Fausto Giunchiglia and Khuyagbaatar Batsuren 96

PaVeDa - Pavia Verbs Database: Challenges and Perspectives
Chiara Zanchi, Silvia Luraghi and Claudia Roberta Combei 99

ParaNames: A Massively Multilingual Entity Name Corpus
Jonne Sälevä and Constantine Lignos 103

Program

Thursday, July 14, 2022

08:30 - 08:40 *Opening Remarks*

08:40 - 09:30 *Grammar Inference for Local Languages: Leveraging Typology for Automatic Grammar Generation (Keynote by Kristen Howell)*

09:30 - 10:00 *Multilingual Representations (Long Talks)*

Multilingualism Encourages Recursion: a Transfer Study with mBERT
Andrea Gregor De Varda and Roberto Zamparelli

Cross-linguistic Comparison of Linguistic Feature Encoding in BERT Models for Typologically Different Languages
Yulia Otmakhova, Karin Verspoor and Jey Han Lau

10:00 - 10:10 *Break*

10:10 - 11:10 *Typology (Short Talks)*

Word-order Typology in Multilingual BERT: A Case Study in Subordinate-Clause Detection
Dmitry Nikolaev and Sebastian Pado

Investigating Information-Theoretic Properties of the Typology of Spatial Demonstratives
Sihan Chen, Richard Futrell and Kyle Mahowald

Tweaking UD Annotations to Investigate the Placement of Determiners, Quantifiers and Numerals in the Noun Phrase
Luigi Talamo

How Universal is Metonymy? Results from a Large-Scale Multilingual Analysis
Temuulen Khishigsuren, Gábor Bella, Thomas Brochhagen, Daariimaa Marav, Fausto Giunchiglia and Khuyagbaatar Batsuren

Typological Word Order Correlations with Logistic Brownian Motion
Kai Hartung, Gerhard Jäger, Sören Gröttrup and Munir Georges

11:10 - 12:00 *Graham Neubig's Keynote Talk*

Thursday, July 14, 2022 (continued)

12:00 - 13:30 *Lunch*

13:30 - 14:50 *Shared Task: Prediction of Cognate Reflexes*

The SIGTYP 2022 Shared Task on the Prediction of Cognate Reflexes
Johann-Mattis List, Ekaterina Vylomova, Robert Forkel, Nathan Hill and Ryan Cotterell

Bayesian Phylogenetic Cognate Prediction
Gerhard Jäger

Mockingbird at the SIGTYP 2022 Shared Task: Two Types of Models forthe Prediction of Cognate Reflexes
Christo Kirov, Richard Sproat and Alexander Gutkin

A Transformer Architecture for the Prediction of Cognate Reflexes
Giuseppe Celano

Approaching Reflex Predictions as a Classification Problem Using Extended Phonological Alignments
Tiago Tresoldi

14:50 - 15:20 *Linguistic Trivia*

15:20 - 15:30 *Break*

15:30 - 16:20 *Learning from our Differences: How Typologically Distinct Modalities of Data Help Demystify Language Models (Keynote by Isabel Papadimitriou)*

16:20 - 17:00 *Databases and Corpora*

A Database for Modal Semantic Typology
Qingxia Guo, Nathaniel Imel and Shane Steinert-Threlkeld

PaVeDa - Pavia Verbs Database: Challenges and Perspectives
Chiara Zanchi, Silvia Luraghi and Claudia Roberta Combei

ParaNames: A Massively Multilingual Entity Name Corpus
Jonne Sälevä and Constantine Lignos

17:00 - 17:10 *Best Paper Awards, Closing*

Multilingualism Encourages Recursion: a Transfer Study with mBERT

Andrea Gregor de Varda
University of Milano-Bicocca
a.devarda@campus.unimib.it

Roberto Zamparelli
CIMeC – University of Trento
roberto.zamparelli@unitn.it

Abstract

The present work constitutes an attempt to investigate the relational structures learnt by mBERT, a multilingual transformer-based network, with respect to different cross-linguistic regularities proposed in the fields of theoretical and quantitative linguistics. We pursued this objective by relying on a zero-shot transfer experiment, evaluating the model's ability to generalize its native task to artificial languages that could either respect or violate some proposed language universal, and comparing its performance to the output of BERT, a monolingual model with an identical configuration. We created four artificial corpora through a Probabilistic Context-Free Grammar by manipulating the distribution of tokens and the structure of their dependency relations. We showed that while both models were favoured by a Zipfian distribution of the tokens and by the presence of head-dependency type structures, the multilingual transformer network exhibited a stronger reliance on hierarchical cues compared to its monolingual counterpart.

1 Introduction

Massively Multilingual Models (MMMs) are neural networks that can perform a NLP task in multiple languages, relying on a shared set of parameters. At the time of writing, the state-of-the-art performance of MMMs is achieved by transformer-based models such as multilingual BERT (mBERT, Devlin et al., 2019), XLM (Conneau and Lample, 2019), and XLM-R (Conneau et al., 2020a). They are usually derived from monolingual language models, trained simultaneously on multilingual text in up 104 languages without major architectural changes nor any reliance on explicit cross-lingual signal. The practical need for MMMs in NLP is undisputed: they drastically reduce resource and maintenance requirements with respect to multiple monolingual models, and benefit in particular low- and mid-resource languages (Dufter and Schütze, 2020). MMMs reach impressive performance levels in zero-shot cross-lingual transfer, enabling the fine-tuning of a model on supervised data in a set of N languages $\{L_i\}_{i=1...N}$ and its application to a different language L_{N+1}, with no additional training[1]. Zero-shot cross-lingual transfer has been shown to be effective across a variety of tasks and languages (Dufter and Schütze, 2020; Liu et al., 2020; Pires et al., 2019; Wu and Dredze, 2019; see Doddapaneni et al., 2021 for a review), and, although performance levels tend to be higher for typologically similar languages, it yields surprising results in languages written in different scripts (Pires et al., 2019) and with little (Karthikeyan et al., 2020) or no (Conneau et al., 2020b; Wang et al., 2019) vocabulary overlap. The distribution of resources available for NLP researchers in the world's languages is extremely skewed, with only a small subset of them being represented in the evolving language technologies (Joshi et al., 2020). MMMs constitute an attempt to mitigate the effects of this uneven allocation of resources by leveraging the knowledge that can be shared across languages.

Besides the obvious practical advantages that MMMs can bring to the NLP community, the nature of the cross-linguistic information extracted by these models is of high theoretical interest from a linguistic standpoint, and can contribute to the domain of artificial intelligence research in relevant subfields such as representation learning and interpretability. A modest but growing body of findings suggests that the structure of the representation space that MMMs exploit is multilingual in nature (Pires et al., 2019; Wu and Dredze, 2019; Hu et al., 2020; Liu et al., 2020; although see Dhar and Bisazza, 2021 for opposite conclusions). For instance, syntactic trees can be retrieved from mBERT's intermediate representational subspaces, with these subspaces being approximately shared

[1] $\{L_i\}_{i=1...N}$ and L_{N+1} are typically resource-rich and resource-poor languages, respectively.

Proceedings of the 4th Workshop on Computational Typology and Multilingual NLP (SIGTYP 2022), pages 1 - 10
July 14, 2022

across languages (Liu et al., 2020). If MMMs learn universal patterns which generalize across languages, the structure of the representations they induce could inform us of the presence of latent regularities in different language spaces. Furthermore, the benefits of the study of the MMMs' behaviour extend to the domain of representation learning, a subfield of AI research focusing on the development of computational representations and the analysis of their properties (Bengio et al., 2013). While the present study will not analyze the internal states of the networks, it will be possible to draw conclusions on the generality of their learned representations through non-parametric probing, by directly examining their behaviour in response to non-linguistic input. More precisely, we will compare the suitability of the representational formats induced by mono- and multilingual models with respect to different properties that are desirable from a linguistic perspective.

The present work aims to analyze the generalizations that BERT and mBERT induced from natural language data in a set of transfer learning experiments. The use of transfer learning methods to shed light on the relational structures learned by neural networks has been recently adopted for monolingual models (Papadimitriou and Jurafsky, 2020). Here, we extended the transfer approach to a multilingual setting, and compare the performance of mBERT and its monolingual counterpart in generalizing their native task (i.e. masked language modelling) to artificial languages that display different degrees of structural similarity with natural languages. We wish to highlight three main differences between our paradigm and the methodologies Papadimitriou and Jurafsky proposed.

1. **Cross-lingualism.** The most significant contribution of our study consists of the transposition of Papadimitriou and Jurafsky's paradigm to a multilingual setting.

2. **Direction of the transfer.** Papadimitriou and Jurafsky (2020) evaluated the performances of several LSTM models trained on non-linguistic data and transferred zero-shot to a natural language corpus in Spanish. We invert the direction of the transfer, testing the pre-trained multilingual model on artificial corpora derived from formal grammars. This choice is desirable for three reasons: first, it allows to test the model once for each experimental condition, and not in different languages. Second, it frees us from the need to train several models – one for each artificial corpus – since we can leverage one single multilingual pre-training. Third, it lets us draw conclusions on the structural generalizations which have been directly induced from natural language data. In the other direction, the models could have extracted helpful generalizations from the artificial dataset which might still not have been visible when looking at natural language alone.

3. **Neural architecture.** Papadimitriou and Jurafsky (2020) have employed LSTM models for all their experiments; however, transformers are gaining increasing popularity in NLP research and applications, and achieve state-of-the-art results across different downstream tasks. Most MMMs are built as transformer architectures, and mBERT is an instance of this class. Hence, our study can be informative also in terms of model comparison. Note that moving to a bidirectional transformer requires a different approach to calculating sequence-level performance, one which eliminates the randomness from the masking process. Our approach, which we name *iterative token-level cloze task* (ITCT) is detailed in Section 2.

Our experiment focused on the Zipf's law and hierarchy, which have been considered as universal linguistic features (Zipf, 1935; Chomsky, 1957). We evaluated the transfer performances of the two transformers in four corpora, characterized by increasing statistical and structural consistency with natural languages. The models were tested on (a) a RANDOM corpus, composed by sequences of tokens sampled from a uniform distribution, (b) a ZIPFIAN corpus, where the tokens were extracted from a Zipfian distribution, (c) a FLAT BRACKETS corpus, composed of sequences of matching parentheses with crossed dependencies, and (d) a NESTED BRACKETS corpus, consisting of paired symbols nested hierarchically. To anticipate the results, we found that both models showed higher performance scores in the ZIPFIAN compared to the RANDOM condition, and in the FLAT BRACKETS as opposed to the ZIPFIAN corpus, while only the multilingual model showed a significant performance advantage in the comparison between the FLAT BRACKETS and the NESTED BRACKETS corpora. We conclude that while mathematical regularities and pairwise head-dependent relationships are detected across model types, the multilingual input favours the reliance on structural cues, and specifically on balanced constituent structures, a hallmark of theoretical linguistic formalisms.

2 Methods

As a testing procedure, we froze all mBERT's weights setting it in evaluation mode, and assessed its structural knowledge by studying its predictive ability. To do so, we employed a non-parametric evaluation procedure, which we named *iterative token-level cloze task* (ITCT). The ITCT consists of an adaptation of mBERT's native functionality, i.e. masked language modelling (MLM). The main difference consists in the fact that while in MLM the model has to predict the tokens corresponding to the masks applied to a randomly selected subpart of the input (15% of the tokens in the sentence), in the ITCT all the tokens are masked iteratively. This mitigates the aleatory dimension in the selection of the tokens that are masked, and provides an index of the predictability of a sequence, where each token has to be predicted by the model given the whole remaining context. After freezing its weights[2], at the first timestep t_0 the model is presented with the input sequence where the first token is masked, i.e. substituted with a mask token, and two special characters – [CLS] and [SEP] – are appended to the beginning and the end of the sequence, to mark the sequence boundaries. The model then predicts the original token relying upon the right context, and the hidden vector corresponding to the masked token is passed through a softmax over the vocabulary, in order to assign it a probability. At t_1, the mask is moved from the first to the second token, and now mBERT's prediction is conditioned by both the right and the left contexts. The process is repeated until the end of the sequence, with the number of timesteps N being equal to the length of the tokenized input (see Figure 1). The mean probability assigned to the masked tokens across all the timesteps is taken as an index of the overall predictability of the sequence. Note that a proper sequence probability metric would require a multiplicative chain rule of the kind that is applicable for auto-regressive models but not for masked language models. The notion of average probability does not correspond to any well-defined notion in probability theory, but it serves the purpose of comparing different structural configurations in the context of our study[3]. The predictions of mBERT were compared with the ones produced by its monolingual counterpart; this comparison provides a crucial element for distinguishing which generalizations are driven by the multilingual input, and which can be extracted by the same model from monolingual data.

t_0 [MASK] should buy a car

t_1 John [MASK] buy a car

t_2 John should [MASK] a car

t_3 John should buy [MASK] car

t_4 John should buy a [MASK]

Figure 1: Unfolding of the iterative token-level cloze task for every timestep *t* in a sample sentence.

3 Data

The corpora on which our analyses were performed were created in a way such that the sequence length varied within each condition, but was identical across all conditions, both in terms of the number of sequences and of the number of tokens within each sequence; they all shared a 50,000 three-letter tokens vocabulary. These design choices were made in order to license pairwise comparisons at the sequence level, so that the difference in probability assigned by the models to a given item of a corpus could be compared with the probability assigned to the corresponding item in the other datasets. This approach allowed us to rule out the effects of intervening variables such as vocabulary and length, so that the differences in the models' predictions could be driven only by structural differences between the corpora. The models were tested on 1,000 sequences in each corpus; within each condition, the mean sequence length was 9.90, with a standard deviation equal to 14.74.

3.1 Nested brackets

A NESTED BRACKETS corpus consisting of sequences of nested matching symbols was created

[2]Freezing the model's weights is a necessary condition for this approach, since if this procedure was implemented during training, the model trying to predict the target token at t_1 would have already seen it at t_0; at the end of the sequence, the prediction would be highly facilitated from having seen *N-1* times the target token in the same context.

[3]We thank Reviewer pYcV for bringing this issue to our attention.

to test the transfer performance of mBERT on hierarchical structures. The corpus was built from a vocabulary of 50,000 three-letter tokens, obtained from random combinations of Latin characters. The tokens were assembled into nested structures through the application of probabilistic rules, defined by a Probabilistic Context-Free Grammar (PCFG). The grammar was composed by a set of recursive rules of the form in (1):

(1) $S \rightarrow tok_i\ S\ tok_i\ S$ [P1]

Where S denotes the start symbol, tok_i a given terminal symbol sampled from the vocabulary, and P1 the probability assigned to the application of the rule. Rules of this form are said to be recursive since the same non-terminal symbol S appears on both sides of the formula, which enables it to be reapplied to its own output. The rule in (1) allows for both right and central recursion, since the non-terminal symbol S is rewritten into itself both within a pair of terminal symbols and in the rightmost part of the formula. The probabilities in P1 followed a Zipfian distribution, so that the terminal symbols were distributed accordingly in the corpus; their distribution summed up to 0.4. This set of rules was complemented by the rule in (2), where the start symbol was rewritten into the empty string ε. The probability assigned to this rule was higher than the sum of all the previous rules, in order to contain the growth of the tree depth. Empty sequences were removed from the corpus.

(2) $S \rightarrow \varepsilon$ [0.6]

The most prominent feature of the sequences generated by this grammar is that the pairwise dependency arcs instantiated between tokens never cross (see Figure 2). In other words, the pairing between tokens can only be nested hierarchically within the overlying dependency relations. This condition is equivalent with respect to this property to the nested parentheses corpus created by Papadimitriou and Jurafsky (2020), although in their work they created the structured sequences with a stack-based grammar, designed to either open a new bracket or close the last one that had been opened at each timestep.

3.2 Flat brackets

A FLAT BRACKETS corpus was created in order to isolate the effects of non-nested dependency pairing from the presence of hierarchical structures

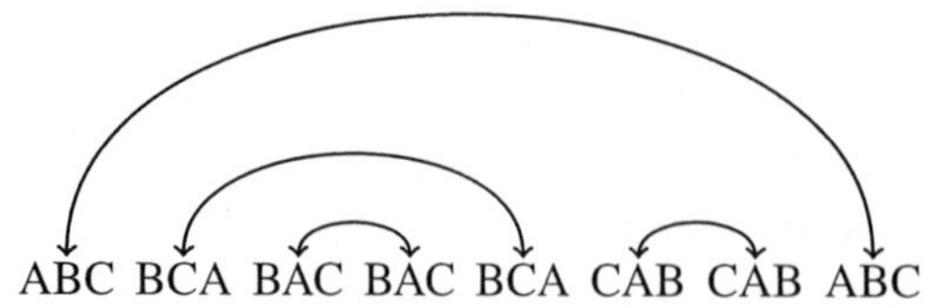

Figure 2: Example of a NESTED BRACKETS sequence.

in the transfer performances. The corpus was derived by randomly shuffling the tokens of each item of the NESTED BRACKETS corpus, a process that creates structures where the dependencies do not necessarily nest, and the pairing arcs instantiated within an entry may cross (see Figure 3). Differently from Papadimitriou and Jurafsky (2020), who created a novel corpus for this condition without any reference to the hierarchical one, we adopted a procedure that kept constant the length of the sequences, and the identity of the tokens within them. We maintain that our methodology licences more meaningful comparisons between the two corpora, since the only difference between them is the hierarchical property of recursive nesting.

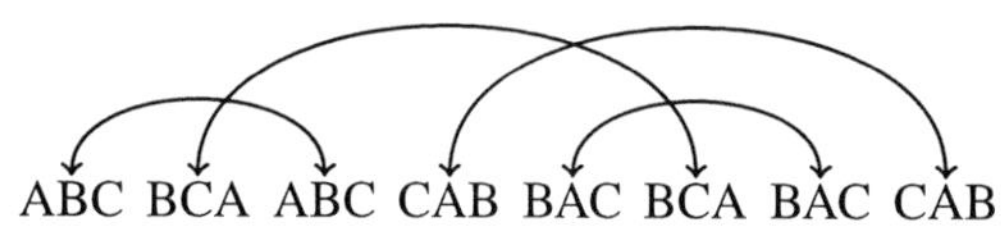

Figure 3: Example of a FLAT BRACKETS sequence.

3.3 Zipf's corpus

The ZIPF'S CORPUS was created in order to evaluate whether BERT and mBERT's performances were affected by the mathematical distribution of the token frequencies in the corpus. The sequences were constructed so that their length had to coincide with the one of the corresponding entry in the previous corpora. For each item in the NESTED BRACKETS corpus, we sampled a number of tokens coinciding with its length from a Zipf's distribution, and conjoined them to form a sequence of tokens. In the creation of this corpus no dependency relation was explicitly encoded. We remark that this corpus is similar to the FLAT BRACKETS corpus, with the only difference that the tokens are not repeated twice within each sequence, and so

				Model			
				BERT		mBERT	
Corpus	Zipf	Pairing	Nesting	Mean	SD	Mean	SD
Random corpus				0.0121	0.0137	0.0094	0.0135
Zipf's corpus	✓			0.0253	0.0457	0.0250	0.0525
Flat brackets	✓	✓		**0.6784**	0.1780	0.6353	0.1558
Nested brackets	✓	✓	✓	0.6576	0.1677	**0.6417**	0.1536

Table 1: Featural summary of the structural and mathematical properties of the four corpora, and descriptive statistics of the results of the transfer. The best performances for each model are highlighted in bold.

there are no structural correspondences between tokens.

3.4 Random corpus

In order to define a baseline for the evaluation of the networks' predictions, we constructed a RANDOM CORPUS where the tokens composing the sequences were sampled from a uniform distribution. As for the ZIPF'S CORPUS, the length of each sequence matched the length of the corresponding entry in the other corpora.

4 Models and experimental setup

All our experiments were performed employing BERT's native masked language modelling component. The configuration of the model was left unaltered with respect to Devlin et al.'s (2019) release. In particular, we relied on the monolingual and multilingual models derived from $\text{BERT}_{\text{BASE}}$, which is composed of 12 layers, 12 self-attention heads, and a hidden size of 768; the overall network comprises 110M parameters. The networks did not undergo any fine-tuning nor adaptation process, as they were employed as out-of-the-box masked language models. As mentioned above, BERT and mBERT only differ in their vocabulary and the weights learned during training, sharing an identical configuration both in terms of architectural choices and learning objectives. While BERT was pre-trained on 800M words of the monolingual BooksCorpus (Zhu et al., 2015) and 2,500 words of the English Wikipedia, mBERT was trained on the entire Wikipedia dump of 104 languages. The two models rely on different tokenizers, each comprising a separate WordPiece vocabulary (Wu et al., 2016). The different tokenizations of the input sequences do not allow us to directly compare the raw probabilities assigned by the two models to a given sequence; for this reason, we will not consider the absolute item-wise difference in the models' predictive performance, but rather the pattern of results between the experimental conditions. This comparative approach is also needed in light of the models' vocabulary. If we simply compared probabilities across models and conditions, our results might be biased by the fact that some of the three-letter tokens might be assigned different probabilities depending on whether they form English meaning-bearing vocabulary items (e.g. "for") or not (e.g. "zyi"). However, since we only compare conditions within models, and the two conditions of main interest (i.e. FLAT and NESTED BRACKETS) are composed by the same tokens in different arrangements, our contrasts are robust with respect to this possible confound.

5 Results

Table 1 reports the mean and the standard deviation of the average probabilities assigned by BERT and mBERT to the token sequences in the four corpora considered in the study, along with a schematic summary of the structural features characterizing each corpus. In line with our expectations, both models assigned on average higher probabilities to the correct tokens in the ZIPF'S CORPUS than in the RANDOM CORPUS, despite a low absolute difference in the scores (0.0132 for the monolingual and 0.0156 for the multilingual model). The substantial increase in performance was obtained with the transition from the ZIPF'S CORPUS to the FLAT BRACKETS corpus, with an average improvement of 0.6531 for BERT and 0.6103 for mBERT in the metric. Interestingly, the two networks started diverging in their behaviour with the subsequent step of the structural hierarchy. While the target tokens of the recursive structures in the NESTED BRACKETS corpus were associated with higher probabilities by the multilingual model, monolingual BERT

		Model					
		BERT			mBERT		
Corpus 1	Corpus 2	t	p	d	t	p	d
Random corpus	Zipf's corpus	8.9740	$\ll .001$	0.3918	9.2296	$\ll .001$	0.4069
Zipf's corpus	Flat brackets	116.9351	$\ll .001$	5.0255	117.4448	$\ll .001$	5.2476
Flat brackets	Nested brackets	-12.7494	$\ll .001$	-0.1205	3.2662	0.0011	0.0415

Table 2: Pairwise comparisons of the results of the transfer to the four corpora. The comparisons are made exclusively between the corpora that are adjacent in the hierarchy of structuredness. The reported p-values are uncorrected, but all the contrasts remain significant when a Bonferroni correction is applied to the α threshold (0.05/3 = 0.0166).

showed no facilitation induced by the presence of nested dependencies. On the contrary, the best performing condition for monolingual BERT was the transfer to the FLAT BRACKETS corpus. While mBERT's results reflected a positive association with the hierarchy of levels of structure that characterizes our four corpora, its monolingual counterpart showed an inverted trend in the last two conditions.

We tested the statistical significance of this dissociation through a set of paired samples t-tests between the mean probability assigned by the models to the sequences of two corpora. We performed the tests only on the pairs of corpora that were adjacent in the structural hierarchy; this choice led us to three comparisons which we summarized in Table 2. The first two columns of the table specify the two conditions being contrasted; the following three columns report the t statistic, the associated p-value, and Cohen's d as a measure of the effect size for BERT; the last three columns indicate the same statistical indexes for mBERT. As can be evinced by the table, the first two contrasts (RANDOM CORPUS-ZIPF'S CORPUS and ZIPF'S CORPUS-FLAT BRACKETS) are highly significant for both models, with an increment in performance attested by the positive sign of the t and d statistics. The effect size associated with the comparisons is modest in the first case and extremely high in the second, with no considerable differences between the models. Nonetheless, as shown in the third row of the table, the pairwise contrast between the FLAT BRACKETS corpus and the NESTED BRACKETS corpus supports the observation of a dissociation between the results of BERT and mBERT. Indeed, while for both models the performance in the NESTED BRACKETS and the FLAT BRACKETS corpus is significantly different, the direction of such difference is the opposite, as shown by the sign of the t statistic and the Cohen's d. While the effect sizes associated with such contrasts are negligible, both dissociations are statistically significant.

6 Discussion

In discussing the present findings, we begin by focusing on the commonalities in the networks' output, and conclude by commenting on the dissociation in their results on the two corpora with token pairing. First, both models showed a preference for sequences where the mathematical distribution of the tokens resembled their empirical distribution in natural languages. We believe that the higher average predictability that characterized the ZIPF'S CORPUS when compared with the RANDOM CORPUS reflects a tendency of the networks to expect a non-uniform distribution of the tokens in input that is coherent with the data on which the pre-training had been performed. Then, we maintain that the substantial gain in performance on the FLAT BRACKET corpus is to be attributed to the paired correspondences between tokens, which in turn might mimic head-dependency type structures in natural language corpora. Arguably, the most surprising result that we obtained is the dissociation between BERT and mBERT's results in the transfer to the two corpora characterized by token pairing. While the multilingual model was facilitated in its native task by the presence of nested structures – although with a minimal effect size –, the same improvement in performance is not found in its monolingual counterpart. On the contrary, the strongest transfer performance is achieved by BERT in the FLAT BRACKETS corpus. These results suggest that the presence of multiple languages in the input during pre-training leads the models to rely on more structured grammatical abstractions. Obviously, this finding does not imply that mBERT does not capture the paired relationships with crossing arcs; the biggest progress is undoubtedly obtained when these simpler one-to-one correspondences are included in the input. Nonetheless, it seems that when more complex structures are instantiated between the tokens in the sequences, the multilingual model is able to capture these configurational regularities, and exploit them in order to make stronger predictions regarding the masked input. This difference should be attributed to the nature of the input that the networks had been presented with during pre-training, since under every other aspect except vocabulary and training set size (e.g. architectures, training regimes, objective functions) the models were identical.

6.1 Follow-up analyses

While the results of mBERT can be given a straightforward interpretation, the fact that the monolingual model showed a preference for the non-recursive corpus needs to be explained. Indeed, if its results had been exclusively driven by the absence of a hierarchical bias, we would have expected no significant difference between its performance scores in the transfer on the two corpora characterized by token pairing. What we found was instead a clear, significant preference for the FLAT BRACKETS corpus, that cannot be explained in terms of sequence length or identity of the tokens, since all these low-level factors were maintained unaltered in the two corpora (see Section 3). Without any clear *a priori* expectation on the factors that might have driven this effect, we inspected the ninety-ninth percentile of the sequences that showed the highest difference between the probability assigned by BERT to the flat and the nested structures. In other words, we computed the difference of the ITCT scores assigned by the model to the nested and the corresponding flat sequences (henceforth Δ score), and selected the first 10 sequences after ranking them in descending order. We remind the reader that the sequences in the two conditions comprised the same tokens, assembled hierarchically and projectively in the NESTED SEQUENCES corpus, and randomly shuffled in the FLAT SEQUENCES corpus. The most salient property of the items with the highest Δ score that we derived was that 80% of them were four-token sequences, with the form *abab* in the FLAT BRACKETS condition and either *aabb* or *abba* in the NESTED BRACKETS condition. We reasoned that a property that distinguishes these three classes of sequences is the presence of identical adjacent tokens, which characterizes both forms of the FLAT BRACKETS corpus, but not the *abab* sequence in the NESTED BRACKETS condition. We speculate that the models – and in particular the monolingual one – might not expect the same token to appear in two immediately adjacent positions within a given sentence, and that this tendency might have driven the higher performance scores of the monolingual model on the FLAT BRACKETS corpus. For this hypothesis to have a plausible theoretical ground, we needed to assess whether the contiguous repetition of identical tokens is indeed a rare phenomenon in natural language. While it is well known that lexical repetition is common at the discourse level – words that have entered the discourse have a higher reuse probability than lexical frequency (Heller et al., 2010) –, the probability of reoccurrence of the same token in two contiguous positions has not been assessed through corpus studies. To do so, we counted the number of such instances of repetition in four corpora of 1M tokens, derived from Wikipedia dumps in three languages (English, Chinese, and Finnish) belonging to three different language families (Indoeuropean, Sino-Tibetan, and Uralic). We tokenized each corpus with mBERT's WordPiece tokenizer, removed punctuation and unknown characters, and counted the number of occurrences of a given token at index i and i+1. Perhaps surprisingly, we found that in two out of three corpora the probability of having the same token k at index i and i+1 was lower than chance (i.e., lower than the probability of having a random token sampled from the corpus' vocabulary; see Table 3). These results support the idea that the juxtaposition of identical tokens is indeed an unusual occurrence in natural language.

Once we verified the low frequency of identical adjacent tokens in three natural languages, we needed to evaluate whether subsequences of this kind had an actual effect on the models' predictions. In order to test this hypothesis, we ran four linear regression models (one for each considered corpus $\times$ model combination) with the score assigned to each sequence as a dependent variable, and the amount of identical adjacent tokens as a predictor. More precisely, we employed as independent variable the ratio of token reoccurrences over the total amount of token pairs in the sequence.[4]

[4]We chose not to employ the raw amount of adjacent pairs as a regressor in order to mitigate the effects of sequence

Language	Family	Repetitions	Vocabulary	P repetitions	P random
English	Indoeuropean	19	24,443	1.9^{-5}	$\mathbf{4.1^{-5}}$
Chinese	Sino-Tibetan	1,891	9,604	$\mathbf{1.8^{-3}}$	1.0^{-4}
Finnish	Uralic	21	17,546	2.1^{-5}	$\mathbf{5.7^{-5}}$

Table 3: Probability of adjacent tokens repetitions and chance level sampling. The probability of the repetitions was computed by dividing the raw count of the repetitions by the number of tokens in the corpus (1M), while the probability of sampling a random token from the vocabulary was obtained dividing 1 by the word types in the corpus.

In line with our expectations, we found a negative, highly significant effect of the ratio of reoccurrences on BERT's scores in the FLAT BRACKETS condition (B = -0.1958, t = -16.098, $p \ll 0.001$, R^2 = 0.206). A similar pattern of results was found in the NESTED condition (B = -0.1667, t = -7.949, $p \ll 0.001$), although the model explained a limited amount of variance (R^2 = 0.06). Crucially, we found no significant effect of the adjacent pairs ratio on the results of the multilingual model neither in the FLAT BRACKETS (B = -0.0214, t = 1.795, p = 0.073, R^2 = 0.003) nor in the NESTED BRACKETS condition (B = 0.0312, t = 1.577, p = 0.115, R^2 = 0.002). These results corroborate our previous suspicion concerning the different performance patterns of the two transformers models. More precisely, they suggest that for the monolingual model, local heuristics relying on linear order prevail, hiding to the model the structural cues that are instantiated in the nested brackets corpus. Conversely, the cross-lingual model seems to be able to rely on more abstract structural features and to exploit them in its predictive behaviour, while not being influenced by shallow linguistic factors such as token repetition.

7 Conclusion

The mathematical regularities of the pre-training input seemed to have been absorbed to the same extent by the monolingual and the multilingual transformer models, since the ZIPF'S CORPUS exerted a similar facilitation effect with respect to the RANDOM CORPUS across model types. Furthermore, token pairing appears to have elicited a much stronger advantage in the predictive task we employed in our study, suggesting that regardless of the mono- or multilingual nature of the input the pre-training procedure had induced a strong structural transfer towards non-hierarchical and non-projective structures. We agree with Papadimitriou and Jurafsky's (2020) conclusion that this facilitation emphasizes the importance of pairing, head-dependency type structures in the linguistic embeddings of neural language models. In addition, our results extend the previous findings to the generalizations employed by pre-trained transformer models, and validate the methodological choice of inverting the direction of the transfer. More importantly, the difference in BERT and mBERT's performances when recursion is implemented in the data suggests that the high surface inconsistency of the input the multilingual model is exposed to during pre-training promotes stronger structural generalizations. This finding directly answers a question raised in the Introduction, concerning the relevance of this study with respect to the domain of representation learning. We noted that the comparison between mono- and multilingual models on linguistic and non-linguistic tasks could have allowed us to draw conclusions on the aptness of their induced representational formats with respect to different properties that are desirable from a linguistic perspective. While the behaviour of the monolingual model seems to be influenced by other non-structural congruences with the pre-training input (such as the presence of adjacent paired tokens), this experiment suggests that multilingual representations are more deeply aligned with the structures posited in theoretical linguistics, showing a hierarchical bias when transferred zero-shot to non-linguistic input.

8 Limitations and further directions

While our results provide empirical evidence for a higher structural awareness in mBERT as opposed to BERT, the generalizability of our findings to natural language is yet to be assessed. In the present paper we employed artificial languages in order to maximize the experimental control over the input; we leave to future research an evaluation of the structural biases operating in mono- and multilingual models in a more naturalistic setting.

length.

References

Y. Bengio, Aaron Courville, and Pascal Vincent. 2013. Representation learning: A review and new perspectives. *IEEE transactions on pattern analysis and machine intelligence*, 35:1798–1828.

Noam Chomsky. 1957. *Syntactic structures*. De Gruyter Mouton.

Alexis Conneau, Kartikay Khandelwal, Naman Goyal, Vishrav Chaudhary, Guillaume Wenzek, Francisco Guzmán, Édouard Grave, Myle Ott, Luke Zettlemoyer, and Veselin Stoyanov. 2020a. Unsupervised cross-lingual representation learning at scale. In *Proceedings of the 58th Annual Meeting of the Association for Computational Linguistics*, pages 8440–8451.

Alexis Conneau and Guillaume Lample. 2019. Cross-lingual language model pretraining. *Advances in neural information processing systems*, 32.

Alexis Conneau, Shijie Wu, Haoran Li, Luke Zettlemoyer, and Veselin Stoyanov. 2020b. Emerging cross-lingual structure in pretrained language models. In *Proceedings of the 58th Annual Meeting of the Association for Computational Linguistics*, pages 6022–6034, Online. Association for Computational Linguistics.

Jacob Devlin, Ming-Wei Chang, Kenton Lee, and Kristina Toutanova. 2019. BERT: Pre-training of deep bidirectional transformers for language understanding. In *Proceedings of the 2019 Conference of the North American Chapter of the Association for Computational Linguistics: Human Language Technologies, Volume 1 (Long and Short Papers)*, pages 4171–4186, Minneapolis, Minnesota. Association for Computational Linguistics.

Prajit Dhar and Arianna Bisazza. 2021. Understanding cross-lingual syntactic transfer in multilingual recurrent neural networks. In *Proceedings of the 23rd Nordic Conference on Computational Linguistics (NoDaLiDa)*, pages 74–85, Reykjavik, Iceland (Online). Linköping University Electronic Press, Sweden.

Sumanth Doddapaneni, Gowtham Ramesh, Anoop Kunchukuttan, Pratyush Kumar, and Mitesh M Khapra. 2021. A primer on pretrained multilingual language models. *arXiv preprint arXiv:2107.00676*.

Philipp Dufter and Hinrich Schütze. 2020. Identifying elements essential for BERT's multilinguality. In *Proceedings of the 2020 Conference on Empirical Methods in Natural Language Processing (EMNLP)*, pages 4423–4437, Online. Association for Computational Linguistics.

Jordana Heller, J Pierrehumbert, and David N Rapp. 2010. Predicting words beyond the syntactic horizon: Word recurrence distributions modulate on-line long-distance lexical predictability. *Architectures and Mechanisms for Language Processing (AMLaP)*.

Junjie Hu, Sebastian Ruder, Aditya Siddhant, Graham Neubig, Orhan Firat, and Melvin Johnson. 2020. Xtreme: A massively multilingual multi-task benchmark for evaluating cross-lingual generalisation. In *International Conference on Machine Learning*, pages 4411–4421. PMLR.

Pratik Joshi, Sebastin Santy, Amar Budhiraja, Kalika Bali, and Monojit Choudhury. 2020. The state and fate of linguistic diversity and inclusion in the NLP world. In *Proceedings of the 58th Annual Meeting of the Association for Computational Linguistics*, pages 6282–6293, Online. Association for Computational Linguistics.

K Karthikeyan, Wang Zihan, Stephen Mayhew, and Dan Roth. 2020. Cross-lingual ability of multilingual bert: An empirical study. In *International Conference on Learning Representations*.

Zihan Liu, Genta Indra Winata, Andrea Madotto, and Pascale Fung. 2020. Exploring fine-tuning techniques for pre-trained cross-lingual models via continual learning. *arXiv preprint arXiv:2004.14218*.

Isabel Papadimitriou and Dan Jurafsky. 2020. Learning music helps you read: Using transfer to study linguistic structure in language models. In *Proceedings of the 2020 Conference on Empirical Methods in Natural Language Processing (EMNLP)*, pages 6829–6839.

Telmo Pires, Eva Schlinger, and Dan Garrette. 2019. How multilingual is multilingual BERT? In *Proceedings of the 57th Annual Meeting of the Association for Computational Linguistics*, pages 4996–5001, Florence, Italy. Association for Computational Linguistics.

Zihan Wang, Stephen Mayhew, Dan Roth, et al. 2019. Cross-lingual ability of multilingual bert: An empirical study. *arXiv preprint arXiv:1912.07840*.

Shijie Wu and Mark Dredze. 2019. Beto, bentz, becas: The surprising cross-lingual effectiveness of BERT. In *Proceedings of the 2019 Conference on Empirical Methods in Natural Language Processing and the 9th International Joint Conference on Natural Language Processing (EMNLP-IJCNLP)*, pages 833–844, Hong Kong, China. Association for Computational Linguistics.

Yonghui Wu, Mike Schuster, Zhifeng Chen, Quoc V Le, Mohammad Norouzi, Wolfgang Macherey, Maxim Krikun, Yuan Cao, Qin Gao, Klaus Macherey, et al. 2016. Google's neural machine translation system: Bridging the gap between human and machine translation. *arXiv preprint arXiv:1609.08144*.

Yukun Zhu, Ryan Kiros, Rich Zemel, Ruslan Salakhutdinov, Raquel Urtasun, Antonio Torralba, and Sanja Fidler. 2015. Aligning books and movies: Towards story-like visual explanations by watching movies and reading books. In *Proceedings of the IEEE international conference on computer vision*, pages 19–27.

George Kingsley Zipf. 1935. *The psycho-biology of language: An introduction to dynamic philology*, volume 21. Psychology Press.

Word-order typology in Multilingual BERT: A case study in subordinate-clause detection

Dmitry Nikolaev **Sebastian Padó**
IMS, University of Stuttgart
dnikolaev@fastmail.com, pado@ims.uni-stuttgart.de

Abstract

The capabilities and limitations of BERT and similar models are still unclear when it comes to learning syntactic abstractions, in particular across languages. In this paper, we use the task of *subordinate-clause detection* within and across languages to probe these properties. We show that this task is deceptively simple, with easy gains offset by a long tail of harder cases, and that BERT's zero-shot performance is dominated by word-order effects, mirroring the SVO/VSO/SOV typology.

1 Introduction

Analysing the ability of pre-trained neural language models, such as BERT (Devlin et al., 2019), to abstract grammatical patterns from raw texts has become a prominent research question (Jawahar et al., 2019; Rogers et al., 2020). Results remain mixed. While BERT-based models have been shown to learn syntactic representations that are similarly structured across languages (Chi et al., 2020), some grammatical patterns, such as discontinuous constituents, remain challenging for them even when training data is plentiful (Kogkalidis and Winholds, 2022). In practical terms, zero-shot performance of BERT-based models is lower for typologically distant languages (Pires et al., 2019), and they can profit from direct exposure to typological features during fine-tuning (Bjerva and Augenstein, 2021).

In this study, we add another datapoint to the conversation by analysing the ability of BERT-based models to capture the *distinction between main and subordinate clauses* across languages. This task is promising for two reasons. First, it highlights variability in the way main and subordinate clauses are structured across languages, thus acting as an informative probe into the relationship between BERT and typological categories. Second, the task is arguably relevant for downstream performance on natural-language understanding, where (some notion of) syntactic scope and compositionality should support tasks such as analysing commitment (Jiang and de Marneffe, 2019; Zhang and de Marneffe, 2021) or factuality (Lotan et al., 2013), text simplification (Sikka and Mago, 2020), or paraphrase detection (Timmer et al., 2021). In order to operationalise it in a cross-lingual fashion, we use the Universal Dependencies framework (UD; Nivre et al., 2020) with its large multilingual collection of corpora.

Our analysis proceeds in two stages. First, we survey the performance of BERT models fine-tuned and tested on the same language across 20 typologically diverse languages (§ 3). For the majority of languages, distinguishing main and subordinate clauses is easily solved with base-size models and relatively small training sets. However, some languages demonstrate a non-negligible number of errors, which we analyse.

Then we study the performance of Multilingual BERT (mBERT) in a zero-shot setting (§ 4), where we fine-tune the model on labeled data in 10 different languages and then test its performance on 31 datasets representing 27 different languages. We find that the performance of mBERT is dominated by word-order effects well known from the typological literature (Comrie, 1981): the Arabic model shows best-in-class performance on Irish, and the Japanese model has best-in-class performance on Korean, while both have poor performance overall. European languages with large training sets provide good inductive bias for typologically diverse languages but fail on SOV languages.

2 Experimental Setup

Data To make our analysis maximally comparable across languages, we start from the Parallel Universal Dependencies (PUD) collection (Zeman et al., 2017), which contains translations for a set of 1000 English sentences. PUD only contains test corpora. As these are too small to be further

Proceedings of the 4th Workshop on Computational Typology and Multilingual NLP (SIGTYP 2022), pages 11 - 21
July 14, 2022 ©2022 Association for Computational Linguistics

Language	Mandarin	Vietnamese	Korean	Arabic	Hindi	German	Armenian	Turkish	Welsh	Indonesian
Accuracy	88.7	90	90.4	91.2	93.6	94.1	94.3	95.1	95.6	96
Language	Basque	Spanish	Irish	English	Hebrew	Afrikaans	French	Japanese	Czech	Russian
Accuracy	96.9	97.1	97.4	97.9	98.2	98.8	99	99.1	99.6	99.7

Table 1: Performance of single-language models.

split into train/test subsets, we use other corpora to fine-tune the models. We also add corpora for languages not covered by PUD for better typological coverage. See Appendix § A.2 for the full list.

Model The experimental setup is identical in the single-language and zero-shot settings. A pre-trained mBERT model (a variant of `bert-base`) and several pre-trained single-language BERT models, all provided by HuggingFace (Wolf et al., 2020), are fine-tuned on the binary classification of predicates into main vs. subordinate clauses. We operationalize main clauses as those headed by predicates with the UD label `root` and subordinate clauses through the UD labels `acl`, `ccomp`, `advcl`, `csubj`, and `xcomp`. The last hidden state of the embedding model for the first subword of each predicate is fed to a two-layer MLP with a tanh activation after the first layer, and the model is fine-tuned using cross-entropy loss. For the single-language setup, the model is fine-tuned for five epochs, and we report the best result on the validation set. Most models begin overfitting after the second epoch, so in the zero-shot setting all models are fine-tuned for two epochs.

3 Single-Language Models

The main results obtained by the models fine-tuned and tested on the same language are shown in Table 1. Results are above 90% for almost all languages, while a majority baseline (always assign subordinate clause) attains an accuracy of 50–70% depending on the language. (Table 3 in the Appendix provides more details about the models and corpora, including exact baseline results.) At first glance, neither the size of the training set nor the size of the model seem to be a major factor: mBERT demonstrates better performance when fine-tuned on the small Afrikaans and Hebrew datasets than when trained on a bigger Chinese dataset. When fine-tuned on the English data, it attains the same performance as an English-only `bert-large`.[1]

[1]The mBERT result is reported in Table 2.

A more fundamental distinction seems to exist between major European languages, the results on which are generally at $> 97\%$ accuracy (except for German), and Mandarin Chinese, Vietnamese, and Korean where results are around 90%. Our analysis indicates that these differences are partly due to discrepancies in UD annotations across corpora but also due to genuine syntactic differences. An example of an annotation-related confound is the treatment of quotations. The PUD corpora that we use preferentially as test sets treat quotations as sentential complements of communication verbs. Some of the corpora we use for fine-tuning, however, analyse the cases where quotation precedes the verb of speech as parataxis. The head predicate of the quotation therefore receives the label `root` and becomes the main predicate of the whole sentence, leading to spurious mistakes in the analysis of PUD corpora, where they are annotated as `ccomp`'s. This discrepancy accounts for the lion's share of classification mistakes in German and some mistakes in Mandarin.

In contrast, an example of genuine ambiguity is provided by the Mandarin *gēnjù* construction. This construction means 'according to' and can incorporate both nominal and verbal constituents. Thus, *gēnjù shàng biǎogé zhōng qī gè yuánsù de guānxì* from the Mandarin GSD corpus, which we used for fine-tuning, means 'based on the relationship of the seven elements in the above table', and the annotation treats this construction as an oblique prepositional phrase. Cf. the following example from the Mandarin PUD corpus: *gēnjù kěxíng xìng yánjiū gūjì* 'according to the feasibility study / the feasibility study estimates that / as the feasbility study estimates'. The analysis of this sentence in PUD makes *gūjì* 'estimate' the main predicate of the sentence, while an alternative analysis would make it the head of an adverbial clause, and yet another analysis would label it as a nominal element. The ability of Mandarin words to act as different parts of speech in different contexts (especially in case of verbs, which can act as clause heads, auxiliaries, complementisers, and compound elements) makes this kind of disambiguation difficult even for human annotators, which in turn makes it hard to formulate the exact rule that language models are supposed to extract from the data. A similar situation holds for Vietnamese.[2]

A different type of systematic ambiguity is presented by Korean, which also demonstrates poorer performance. Korean has about sixty markers connecting two clauses, and many of those allow for both coordinative and conjunctive readings, which makes either the first or the second clause the main one, respectively (Cho and Whitman, 2020, 220–227). Examples of this type are responsible for a large share of mistakes in Korean.

Overall, these results indicate that subordinate-clause detection is a long-tail task: major easily learnable patterns account for more than 90% of test cases for all languages, but in some languages there is an assortment of harder cases that prevent language models from efficiently generalising.

4 Zero-Shot Setting

4.1 Quantitative Results

We now turn to the analysis of the performance of the models in the zero-shot setting. The model described in § 2 is fine-tuned for two epochs on five European languages (English, Russian, Czech, French, and German) and five Eurasian languages (Standard Arabic, Mandarin Chinese, Turkish, Korean, and Japanese) with larger training corpora (the ones shown in Table 3). Each of the fine-tuned models is then applied in a zero-shot way to a range of test corpora from the UD collection.[3]

Based on the results in Table 2, several observations can be made. First, there is a set of European languages with large training corpora that can act as 'general approximators': they demonstrate high performance across the board. The best overall performance is attained by Russian, which has the second-largest training corpus (nearly 33k sentences). German, with the largest training corpus (nearly 56k sentences) performs worse than both Russian and English (the second best, with only circa 6k training sentences). While this good result for English may be attributed to more informative pre-training (English Wikipedia is much larger than the German one), such a bias would also have favoured German compared to Russian. An alternative explanation is provided by the more idiosyncratic German word-order patterns (V2 in main clauses vs. V-last in subordinate clauses), which help it achieve best-in-class performance on the similar Afrikaans. Notably, Russian beats English even though PUD corpora were translated from English and therefore should contain some traces of its morphosyntactic patterns (Rabinovich et al., 2017; Nikolaev et al., 2020).

At the other end of the spectrum, we find mediocre general approximators (Arabic, Turkish) and outright bad ones (Japanese and Korean). At first glance, their performance could be an artefact of lower-quality annotations or suboptimal tokenisation (Mielke et al., 2021). This, however, does not explain a remarkable set of results that is clearly due to word-order patterns. While the fine-tuned model for Arabic, a VSO language, performs worse on its own test corpus than models fine-tuned on European languages, it provides best-in-class performance on Irish, another VSO language (96% accuracy). The English-based model is not far behind (95%), but given the overall large gap in performance between them across the board, it seems that congruent word-order patterns provide a strong inductive bias for subordinate-clause identification.

Unfortunately, VSO languages are rare,[4] and it is impossible to check if this pattern generalises to other language pairs. However, our test-corpus suite includes data on strict SOV languages (Japanese, Korean) and languages where SOV is the dominant (Hindi, Turkish) or a common (Mandarin, Basque) pattern. These provide us with a large number of language pairs with different degrees of word-order congruence and fairly clear patterns of model performance. First, universal approximators, despite good performance on VSO languages, struggle on strict SOV languages, especially Japanese, while SOV languages demonstrate consistently good performance among themselves. E.g., Korean demonstrates best-in-class performance on Turkish, tied with Turkish itself, while Japanese has best-in-class performance on Korean. Turkish also demonstrates decent perfor-

[2] 'Syntactic category classification for Vietnamese is still in debate. That lack of consensus is due to the unclear limit between the grammatical roles of many words as well as the frequent phenomenon of syntactic category mutation' (Nguyen et al., 2004).

[3] Where available, we experiment with two test sets for the same language to assess domain-induced variance. As Table 2 shows, the difference in scores between different testing corpora for the same language can reach 5–6%, but it does not change the overall pattern.

[4] Out of 1376 languages in WALS (Dryer and Haspelmath, 2013), 95 are VSO, 564 are SOV and 488 are SVO.

	ar padt	ga idt	af booms	de pud	cs pud	cy ccg	en ewt	en pud	es pud	fi pud	fr pud	he hdt	hy arm	id pud	is pud	it pud
English	**96**	95	93	94	94	86	**98**	**98**	**96**	96	96	93	93	**95**	**96**	**98**
Russian	95	94	86	93	95	90	94	96	95	**97**	**99**	94	**94**	93	**96**	96
Czech	94	94	83	**95**	**100**	**92**	92	93	94	94	98	**95**	88	89	92	94
French	94	91	84	92	95	90	92	97	95	95	**99**	94	87	93	**96**	96
German	94	87	**95**	94	88	82	90	95	94	92	93	91	90	89	95	96
Arabic	90	**96**	76	85	84	90	85	87	86	85	84	87	84	85	89	85
Mandarin	86	84	85	87	87	85	85	86	86	89	87	87	81	83	86	87
Turkish	67	61	61	65	71	62	64	69	75	77	71	73	73	68	68	74
Korean	51	53	63	53	61	52	51	54	59	65	59	59	57	55	54	61
Japanese	55	56	41	39	52	63	51	52	52	54	55	54	58	53	51	54

	pl pud	pt pud	ru pud	ru syntag	sv pud	eu bdt	hi pud	tr pud	ja gsd	ja pud	ko pud	vi vtb	th pud	zh gsd	zh pud	mean
English	95	**97**	93	93	96	**88**	87	83	66	70	67	**82**	**84**	67	71	88.9
Russian	**98**	95	**100**	**99**	95	**88**	90	90	68	72	70	79	80	64	69	**89.2**
Czech	97	93	94	96	92	87	88	88	64	66	68	78	79	65	71	87.5
French	**98**	96	96	97	94	85	**89**	86	54	61	66	77	76	63	69	87.0
German	89	94	93	88	**97**	81	86	78	59	62	57	78	78	67	68	85.2
Arabic	85	86	88	85	89	71	70	65	63	66	59	74	79	66	65	80.3
Mandarin	85	85	86	85	86	82	87	89	80	78	77	74	80	**91**	**86**	84.6
Turkish	76	73	71	71	69	79	83	**94**	82	83	88	63	68	72	71	72.3
Korean	66	58	59	59	53	74	76	**94**	87	88	88	52	61	67	66	63.1
Japanese	54	52	55	55	50	57	63	88	**99**	**98**	**95**	54	70	72	66	60.3

Table 2: Performance of zero-shot models. Rows: source languages; columns: target languages and corpora. Underlined values fail to beat the majority-class baseline (always predict subordinate clause). See § A.1 for language abbreviations and § A.2 for details about corpora.

mance on Hindi, with which it shares a relatively flexible SOV order.

Another language with strong SOV tendencies is Mandarin Chinese, which has been argued to be in transition from SVO to SOV order (Sun and Givón, 1985). Mandarin, which we already found difficult to model in § 3, is very hard to generalise to, with no source languages attaining accuracy above 71–72%. Tellingly, Turkish is the only other language with decent results on both Mandarin test sets. Mandarin is also the only language to always beat the majority-class baseline.

4.2 Case Study: English–Mandarin

In order to get a better understanding of the difficulties that models face in the zero-shot setting we analysed the mistakes that the English-based fine-tuned model made when making predictions on Mandarin data.

Setting aside errors stemming from annotation discrepancies,[5] the major source of model mistakes seems to be the fact that Mandarin complex sentences are predominantly right-headed: 99% of `advcl`, 100% of `acl`, and 96% of `dep`[6] have their parent node to the right. In contrast, 75% of English `advcl` and 98% of English `acl` are left-headed in PUD. This makes an English-based zero-shot model prejudiced against finding `root` nodes in the final clause of the sentence, and it incorrectly analyses a wide range of right-headed Mandarin complex clauses. Statistically, there are 142 sentence-initial subordinate clauses mistakenly analysed as main clauses and only 6 reverse errors. By contrast, there are 278 sentence-final main clauses mistakenly analysed as subordinate ones and 82 reverse errors.

Sometimes this divergence further interacts with ways in which English and Mandarin alternate between clause coordination and subordination. Thus, Mandarin tends to describe sequences of events as a pair of an adverbial clause and a main clause (*after having taken a shower, he dried himself*) instead of as two coordinated clauses (*he took a shower and dried himself*). English UD treats the first conjoined clause as the matrix one, while it is often `advcl` in Mandarin, and the absence of overt unambiguous complementisers makes it hard

[5] E.g., as discussed in §3, the model expects direct quotes to have the form `ccomp` (quote) + `root` (verb of speech) and not `root` (quote) + `parataxis` (verb of speech).

[6] `dep` labels different kinds of hard-to-analyse relations and is frequent in Mandarin PUD (397 occurrences).

for the model to see beyond mere frequencies.

A similar situation obtains with some English postposed descriptive subordinate clauses, such as *it's X–that Y* constructions[7] and non-restrictive relative clauses.[8] In these cases, Mandarin uses a coordinative construction, in which the head, according to the UD analysis, is on the right conjunct, corresponding to the English `acl`, and the first conjunct is attached to it using the `dep` label. Again, the English-based model expects to find the root in the first of the two clauses, and there is no overt complementiser to suggest otherwise.

4.3 Attention Patterns

An analysis of the properties of the models underlying these findings is beyond the scope of this paper, but preliminary checks of the attention patterns show that successful models strongly attend to complementisers in the last two layers. As SVO and VSO languages tend to have complementisers before subordinate clauses and SOV languages after (Hawkins, 1990), fine-tuning biases models towards looking for them in only one direction. The attention of subordinate-clause heads to main-clause heads is weaker, presumably due to higher lexical variety in that position.

5 Related Work

Both aspects of our analysis – subordinate-clause detection and the study of word-order effects – have been addressed but not in conjunction and not in a multiple-source-language setting. Our study extends previous approaches by providing a ZS 'upper baseline' derived from the study of the performance of several monolingual models and then conducting a novel many-sources-to-many-target analysis of zero-shot performance.

Lin et al. (2019) test BERT on the auxiliary-classification task (main vs. subordinate clause) as part of their investigation of BERT's linguistic knowledge. Rönnqvist et al. (2019) extend this analysis to the multilingual setting with a focus on Nordic languages.

Word-order differences have been shown to impact the performance of English-based cross-lingual models, especially in the domain of syntactic parsing (Ahmad et al., 2019) and with tasks that rely on syntactic information (Liu et al., 2020; Arviv et al., 2021), while reordering has been long known to be an efficient preprocessing step in syntactic transfer (Rasooli and Collins, 2019) and machine translation, both statistical (Wang et al., 2007) and neural (Chen et al., 2019).

6 Conclusion

We extend previous work on syntactic capabilities of BERT, mostly focusing on English, by providing a more comprehensive analysis of its performance on the task of subordinate-clause detection in multiple languages and language pairs in the zero-shot setting. We show that the performance of single-language models is uneven across languages: East and Southeast Asian languages with less rigid boundaries between POS categories and coordination and subordination prove harder to model. We also show that mBERT's performance in the zero-shot setting, while being largely correlated with the size of the pre-training and fine-tuning corpora, with Russian being the best source language across the board, is well aligned with the word-order typology: language pairs with congruent word orders demonstrate better results, with both SVO and SOV orders having higher in-group than across-group accuracies. A single pair of VSO languages in the data further corroborates this finding, showing that the verb-final order is not important *per se*.

The clause-initial position of complementisers in VSO languages partly blurs this effect and helps SVO languages with large training corpora serve as good sources for fine-tuning, but even Russian and English fail on SOV languages, where complementisers tend to be postposed and dependent-clause predicates never appear in the sentence-final position. This shows that at least for some tasks, training on a single source language is not enough. Moreover, our results from single-language modelling seem to indicate that even superficially simple syntactic tasks vary in difficulty across languages, which imposes a hard limit on how well cross-lingual projection can perform.

Acknowledgements

We thank Lilja Maria Sæbø and Chih-Yi Lin for their help with the analysis of Mandarin Chinese data and Dojun Park for his help with the analysis of Korean.

[7] *It's fantastic that they got the Paris Agreement, but...*

[8] *However, they could not find this same pattern in tissues such as the bladder, which are not directly exposed.*

References

Wasi Ahmad, Zhisong Zhang, Xuezhe Ma, Eduard Hovy, Kai-Wei Chang, and Nanyun Peng. 2019. On difficulties of cross-lingual transfer with order differences: A case study on dependency parsing. In *Proceedings of the 2019 Conference of the North American Chapter of the Association for Computational Linguistics: Human Language Technologies, Volume 1 (Long and Short Papers)*, pages 2440–2452, Minneapolis, Minnesota. Association for Computational Linguistics.

Ofir Arviv, Dmitry Nikolaev, Taelin Karidi, and Omri Abend. 2021. On the relation between syntactic divergence and zero-shot performance. In *Proceedings of the 2021 Conference on Empirical Methods in Natural Language Processing*, pages 4803–4817, Online and Punta Cana, Dominican Republic. Association for Computational Linguistics.

Eduard Bejček, Eva Hajičová, Jan Hajič, Pavlína Jínová, Václava Kettnerová, Veronika Kolářová, Marie Mikulová, Jiří Mírovský, Anna Nedoluzhko, Jarmila Panevová, Lucie Poláková, Magda Ševčíková, Jan Štěpánek, and Šárka Zikánová. 2013. Prague dependency treebank 3.0. LINDAT/CLARIAH-CZ digital library at the Institute of Formal and Applied Linguistics (ÚFAL), Faculty of Mathematics and Physics, Charles University.

Riyaz Ahmad Bhat, Rajesh Bhatt, Annahita Farudi, Prescott Klassen, Bhuvana Narasimhan, Martha Palmer, Owen Rambow, Dipti Misra Sharma, Ashwini Vaidya, Sri Ramagurumurthy Vishnu, et al. 2017. The Hindi/Urdu treebank project. In *Handbook of Linguistic Annotation*. Springer Press.

Johannes Bjerva and Isabelle Augenstein. 2021. Does typological blinding impede cross-lingual sharing? In *Proceedings of the 16th Conference of the European Chapter of the Association for Computational Linguistics: Main Volume*, pages 480–486, Online. Association for Computational Linguistics.

Emanuel Borges Völker, Maximilian Wendt, Felix Hennig, and Arne Köhn. 2019. HDT-UD: A very large Universal Dependencies treebank for German. In *Proceedings of the Third Workshop on Universal Dependencies (UDW, SyntaxFest 2019)*, pages 46–57, Paris, France. Association for Computational Linguistics.

Kehai Chen, Rui Wang, Masao Utiyama, and Eiichiro Sumita. 2019. Neural machine translation with reordering embeddings. In *Proceedings of the 57th Annual Meeting of the Association for Computational Linguistics*, pages 1787–1799, Florence, Italy. Association for Computational Linguistics.

Ethan A. Chi, John Hewitt, and Christopher D. Manning. 2020. Finding universal grammatical relations in multilingual BERT. In *Proceedings of the 58th Annual Meeting of the Association for Computational Linguistics*, pages 5564–5577, Online. Association for Computational Linguistics.

Sungdai Cho and John Whitman. 2020. *Korean: A linguistic introduction*. Cambridge University Press, Cambridge; New York.

Jayeol Chun, Na-Rae Han, Jena D. Hwang, and Jinho D. Choi. 2018. Building Universal Dependency treebanks in Korean. In *Proceedings of the Eleventh International Conference on Language Resources and Evaluation (LREC 2018)*, Miyazaki, Japan. European Language Resources Association (ELRA).

Bernard Comrie. 1981. *Language universals and linguistic typology*. University of Chicago Press, Chicago, IL.

Jacob Devlin, Ming-Wei Chang, Kenton Lee, and Kristina Toutanova. 2019. BERT: Pre-training of deep bidirectional transformers for language understanding. In *Proceedings of the 2019 Conference of the North American Chapter of the Association for Computational Linguistics: Human Language Technologies, Volume 1 (Long and Short Papers)*, pages 4171–4186, Minneapolis, Minnesota. Association for Computational Linguistics.

Matthew S. Dryer and Martin Haspelmath, editors. 2013. *WALS Online*. Max Planck Institute for Evolutionary Anthropology, Leipzig.

Bruno Guillaume, Marie-Catherine de Marneffe, and Guy Perrier. 2019. Conversion et améliorations de corpus du français annotés en universal dependencies. *Revue TAL*, 60(2):71–95.

Jan Hajič, Otakar Smrž, Petr Zemánek, Petr Pajas, Jan Šnaidauf, Emanuel Beška, Jakub Kracmar, and Kamila Hassanová. 2009. Prague arabic dependency treebank 1.0. LINDAT/CLARIAH-CZ digital library at the Institute of Formal and Applied Linguistics (ÚFAL), Faculty of Mathematics and Physics, Charles University.

John A Hawkins. 1990. A parsing theory of word order universals. *Linguistic inquiry*, 21(2):223–261.

Ganesh Jawahar, Benoît Sagot, and Djamé Seddah. 2019. What does BERT learn about the structure of language? In *Proceedings of the 57th Annual Meeting of the Association for Computational Linguistics*, pages 3651–3657, Florence, Italy. Association for Computational Linguistics.

Nanjiang Jiang and Marie-Catherine de Marneffe. 2019. Evaluating BERT for natural language inference: A case study on the CommitmentBank. In *Proceedings of the 2019 Conference on Empirical Methods in Natural Language Processing and the 9th International Joint Conference on Natural Language Processing (EMNLP-IJCNLP)*, pages 6086–6091, Hong Kong, China. Association for Computational Linguistics.

Konstantinos Kogkalidis and Gijs Winholds. 2022. Discontinuous constituency and BERT: A case study of Dutch. *arXiv preprint arXiv:2203.01063*.

Yongjie Lin, Yi Chern Tan, and Robert Frank. 2019. Open sesame: Getting inside BERT's linguistic knowledge. In *Proceedings of the 2019 ACL Workshop BlackboxNLP: Analyzing and Interpreting Neural Networks for NLP*, pages 241–253, Florence, Italy. Association for Computational Linguistics.

Zihan Liu, Genta Indra Winata, Samuel Cahyawijaya, Andrea Madotto, Zhaojiang Lin, and Pascale Fung. 2020. On the importance of word order information in cross-lingual sequence labeling. *arXiv preprint arXiv:2001.11164*.

Amnon Lotan, Asher Stern, and Ido Dagan. 2013. TruthTeller: Annotating predicate truth. In *Proceedings of the 2013 Conference of the North American Chapter of the Association for Computational Linguistics: Human Language Technologies*, pages 752–757, Atlanta, Georgia. Association for Computational Linguistics.

Sabrina J Mielke, Zaid Alyafeai, Elizabeth Salesky, Colin Raffel, Manan Dey, Matthias Gallé, Arun Raja, Chenglei Si, Wilson Y Lee, Benoît Sagot, and Samson Tan. 2021. Between words and characters: A brief history of open-vocabulary modeling and tokenization in NLP. *arXiv preprint arXiv:2112.10508*.

Phuong-Thai Nguyen, Xuan-Luong Vu, Thi-Minh-Huyen Nguyen, Van-Hiep Nguyen, and Hong-Phuong Le. 2009. Building a large syntactically-annotated corpus of Vietnamese. In *Proceedings of the Third Linguistic Annotation Workshop (LAW III)*, pages 182–185, Suntec, Singapore. Association for Computational Linguistics.

Thanh Bon Nguyen, Thi Minh Huyen Nguyen, Laurent Romary, and Xuan Luong Vu. 2004. Lexical descriptions for Vietnamese language processing. In *The 1st International Joint Conference on Natural Language Processing - IJCNLP'04 / Workshop on Asian Language Resources*, Sanya, Hainan Island, China. Colloque avec actes et comité de lecture. internationale.

Dmitry Nikolaev, Taelin Karidi, Neta Kenneth, Veronika Mitnik, Lilja Saeboe, and Omri Abend. 2020. Morphosyntactic predictability of translationese. *Linguistics Vanguard*, 6(1).

Joakim Nivre, Marie-Catherine de Marneffe, Filip Ginter, Jan Hajič, Christopher D. Manning, Sampo Pyysalo, Sebastian Schuster, Francis Tyers, and Daniel Zeman. 2020. Universal Dependencies v2: An evergrowing multilingual treebank collection. In *Proceedings of the 12th Language Resources and Evaluation Conference*, pages 4034–4043, Marseille, France. European Language Resources Association.

Telmo Pires, Eva Schlinger, and Dan Garrette. 2019. How multilingual is multilingual BERT? In *Proceedings of the 57th Annual Meeting of the Association for Computational Linguistics*, pages 4996–5001, Florence, Italy. Association for Computational Linguistics.

Ella Rabinovich, Noam Ordan, and Shuly Wintner. 2017. Found in translation: Reconstructing phylogenetic language trees from translations. In *Proceedings of the 55th Annual Meeting of the Association for Computational Linguistics (Volume 1: Long Papers)*, pages 530–540, Vancouver, Canada. Association for Computational Linguistics.

Mohammad Sadegh Rasooli and Michael Collins. 2019. Low-resource syntactic transfer with unsupervised source reordering. In *Proceedings of the 2019 Conference of the North American Chapter of the Association for Computational Linguistics: Human Language Technologies, Volume 1 (Long and Short Papers)*, pages 3845–3856, Minneapolis, Minnesota. Association for Computational Linguistics.

Anna Rogers, Olga Kovaleva, and Anna Rumshisky. 2020. A primer in BERTology: What we know about how BERT works. *Transactions of the Association for Computational Linguistics*, 8:842–866.

Samuel Rönnqvist, Jenna Kanerva, Tapio Salakoski, and Filip Ginter. 2019. Is multilingual BERT fluent in language generation? In *Proceedings of the First NLPL Workshop on Deep Learning for Natural Language Processing*, pages 29–36, Turku, Finland. Linköping University Electronic Press.

Punardeep Sikka and Vijay Mago. 2020. A survey on text simplification. *arXiv preprint arXiv:2008.08612*.

Chao-Fen Sun and Talmy Givón. 1985. On the so-called SOV word order in Mandarin Chinese: A quantified text study and its implications. *Language*, pages 329–351.

Roelien C Timmer, David Liebowitz, Surya Nepal, and Salil S Kanhere. 2021. Can pre-trained transformers be used in detecting complex sensitive sentences? – A Monsanto case study. In *2021 Third IEEE International Conference on Trust, Privacy and Security in Intelligent Systems and Applications (TPS-ISA)*, pages 90–97. IEEE.

Reut Tsarfaty. 2013. A unified morpho-syntactic scheme of Stanford dependencies. In *Proceedings of the 51st Annual Meeting of the Association for Computational Linguistics (Volume 2: Short Papers)*, pages 578–584, Sofia, Bulgaria. Association for Computational Linguistics.

Chao Wang, Michael Collins, and Philipp Koehn. 2007. Chinese syntactic reordering for statistical machine translation. In *Proceedings of the 2007 Joint Conference on Empirical Methods in Natural Language Processing and Computational Natural Language Learning (EMNLP-CoNLL)*, pages 737–745, Prague, Czech Republic. Association for Computational Linguistics.

Thomas Wolf, Lysandre Debut, Victor Sanh, Julien Chaumond, Clement Delangue, Anthony Moi, Pierric Cistac, Tim Rault, Remi Louf, Morgan Funtowicz, Joe Davison, Sam Shleifer, Patrick von Platen,

Clara Ma, Yacine Jernite, Julien Plu, Canwen Xu, Teven Le Scao, Sylvain Gugger, Mariama Drame, Quentin Lhoest, and Alexander Rush. 2020. Transformers: State-of-the-art natural language processing. In *Proceedings of the 2020 Conference on Empirical Methods in Natural Language Processing: System Demonstrations*, pages 38–45, Online. Association for Computational Linguistics.

Daniel Zeman, Martin Popel, Milan Straka, Jan Hajič, Joakim Nivre, Filip Ginter, Juhani Luotolahti, Sampo Pyysalo, Slav Petrov, Martin Potthast, Francis Tyers, Elena Badmaeva, Memduh Gokirmak, Anna Nedoluzhko, Silvie Cinková, Jan Hajič jr., Jaroslava Hlaváčová, Václava Kettnerová, Zdeňka Urešová, Jenna Kanerva, Stina Ojala, Anna Missilä, Christopher D. Manning, Sebastian Schuster, Siva Reddy, Dima Taji, Nizar Habash, Herman Leung, Marie-Catherine de Marneffe, Manuela Sanguinetti, Maria Simi, Hiroshi Kanayama, Valeria de Paiva, Kira Droganova, Héctor Martínez Alonso, Çağrı Çöltekin, Umut Sulubacak, Hans Uszkoreit, Vivien Macketanz, Aljoscha Burchardt, Kim Harris, Katrin Marheinecke, Georg Rehm, Tolga Kayadelen, Mohammed Attia, Ali Elkahky, Zhuoran Yu, Emily Pitler, Saran Lertpradit, Michael Mandl, Jesse Kirchner, Hector Fernandez Alcalde, Jana Strnadová, Esha Banerjee, Ruli Manurung, Antonio Stella, Atsuko Shimada, Sookyoung Kwak, Gustavo Mendonça, Tatiana Lando, Rattima Nitisaroj, and Josie Li. 2017. CoNLL 2017 shared task: Multilingual parsing from raw text to Universal Dependencies. In *Proceedings of the CoNLL 2017 Shared Task: Multilingual Parsing from Raw Text to Universal Dependencies*, pages 1–19, Vancouver, Canada. Association for Computational Linguistics.

Xinliang Frederick Zhang and Marie-Catherine de Marneffe. 2021. Identifying inherent disagreement in natural language inference. In *Proceedings of the 2021 Conference of the North American Chapter of the Association for Computational Linguistics: Human Language Technologies*, pages 4908–4915, Online. Association for Computational Linguistics.

A Appendix

A.1 Abbreviations

af Afrikaans

ar Standard Arabic

cs Czech

cy Welsh

de German

en English

es Spanish

eu Basque

ga Irish

fi Finnish

fr French

he Hebrew

hi Hindi

hy Eastern Armenian

id Indonesian

is Icelandic

it Italian

ja Japanese

ko Korean

pl Polish

pt Portuguese

ru Russian

sv Swedish

th Thai

tr Turkish

vi Vietnamese

zh Mandarin Chinese

A.2 Corpora

In addition to the Parallel Universal Dependencies collection (Zeman et al., 2017), the following corpora were used to train and/or validate models:

- Afribooms: UD Afrikaans-AfriBooms, `https://github.com/UniversalDependencies/UD_Afrikaans-AfriBooms`
- ArmTDP: Universal Dependencies treebank for Eastern Armenian, `https://github.com/UniversalDependencies/UD_Armenian-ArmTDP`
- BDT: Basque UD treebank, `https://github.com/UniversalDependencies/UD_Basque-BDT`
- CCG: Corpws Cystrawennol y Gymraeg (Syntactic Corpus of Welsh), `https://github.com/UniversalDependencies/UD_Welsh-CCG`
- EWT: Universal Dependencies English Web Treebank, `https://github.com/UniversalDependencies/UD_English-EWT`
- GSD (French): UD French GSD, `https://github.com/UniversalDependencies/UD_French-GSD` (Guillaume et al., 2019)
- GSD (Japanese): UD Japanese Treebank, `https://github.com/UniversalDependencies/UD_Japanese-GSD`
- GSD (Korean): Google Korean Universal Dependency Treebank, `https://github.com/UniversalDependencies/UD_Korean-GSD` (Chun et al., 2018)
- GSD (Mandarin): Traditional Chinese Universal Dependencies Treebank, `https://github.com/UniversalDependencies/UD_Chinese-GSD`

- GSD (Spanish): Spanish UD treebank, `https://github.com/UniversalDependencies/UD_Chinese-GSD`

- HDT: UD version of the Hamburg Dependency Treebank, `https://github.com/UniversalDependencies/UD_German-HDT` (Borges Völker et al., 2019)

- HDTB: Hindi Universal Dependency Treebank, `https://github.com/UniversalDependencies/UD_Hindi-HDTB` (Bhat et al., 2017)

- HTB: Universal Dependencies Corpus for Hebrew, `https://github.com/UniversalDependencies/UD_Hebrew-HTB` (Tsarfaty, 2013)

- IDT: Irish UD Treebank, `https://github.com/UniversalDependencies/UD_Irish-IDT`

- KENET: Turkish-Kenet UD Treebank, `https://github.com/UniversalDependencies/UD_Turkish-Kenet`

- PADT: UD version of the Prague Arabic Dependency Treebank, `https://github.com/UniversalDependencies/UD_Arabic-PADT` (Hajič et al., 2009)

- PDT: UD version of the Prague Dependency Treebank, `https://github.com/UniversalDependencies/UD_Czech-PDT` (Bejček et al., 2013)

- Syntagrus: SynTagRus Dependency Treebank, `https://github.com/UniversalDependencies/UD_Russian-SynTagRus`

- VTB: UD version of the VLSP constituency treebank, `https://github.com/UniversalDependencies/UD_Vietnamese-VTB` (Nguyen et al., 2009)

A.3 Single-language model results

The results attained by the models fine-tuned and tested on the same language are shown in Table 3. See § A.2 for the details about the train and test corpora.

Language	Train corpus	Test corpus	Model	#Train	#Test	Main-Main	Main-Sub	Sub-Main	Sub-Sub	Acc.
Mandarin	GSD-Train	PUD	mBERT	3196	736	556	180	122	1364	86.4
Mandarin	GSD-Train	PUD	HFL-BERT-WWM	3196	736	570	166	85	1401	88.7
Vietnamese	VTB-Train	VTB-Dev	mBERT	1105	619	510	109	90	1283	90
Korean	GSD-Train	PUD	mBERT	2201	618	603	15	149	936	90.4
Arabic	PADT-Train	PUD	mBERT	3755	520	436	84	31	752	91.2
Hindi	HDTB-Train	PUD	mBERT	5167	565	506	59	32	831	93.6
German	HDT-Train	PUD	mBERT	55938	441	427	14	49	578	94.1
Armenian	ArmTDP-Train	ArmTDP-Dev	mBERT	1165	149	145	4	21	269	94.3
Turkish	KENET-Train	PUD	mBERT	6784	731	653	78	25	1338	95.1
Welsh	CCG-Train	CCG-Dev	mBERT	377	341	315	26	27	824	95.6
Indonesian	GSD-Train	PUD	mBERT	2770	572	553	19	42	923	96
Basque	BDT-Train	BDT-Dev	mBERT	3181	1029	979	50	39	1758	96.9
Spanish	GSD-Train	PUD	mBERT	7247	548	513	35	5	824	97.1
Irish	IDT-Train	IDT-Dev	mBERT	2323	236	226	10	8	441	97.4
English	EWT-Train	PUD	BERT-LARGE-CASED	5968	556	529	27	4	915	97.9
Hebrew	HTB-Train	HTB-Dev	mBERT	2342	206	201	5	4	297	98.2
Afrikaans	Afribooms-Train	Afribooms-Train	mBERT	643	97	96	1	2	142	98.8
French	GSD-Train	PUD	mBERT	7712	572	563	9	6	956	99
Japanese	GSD-Train	PUD	TOHOKU-BERT-LARGE	5101	844	838	8	18	2090	99.1
Czech	PDT-Train	PUD	mBERT	26277	504	502	2	3	779	99.6
Russian	Syntagrus-Train	PUD	mBERT	32851	595	593	2	2	961	99.7

Table 3: Performance of single-language models across languages. #Train and #Test denote the number of sentences in the train and test corpus respectively. In the 'Main-Main', 'Main-Sub', 'Sub-Main', and 'Sub-Sub' columns, the part before the hyphen is the gold label of a predicate (main/subordinate clause) and the second part is the guessed label. Acc: Accuracy.

Typological Word Order Correlations with Logistic Brownian Motion

Kai Hartung[1], Gerhard Jäger[2], Sören Gröttrup[1], and Munir Georges[1,3,4]

[1]Technische Hochschule Ingolstad, Germany
[2]Universität Tübingen, Germany
[3]Research Institute AImotion Bavaria, Ingolstadt, Germany
[4]Intel Labs, Munich, Germany
{kai.hartung, soeren.groettrup, munir.georges}@thi.de
gerhard.jaeger@uni-tuebingen.de

Abstract

In this study we address the question to what extent syntactic word-order traits of different languages have evolved under correlation and whether such dependencies can be found universally across all languages or restricted to specific language families. To do so, we use logistic Brownian Motion under a Bayesian framework to model the trait evolution for 768 languages from 34 language families. We test for trait correlations both in single families and universally over all families.

Separate models reveal no universal correlation patterns and Bayes Factor analysis of models over all covered families also strongly indicate lineage specific correlation patters instead of universal dependencies.

1 Introduction

Over the long time of their history, humans have come to develop a wide variety of languages. Overall, these languages share basic structural similarities. The nature and extent of these similarities have been subject of many theories. As language structure is mostly described in terms of syntax trees, these are often used as explanatory models for structural confines of possibly observable word orders in different languages. The explanations for such confines differ from Chomskian innate universal grammar (Chomsky, 1986), to more general aspects of computational ease of for the brain (Hawkins, 2009). On the other hand, increasing data about languages and computational means have prompted examinations of which structural universalities can be found empirically (Greenberg, 1963; Dryer, 1992; Dunn et al., 2011; Jäger, 2018).

More recent representatives of this start also to account for the historical evolution and relationships of the researched languages (Dunn et al., 2011; Jäger, 2018). By treating the evolution of languages analogous to biological evolution, they apply a method from bioinformatics (Pagel et al., 2004) to model historical transition rates between word-order traits. For Dunn et al (2011) the focus lay on four language families: Austronesian, Bantu, Indo-European and Uto-Aztecan. Across those they found widely differing trait correlations, proposing that correlations arise only specific to lineages and not from cognitive factors universally determining language evolution, but instead due to more local cultural evolution.

Jäger (2018) applied the models on a set of 34 families including models which cover all families at once comparing universal with lineage-specific correlations. This comparison resulted in a group of word-order traits being correlated universally. This suggests that phylogenetic models for individual language families cannot fully capture the universal correlations between different families.

In this work, we attempted to test this assumption with a different phylogenetic model. We used Brownian Motion to describe the evolutionary process of the trait change over time. This type of application is common in a biological phylogenetic context. It is described by, e.g., Harmon (2018). The Brownian Motion part of the model below is also based on this description. We then applied logistic linkage to model the observed categorical features of word order with a binomial distribution.

The paper is structured as follows. Section 2 describes the Brownian Motion models used. Section 3 will give a short overview of the data. The experimental setup is described in Section 4. Finally, we present the results in Section 5, followed by the conclusions in Section 6.

2 Brownian Motion Model

A Brownian Motion model is used in this study. It describes the process of evolutionary change of specified traits through time as a multivariate normal distribution. We denote it here as

$$x \sim MultiNormal(a, V) \qquad (1)$$

Proceedings of the 4th Workshop on Computational Typology and Multilingual NLP (SIGTYP 2022), pages 22 - 26
July 14, 2022 ©2022 Association for Computational Linguistics

with means a and Variance-Covariance matrix V, describing the distribution of the observed traits x.

Let V be the variance-covariance matrix which is computed of two matrices C and R. C encodes the degree of relation t between species such that languages with a longer shared history in a phylogenetic tree have a stronger covariance. We then define R as the correlation matrix. It is composed of the traits' evolutionary rates σ_n^2 and their correlations σ_{12}:

$$R = \begin{pmatrix} \sigma_1^2 & \sigma_{12} \\ \sigma_{12} & \sigma_2^2 \end{pmatrix} \quad (2)$$

V is computed by the Kronecker product as shown below on the example of a family with two traits and two species:

$$V = R \otimes C = \begin{pmatrix} \sigma_1^2 & \sigma_{12} \\ \sigma_{12} & \sigma_2^2 \end{pmatrix} \otimes \begin{pmatrix} t_1 & t_{12} \\ t_{12} & t_2 \end{pmatrix}$$

$$= \begin{pmatrix} \sigma_1^2 \cdot t_1 & \sigma_{12} \cdot t_1 & \sigma_1^2 \cdot t_{12} & \sigma_{12} \cdot t_{12} \\ \sigma_{12} \cdot t_1 & \sigma_2^2 \cdot t_1 & \sigma_{12} \cdot t_{12} & \sigma_2^2 \cdot t_{12} \\ \\ \sigma_1^2 \cdot t_{12} & \sigma_{12} \cdot t_{12} & \sigma_1^2 \cdot t_2 & \sigma_{12} \cdot t_2 \\ \sigma_{12} \cdot t_{12} & \sigma_2^2 \cdot t_{12} & \sigma_{12} \cdot t_2 & \sigma_2^2 \cdot t_2 \end{pmatrix}$$

The means a and the correlation R are parameters to be estimated. The traits x and phylogenetic matrix C are observed data as described in the following section.

Finally, logistic linking is introduced to model the categorical word-order traits x as a binomial distribution with probabilities p. Their logits, $logistic(p)$ are modelled as Brownian Motion:

$$x \sim Binomial(p) \quad (3)$$

$$logistic(p) \sim MultiNormal(a, V) \quad (4)$$

3 Word-order Traits & language families

The data used in this paper are of two kinds. The first are language features that are to be modeled. The second are phylogenetic data used as basis for the evolutionary model. Combined, these provide data for 768 languages from 34 language families as described in more detail by Wichman et al. (Wichman et al., 2016). All data were kindly provided by Gerhard Jäger(2018). We provide the data as part of this work[1].

We considered the same eight word-order traits (table 1) as in Dunn et al.(2011) and Jäger (2018).

[1] https://github.com/Hartunka/TypologicalWordOrderCorrelations/tree/main/dataprep/dat

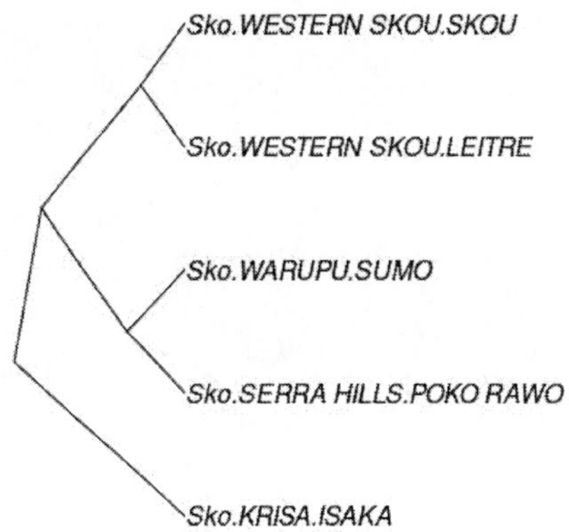

Figure 1: Example phylogenetic tree of the Sko language family.

These word order traits are based on the World Atlas of Languages (Dryer and Haspelmath, 2013), but their respective values are summarized into three possible values per trait. Each of these three values represents order configurations for the concerned syntactic elements. The first two classes represent the most dominant values. The third class summarizes all alternative configurations, appearing more rarely overall. For this work, we summarized the data as binary to be used in the binomial model. The distinction is only between a language having a value of the first majority class or not.

The phylogenetic data represent the languages' historical relations in the form of binary trees as for example in Figure 1. The trees' edge lengths represent the time since the last common ancestor split up. They have been estimated by Jäger (2018) and range from 10 to 1000 samples per family.

4 Experiments

In our experiments, we compared variations of this model with different base assumptions:

(A), we fitted two models to each of the 34 language families separately and pairwise to each of the eight traits. One version assumes strict independence of the traits by defining the trait correlations σ_{12} in R as constants with value 0. In the other version, the correlation between the characteristics is taken into account by keeping the values in R as parameters to be estimated. In this way, we could test whether we could find any correlation patterns by examining the families separately.

(B), we fitted three models for each trait pair, describing all language families together. Here

trait	0	1
AN	!adjective-noun	adjective-noun
PN	!postpositions	postpositions
ND	!demonstrative-noun	demonstrative-noun
NG	!genitive-noun	genitive-noun
NNum	!numeral-noun	numeral-noun
VO	!object-verb	object-verb
NRc	!relative clause-noun clause	relative clause-noun
VS	!subject-verb	subject-verb

Table 1: Word-order features based on WALS (Dryer and Haspelmath, 2013). The features are summarised as binary such that every feature is given either '1' for the listed value being present, or '0' for it being absent.

the first version assumes the same universal correlation R over all families. The second assumes distinct lineage-specific correlation R_F for each family. The last assumes strict universal independence for all families. The different versions were each compared with three different metrics. The first of these are Bayes Factors (Kass and Raftery, 1995), which allow a comparison with previous works (Dunn et al., 2011; Jäger, 2018). Bayes Factors above 10 indicate strong, values above 100 decisive evidence (Kass and Raftery, 1995). Further, we adopted 5 as minimum threshold for meaningful comparisons from Dunn et al. (2011). The Bayes Factors were obtained using bridgesampling (Gronau et al., 2020).

In addition, we used the information criteria WAIC (Watanabe and Opper, 2010) & LOOIC (Vehtari et al., 2016). These were added to test for consistency across different metrics. They are both based on pointwise log-likelihoods and can become unreliable, when dealing with strongly dependent data points (McElreath, 2020). Both express model comparisons primarily in differences where the value of the difference is not directly amenable to assess how strongly one model is favoured over another. To address this, we utilized the `rethinking` package by McElreath (2020). This offers a convenient function to compare models via WAIC including the assignment of weights ranging from 0 to 1 to give an accessible overview over the relative quality of the models.

The models were implemented in the Stan Modeling Language (2020) which uses the NUTS sampler (Hoffman et al., 2014) for parameter estimation. The code is available here[2] . Based on the suggestion of (Gronau et al., 2020) the models are run for 21,000 iterations after warm-up, to achieve reliable Bayes factors. Distributed on 14 chains, this becomes 1.500 iterations per chain, in addition to 1,500 warm-up iterations each. The sampling was done with the default control parameters for Stan's sampler. With these parameters the lineage-specific models of the ND-NNum trait pair and the independent models of the NG-VO & AN-VO trait pairs did return a too small effective sample size for the bridgesampling to be effective. So these models were rerun with `max_treedepth` raised from 10 to 15.

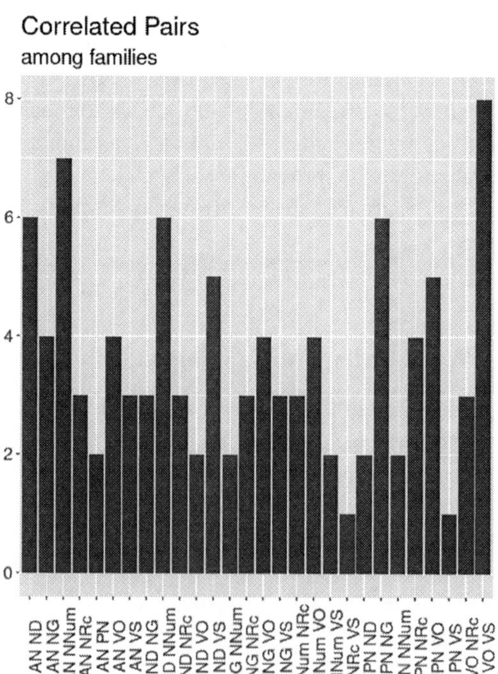

Figure 2: Numbers of families for which each trait pair was estimated to be correlated. Counts all cases for which Bayes Factors in favour of the dependent model have a value of at least five.

[2] `https://github.com/Hartunka/TypologicalWordOrderCorrelations`

5 Results

For the single-family models, the comparisons did not yield Bayes factors above 5 for 15 of the 34 families. Therefore, no conclusions about preferred models are possible in those cases. Those trait correlations that did come up, only appeared in a minority of the covered families, not providing any pattern for universal correlations. Figure 2 shows for each trait pair in how many families it was estimated to be correlated.

The information criteria at face value find up to 22 families for which the same trait-pair is correlated. We filtered cases close to equivalence with WAIC weights to test how many cases have a robust preference. We chose the cutoff at 0.6. Filtering such cases results in less cross-family similarities, with no more than 3 families sharing the same trait pair as correlated. Cross-metric agreement: The percentage of model comparisons where Bayes Factors & WAIC weights favoured the same model or both don't favour any model at all is 85.5% with a LOOIC & WAIC agreement of 99.8%.

The model comparison between universal and lineage specific models strongly favour lineage specificity, with Bayes Factors favouring lineage-specific correlation for each trait pair (Figure 3).

In contrast to single family models, Bayes Factors and information criteria strongly disagree. Both WAIC & LOOIC strongly favour universal correlation models for each trait pair. WAIC weights are fully assigned to the universal models. Comparing lineage specificity with universal independence shows similar results. Bayes Factors strongly favour lineage-specificity but information criteria favour independence.

Universal trait pair correlations, based on the dependent-independent model comparisons center around the Adposition-Noun order (Figure 4).

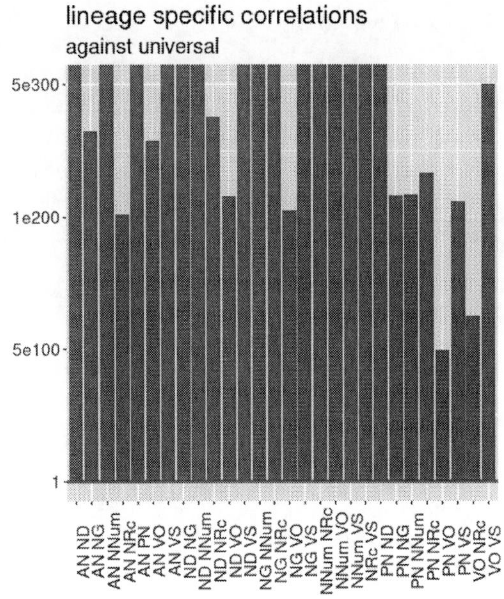

Figure 3: Model comparisons of lineage-specific vs universal correlations. The y-axis shows the strength of the Bayes Factors in favour of the models with lineage-specific correlations for each trait pair on the x-axis.

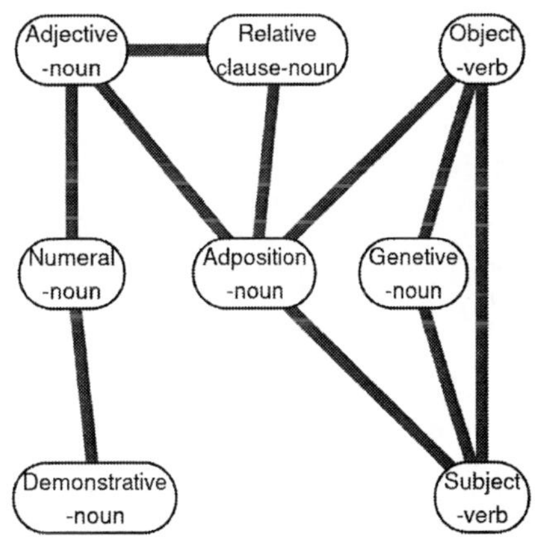

Figure 4: Universal trait correlations from directly comparing dependence and independence assumptions. For connected trait pairs, the dependence assumption is stronger in terms of Bayes Factors.

6 Conclusions

We applied logistic Brownian Motion under a Bayesian framework to model the trait evolution for 768 languages from 34 language families. The models for single language families and those across all families indicate no universal word-order trait correlations across language families when compared using Bayes Factors.

This result matches with the observations made by Dunn et al.(2011), but contradicts the results over all families presented by Jäger (2018). Thus, representing all families in one model did not add much information to single family models.

It is noteworthy, that the results from the information criteria contradict those from the Bayes Factors regarding the universal models. Although this could be attributed to some unreliability of the information criteria given the data and the nature of the model, it is still worth further investigation.

Acknowledgements

This research was supported by the DFG Centre for Advanced Studies in the Humanities Words, Bones, Genes, Tools (DFG-KFG 2237) and by the European Research Council (ERC) under the European Union's Horizon 2020 research and innovation programme (Grant agreement 834050).

References

Noam Chomsky. 1986. *Knowledge of language: Its nature, origin, and use*. Greenwood Publishing Group.

Matthew S Dryer. 1992. The greenbergian word order correlations. *Language*, pages 81–138.

Matthew S. Dryer and Martin Haspelmath, editors. 2013. *WALS Online*. Max Planck Institute for Evolutionary Anthropology, Leipzig.

Michael Dunn, Simon J Greenhill, Stephen C Levinson, and Russell D Gray. 2011. Evolved structure of language shows lineage-specific trends in word-order universals. *Nature*, 473(7345):79–82.

Joseph Greenberg. 1963. Some universals of grammar with particular reference to the order of meaningful elements. *In J. Greenberg, ed., Universals of Language. 73-113. Cambridge, MA.*

Quentin F. Gronau, Henrik Singmann, and Eric-Jan Wagenmakers. 2020. bridgesampling: An R package for estimating normalizing constants. *Journal of Statistical Software*, 92(10):1–29.

Luke Harmon. 2018. *Phylogenetic comparative methods: learning from trees*. EcoEvoRxiv.

John A Hawkins. 2009. Language universals and the performance-grammar correspondence hypothesis. *Language universals*, pages 54–78.

Matthew D Hoffman, Andrew Gelman, et al. 2014. The no-u-turn sampler: adaptively setting path lengths in hamiltonian monte carlo. *J. Mach. Learn. Res.*, 15(1):1593–1623.

Gerhard Jäger. 2018. A bayesian test of the lineage-specificity of word order correlations. In *12th International Conference on Language Evolution (Evolang XII), Torun.*

Robert E Kass and Adrian E Raftery. 1995. Bayes factors. *Journal of the american statistical association*, 90(430):773–795.

Richard McElreath. 2020. *Statistical rethinking: A Bayesian course with examples in R and Stan*. CRC press.

Mark Pagel, Andrew Meade, and Daniel Barker. 2004. Bayesian estimation of ancestral character states on phylogenies. *Systematic biology*, 53(5):673–684.

Stan Development Team. 2020. Stan Modeling Language Users Guide and Reference Manual, Version 2.21.0. `https://mc-stan.org`.

Aki Vehtari, Andrew Gelman, and Jonah Gabry. 2016. Practical bayesian model evaluation using leave-one-out cross-validation and waic. *Statistics and Computing*, 27(5):1413–1432.

Sumio Watanabe and Manfred Opper. 2010. Asymptotic equivalence of bayes cross validation and widely applicable information criterion in singular learning theory. *Journal of machine learning research*, 11(12).

Søren Wichman, Eric W. Holman, and Cecil H. Brown. 2016. The asjp database (version 17). `https://asjp.clld.org/`.

Cross-linguistic comparison of linguistic feature encoding in BERT models for typologically different languages

Yulia Otmakhova[1], **Karin Verspoor**[2], **Jey Han Lau**[1]
[1]The University of Melbourne, [2]RMIT University
yotmakhova@student.unimelb.edu.au, karin.verspoor@rmit.edu.au,
jeyhan.lau@gmail.com

Abstract

Though recently there have been an increased interest in how pre-trained language models encode different linguistic features, there is still a lack of systematic comparison between languages with different morphology and syntax. In this paper, using BERT as an example of a pre-trained model, we compare how three typologically different languages (English, Korean, and Russian) encode morphology and syntax features across different layers. In particular, we contrast languages which differ in a particular aspect, such as flexibility of word order, head directionality, morphological type, presence of grammatical gender, and morphological richness, across four different tasks.

1 Introduction

Transformers (Vaswani et al., 2017) and especially pre-trained language models based on them, such as BERT (Devlin et al., 2019), had a revolutionary impact on the field of Natural Language Processing (NLP), allowing to achieve new heights in classification, retrieval, text understanding, and generation tasks. However, though major progress was made in adapting Transformers to different downstream tasks, they largely remain black-box models, especially from the linguistic point of view. In particular, though we know that they roughly follow the same pipeline as human-made natural language processing (NLP) systems when encoding the features (the lower layers of a Transformer encode part-of-speech information, the middle layers perform syntax parsing, while the top layers enable such tasks as coreference resolution) (Tenney et al., 2019), it is still unclear if there is a systematic relation between the type of morphological, syntactical and discourse features encoded and particular layers of Transformer-based models. More importantly, though there have been some attempts to examine this for languages other than English (see, for example, a study by de Vries et al. (2020) for Dutch), we still do not know if there is a consistency between models for different languages in encoding such features, especially if the languages in question are typologically different. Thus it is important to analyse how Transformers encode different linguistic features for dissimilar languages, as it would help us to better understand how they work and ultimately allow to improve their performance in such tasks as translation or multi-lingual information retrieval and summarisation.

In this study, we compare how Transformers encode particular linguistic features for the following languages: English, Russian, and Korean. The choice of languages are motivated linguistically: English, Russian and Korean are morphologically very distant languages (analytical, fusional and agglutinative respectively) which are also different in term of syntax such as word order. To examine Transformers encodings more systematically, we conduct a series of pairwise comparisons of languages which contrast in a particular linguistic feature, similarly to how it is performed in theoretical linguistics. In particular, using targeted manipulation of inputs to produce a binary correctness classification or a masked token prediction task, we examine the following research questions:

1. How sensitive are the encoders and their particular layers to correct word orders in languages with fixed and free word order?

2. Does the encoding of word order depend on the morphological type of the language (agglutinative vs inflected) and on its head directionality (head-initial vs head-final)?

3. How well is long-distance agreement encoded for languages with rich and poor morphology and agreement patterns?

4. Are gender biases encoded more strongly in languages with agreement in gender?

Proceedings of the 4th Workshop on Computational Typology and Multilingual NLP (SIGTYP 2022), pages 27 - 35
July 14, 2022

In the following sections we describe our experiments for these tasks and present our findings.

2 Sensitivity to word order in languages with fixed vs free word order

In this section we compare the ability of a BERT-based classification model to detect the corruption of word order in languages with fixed vs free word order. We hypothesise that as languages with free word order allow for more permutations in terms of token positions in the sentences, it would be more difficult for the model to detect word order corruption.

2.1 Fixed and free word order

We use English as an example of a fixed word order language and Russian as a free word order language as they are related languages which typologically differ in one aspect: while in Russian the grammatical and syntactical meaning is mostly expressed through morphological means such as suffixes and particles which allows the words to be relatively unconstrained in terms of their position in the sentence, in English due to limited morphology the grammatical and syntactical meaning is linked to the position of a word in a sentence and thus the word order is fixed. For example, to show that the word "apples" is an object rather than a subject, it should occupy the position after the predicate (verb) in English:

Emma	ate	apples.
Subject	*Verb*	*Object*

On the other hand, in Russian the word "apples" can potentially occupy both the position before and after the verb without changing the meaning[1]:

Эмма	ела	яблоки
Emma	ate	apples.
Subject	*Verb*	*Object (normal word order)*
Яблоки	ела	Эмма.
Apples	ate	Emma.
Object	*Verb*	*Subject*
(inverted word order, more focus on "Emma")		

Despite this flexibility, the word order in Russian is not random or arbitrary: there is still a strong tendency for constituents (such as noun phrases and predicates) to occupy a particular position, and the movement of words across the constituent borders is very limited. However, as there is still more word movement allowed compared to English, we postulate that it would be more difficult to automatically detect ungrammatical word order changes in Russian than in English.

2.2 Dataset

For the experiments in this section we use UMC 0.1, a Czech-Russian-English corpus of news articles automatically aligned at sentence level (Klyueva and Bojar, 2008). We chose to use a parallel corpus for this task to ensure that the difficulty of classification is not affected by the syntactic complexity or the length of the sentences. We use the train/test data split provided by the authors of the corpus. For both the train and test data we remove the pairs where either the English or Russian sentence contains less than two tokens, since otherwise it is impossible to swap tokens. We also remove pairs where either of the sentences has over 100 tokens, as the task's difficulty would increase in case of very long inputs. The statistics of the resulting dataset are provided in Table 1.

2.2.1 Model and experiments

The *bigram shift* (BShift) probing task introduced by Conneau et al. (2018) allows to check the capability of a model to distinguish between sentences with correct and incorrect word orders. Specifically, it is a binary classifier which has to distinguish between intact sentences and sentences where some two random adjacent tokens were swapped. For this task, we randomly sample half of the sentences in the training and test datasets and corrupt the token order in them at a random position.

We use BERT-Base Cased (Devlin et al., 2019)[2] as a pre-trained model for English and RuBERT (Kuratov and Arkhipov, 2019)[3], which was initialized with the multilingual version of BERT-Base and trained on the Russian Wikipedia and news, for Russian. We choose these particular models as the most closely matching in terms of their architecture and parameters (12-layer, 768-hidden, 12-heads for both models, 110M parameters for BERT-Base Cased and 180M Parameters for RuBERT). Unlike most studies which use the uncased version of BERT, we choose the cased one, as only

[1]Though, as we explain in Section 3, there is a strong preference for the position after the verb.

[2]`https://huggingface.co/bert-base-cased`

[3]`https://huggingface.co/DeepPavlov/rubert-base-cased`

cased models are available for Russian.

To ensure that the classification results reflect the performance of the pre-trained model itself on the task, we add a only single linear layer on top of the pre-trained model, freeze the BERT layers, and train the model only for 1 epoch. For the training optimization we use Adam (Kingma and Ba, 2014) with the learning rate of 2e^{-5}. As usual for the classification tasks, we use the embedding of the first token [CLS] as the input to the linear layer. However, to explore how well the word order information is encoded in the different layers of the pre-trained model, we do this not only for the last layer, but for all layers in the pre-trained model.

2.3 Results

The results of the BShift classification tasks for all layers of BERT-Base Cased and RuBERT models are shown in Table 2. We report classification accuracy averaged over 5 runs with various random seeds. For all layers, the difference between the accuracy of the models was statistically significant, while the variation among the different runs was minimal, which shows that there is a visible difference in the ability of the Russian and English models to encode the correct word order.

In particular, though at lower layers the Russian model underperforms in terms of accuracy, it performs better than the English one at middle and higher layers. The English model also achieves its maximum performance at an earlier layer (5) than the Russian one (11). Both of these phenomena can be largely explained by the fact that the models' layers follow the so-called classic NLP pipeline (Tenney et al., 2019), where the lower layers specialize in lower-level language features such as parts of speech and other morphological information, the middle layers are responsible for more complex syntactic relations, while the higher layers deal with even more high-level language phenomena such as anaphora and coreference. Therefore, we might conclude that though it takes more layers for the Russian model to encode more complex morphology and syntax relations which are necessary to detect if the word order was corrupted, once it does that, it performs better on the task since the morphology of the inflected language binds the words together by the means of suffixes showing their gender, number, aspect, or tense. Thus, in contrast to our expectations, the free word order is not that free, as moving a word arbitrarily has a high probability of breaking such rich morphological and syntactical ties.

	Train		Test	
	EN	RU	EN	RU
Sentences	85663		2753	
Tokens	1798267	1599786	49642	44006

Table 1: Dataset statistics for the English vs Russian BShift task.

	EN	RU
Layer 1	0.786	0.903
Layer 2	0.902	0.867
Layer 3	0.893	0.824
Layer 4	0.926	0.855
Layer 5	0.931	0.937
Layer 6	0.903	0.944
Layer 7	0.895	0.945
Layer 8	0.893	0.935
Layer 9	0.875	0.935
Layer 10	0.869	0.944
Layer 11	0.873	0.948
Layer 12	0.863	0.911

Table 2: The accuracy of detecting word order corruption for the languages with fixed and free word order.

3 Sensitivity to word order corruption in agglutinative and inflected languages with different head directionality

In this section we compare the ability of pre-trained models to recognize word order corruption in such languages as Russian and Korean. We originally chose to analyse these languages as they differ in terms of head directionality (Haider, 2015) (see below) while both having a free word order. We hypothesized that since the attention mechanism in Transformer models (Vaswani et al., 2017) is able to capture the context to the both sides of a focus token, the performance on the word order corruption task should be comparable between these two languages. However, our experiments showed that some other aspects of these languages are affecting the task, namely the type of their morphology (inflected for Russian vs agglutinative for Korean).

3.1 Head directionality

Head directionality refers to the position of a head (main) word in a phrase relative to its subordinate word (Haider, 2015), and languages can be roughly categorized into head-initial and head-final. In head-initial languages such as Russian the verb (predicate) normally precedes the object (VO word order), while in head-final languages such as Korean they follow the object (OV word order) (Lehmann, 1973)[4]:

Эмма	ела	яблоки.
Emma	ate	apples.
Subject	*Verb*	*Object*

엠마는	사과를	먹었다
Emma	apples	ate.
Subject	*Object*	*Verb*

As head directionality essentially refers to the expected position of subordinates relative to head words, it affects the importance of right-hand and left-hand context of a focus (head) word in representing the input text. However, as the attention mechanism (Vaswani et al., 2017) allows to capture both the right-hand and left-hand context equally well, we hypothesised that there should not be a remarkable difference in word corruption detection between these two languages, i.e. neither VO nor OV syntax should make it more difficult for a direction-agnostic model.

3.2 Inflection vs agglutination

Both Korean and Russian are morphologically rich synthetical languages, that is, grammatical meaning is expressed by adding a diverse variety of morphemes to the lexical root. However, while in Russian morphemes expressing tense, aspect, gender, person, number etc are fused together and one suffix can thus carry several grammatical meanings, in Korean morphemes can be stacked on top of each other in various combinations. For example, while in Russian the verb иду ("I am going") is a fusion of a stem ид- and a morpheme у which simultaneously signifies present tense, inperfect aspect, single number, and 1st person, in Korean the verb 가고있어요 with the same meaning can be split into a stem 가 and a stack of morphemes: 고 (continuous aspect), 있어 (present tense), 요 (politeness marker). Such difference in morphology is reflected in approaches to tokenization: while in Russian texts are normally tokenized by space, i.e. each token represents a lexical item together with its grammatical meanings, in Korean words are usually split into stems and particles, each representing a distinct lexical or grammatical meaning. Thus, in this experiment we also compare how the tokenization before word order corruption affects the model's ability to recognize the latter.

3.3 Dataset

For this task, similar to Section 2, we use a parallel corpus of Russian and Korean sentences, this time based on TED talk subtitles[5]. We apply the same preprocessing steps, and randomly sample 10% of the sentences to create the training/test split. The statistics of the dataset are presented in Table 3.

3.4 Model and experiments

For this set of experiments we use the same RuBERT model for Russian as in Section 2; for Korean we use a similar BERT-Kor-base model[6]. We follow the same method for corrupting the word order, training and evaluation as in Section 2. However, for this task we restrict BShift to VO chunks for Russian and OV chunks for Korean. To do that, we apply part-of-speech tagging using morphological analysers for Russian (Korobov, 2015)[7] and Korean[8], and then restrict the application of BShift only to spans with a verb and the following (for Russian) or preceding (for Korean) noun.

We also experiment with two types of tokenization for BShift in Korean. For the first experiment, we tokenize the text using Kkma parser[8] and then swap the resulting tokens which can be lexical stems or grammatical particles; for the second one, we apply the usual whitespace tokenization and thus swap the whole words with grammatical particles attached to them. The reason for such setup is that we intend to compare the effect of swapping the entire lexical units vs swapping subunits, potentially including grammatical ones.

3.5 Results and discussion

Table 4 reports the accuracy of detecting the sentences which underwent BShift in Korean and Russian. For Korean, we report the results for two approaches to word order corruption described above.

The most striking finding is probably an almost perfect accuracy even at the lowest layers achieved by the Korean model with the native (morphology-based) tokenization, where morphological particals/subunits could potentially be switched. This

[4]As both languages are relatively free in their word order, VO structures are possible in Korean while OV structures are legal in Russian, but such word order is inverted or emphatic.

[5]https://github.com/ajinkyakulkarni14/TED-Multilingual-Parallel-Corpus

[6]https://huggingface.co/kykim/bert-kor-base

[7]https://pypi.org/project/pymorphy2/

[8]https://konlpy.org/en/v0.4.4/api/konlpy.tag

	Train			Test		
	KO1	KO2	RU	KO1	KO2	RU
Sentences		299769			33308	
Tokens	7477635	3597639	4283921	826887	397301	473650

Table 3: Dataset statistics for the Korean vs Russian BShift task. KO1 refers to BShift using morphology-based tokenization; KO2 refers to BShift based on whitespace tokenizer.

shows that the order of particles that are attached to the stem is strongly encoded even at the lowest layers of the model, i.e. the pre-trained model is aware of agglutination and learned the correct slots for suffixes with a particular meaning. On the other hand, compared to the Korean model with the native tokenization, the performance of the model where the BShift occurred after whitespace tokenization is considerably lower and worsens even more at higher levels. This shows that whitespace tokenization makes it much harder to recognize word swaps, as in that case the whole word moves together with its suffixes and thus the basic morphology is preserved.

Interestingly, the performance of the Russian model and the Korean model with whitespace-based corruption is very similar at the lowest (morphology) layers, which supports our claim that the attention mechanism is agnostic to head directionality at lower levels and can recognize incorrect word order equally well for both OV and VO languages. However, at higher layers, with more syntactic information taken into account, it becomes easier for the Russian model to recognize corruption, while the performance of the Korean model falls significantly.

Another thing to note is that the accuracy of classification for the Russian model is higher here than reported in Section 2, and the best results are achieved at lower RuBERT layers. This can be explained by the fact that we restricted possible movements to one type of structure, so the task is inherently easier and potentially requires less information about the syntactic structure; another reason for such discrepancy can simply be a much larger training dataset available for this task. Thus, though these experiments provide some intuition into the abilities of the models to encode word order information and detect different types of word order shift, more rigorous experiments across different datasets and with more exact and diverse chunking strategies are in order.

	KO1	KO2	RU
Layer 1	0.988	0.940	0.948
Layer 2	0.989	0.928	0.928
Layer 3	0.995	0.942	0.886
Layer 4	0.996	0.921	0.899
Layer 5	0.994	0.896	0.981
Layer 6	0.991	0.895	0.983
Layer 7	0.990	0.902	0.982
Layer 8	0.987	0.888	0.977
Layer 9	0.985	0.863	0.976
Layer 10	0.989	0.844	0.979
Layer 11	0.990	0.888	0.979
Layer 12	0.990	0.875	0.921

Table 4: The accuracy of word order corruption for an agglutinative SOV language vs inflected SVO language. KO1 refers to BShift using morphology-based tokenization; KO2 refers to BShift based on whitespace tokenization.

4 Long-distance agreement in morphologically rich and poor languages

In this task we test the ability of attention-based models to encode long-distance agreement, in particular the agreement in number (plural vs singular). We choose this task as it tests the model's ability to encode hierarchical syntactic structure, for example to determine the number of a verb based on the form of the noun related to it in the syntactic tree, rather than on the form of the closest noun.

4.1 Long-distance agreement

Agreement refers to a linguistic phenomenon where the grammatical form of one word depends on the form of another word. While in English agreement is restricted only to nouns and verbs in the present tense, in Russian nouns agree with verbs in all tenses and also with adjectives and some pronouns. Though in Russian words agree in several different grammatical aspects such as gender, person, case, and number, in this task we focus only on the number agreement as it is the only agreement type present in English. In particular, we focus on long-distance agreement, which occurs when a head word (cue) that determines the form of a dependent (target) is separated from it by intervening words (context). As such agreement requires the model to consider not only the nearby context but often far removed tokens that are nevertheless closely connected with the cue in terms of their position in the syntactic tree, it should be able to encode at least some hierarchical syntactic structure. We hypothesise that a higher performance can be achieved on this task for Russian, since the majority of parts of speech are marked for number there. Thus it is highly likely that there are some words in the context between the cue and target words that provide some clues for the correct long-distance agreement. Consider the following example:

Выросли	любимые	мамой	розы
Have grown	loved	by mom	roses
pl verb	*pl adj*	*sing noun*	*pl noun*

In this sentence, the words выросли (*have grown*) and розы (*roses*) should both have the plural form as they agree in number, but there is a noun in singular (*mom*) between them which can potentially interfere with the ability of the model to assign the correct plural number. However, unlike English, in Russian there is another word in the context between the cue and the target (любимые, *loved*) which has plural number and thus allows to infer the correct form.

4.2 Dataset

For this task we use the long-distance agreement test set created by Gulordava et al. (2018)[9]. We choose this dataset rather than a more popular agreement dataset by Linzen et al. (2016) as in addition to regular sentences with long-distance agreement the authors generate nonce sentences which retain the same syntactic structure but have no meaning. They do so by replacing all content words in a sentence by random words with the same grammatical properties; 9 nonce sentences are generated for each normal sentence in this manner. Gulordava et al. (2018) do so in attempt to disentangle the abilities of the model to capture syntactic and semantic information, as they notice that models tend to rely on semantic and lexical features such as frequency of co-occurance when resolving long-distance relationships. Thus, in the example above the model can choose the plural form of "have grown" for "roses" not because it learned to abstract such features as number and detect the long-distance relationships, but simply because "have grown" occurs more frequently around "roses" than "has grown" in the corpus it was trained on. To see how much of the performance on the task is due to such effect, the nonce sentences contain random words which are unlikely to frequently co-occur. Overall, the dataset contains 41 original vs 369 generated sentences for English and 442 original vs 3978 generated sentences for Russian.

4.3 Model and experiments

For this set of experiments we use BERT-Base Cased and RuBERT models introduced above, and BERT-Base Uncased model in addition to them. We compare the cased and uncased variants of the model to estimate the effect of capitalization on the encoding and detection of long-distance agreement.

We adapt the evaluation protocol proposed by Goldberg (2019) for our task. Namely, we cast it as a masked token prediction task where we replace the word which form we are trying to predict by [MASK]. To predict the token, we use a masked language model which is essentially a BERT model with a feed-forward network projecting onto the vocabulary. Then for each masked token we compare the probability of the word in the correct form (plural or singular) with the probability of the incorrect form (opposite in number). We consider the prediction to be correct if the probability of the expected token is strictly higher than then probability of the alternative form. As in the tasks above, we perform the experiments for all layers of the pre-trained models.

4.4 Results and discussion

	EN uncased		EN cased		RU cased	
	orig.	gen.	orig.	gen.	orig.	gen.
L 1	0.683	0.477	0.683	0.423	0.464	0.471
L 2	0.659	0.477	0.756	0.439	0.489	0.481
L 3	0.707	0.485	0.707	0.472	0.502	0.485
L 4	0.707	0.458	0.659	0.496	0.500	0.501
L 5	0.659	0.466	0.683	0.520	0.523	0.518
L 6	0.732	0.499	0.757	0.537	0.539	0.543
L 7	0.805	0.623	0.780	0.602	0.559	0.538
L 8	0.780	0.612	0.854	0.664	0.520	0.515
L 9	0.878	0.737	0.951	0.734	0.568	0.531
L 10	0.927	0.770	0.976	0.797	0.586	0.558
L 11	0.951	0.816	0.976	0.824	0.618	0.569
L 12	0.951	0.810	0.976	0.821	0.991	0.919

Table 5: The accuracy of long-distance agreement.

Table 5 shows the accuracy of grammatical form

[9]https://github.com/facebookresearch/colorlessgreenRNNs

prediction related to long-distance agreement for both semantically correct and nonce sentences. First, we can observe a clear gap in performance between the original and generated (nonce) test sets for all three models, which shows that the ability to assign the correct number is largely due to the co-occurrence and frequency effects rather than recognizing syntactic structure. However, it can be noticed that as the number of layers grow, the gap in accuracy for normal and nonce sentences diminishes, which means that at higher layers the models do learn to abstract from the lexical information and encode long-distance syntactic relations even when they cannot rely on co-occurrence.

When comparing the three models, it can be observed that, as expected, the Russian model performs better at the last layer than both English ones, which shows that rich morphology helps to encode long-distance relationships. Interestingly, the cased variant of BERT-Base had a higher accuracy than the uncased one, especially at some intermediate layers, which can mean that capitalization helps to encode morphological and syntactic relationships. Another thing to note is a remarkable difference in the progression of accuracy across layers between the Russian and English models: while in BERT-Base Cased and Uncased there is a consistent improvement with moving to higher layers, in RuBERT the accuracy grows very slowly at all but the last layer, where there is a huge jump in performance. It can be explained by the fact that due to complex morphology of the Russian language it takes more layers to encode some lower-level morphology and syntactic features before the model is ready to handle long-distance agreement. Lastly, compared to lower-level morphology tasks in Sections 2 and 3, where the performance actually downgraded at the last layer, here the last layers are important, especially for Russian.

5 Gender bias encoding in languages with and without gender marking

Though gender bias is a wide-known issue affecting such down-stream tasks as machine translation or text generation, it has been mostly studied only through such phenomena as co-reference and pronoun resolution (Rudinger et al., 2018). In this task we aim to explore if the gender bias is more prominent in languages such as Russian where nouns, adjectives and verbs can be marked for gender, i.e. have masculine, neutral or feminine gender. We hypothesise that the gender bias would be even more pronounced in such languages.

5.1 Dataset

For this task we construct the test set using the dataset provided by Stanovsky et al. (2019)[10] as a starting point. In particular, we extract the mentions of professions (triggers) and the relevant sentences from their English dataset and modify them as follows:

- We remove triggers that have a strong feminine gender (i.e. feminine ending) since they can only be used with feminine forms of words according to grammar rules. For example, referring to a nurse (медсестра) as "her" is the only correct way in Russian as the feminine ending of the word requires such agreement. Therefore, agreement with such words is due to grammatical conventions rather than bias. For the same reason, we remove triggers which can be translated both in a masculine and feminine form, as that would pre-determine the agreement.[11] As the result we selected 30 triggers (see Appendix A).
- We simplify the sentences so that there is only one trigger and it is referred to unambiguously. We do this to ensure that any discrepancy in gender usage is due to the model attending to the trigger noun rather than other nouns.
- For English we mask the pronoun referring to the trigger to test the assumed gender of co-reference resolution.
- For Russian, we modify the sentence to create three variants: with a masked pronoun, as in English, with a masked adjective referring to the trigger, and with a masked verb referring to it, to compare the degree of bias for these parts of speech. While doing so we ensure that other words in the sentence do not reveal the assumed gender; for instance, we change the past tense verbs (marked for gender) into their present tense forms (which are the same for both genders). On the other hand, we try to ensure that the masked word is predicted in a form marked for gender, such as past tense, by adding adverbs such as "yesterday".

[10]https://github.com/gabrielStanovsky/

[11]Some of nouns can have both neutral-style masculine forms and derogative feminine forms; we included them as we expect neutral forms also to be used for women.

5.2 Model and experiments

We use the same approach to evaluation as in Section 4, but here instead of comparing probabilities of two tokens we extract the list of 50 most prominent candidates and compare the probabilities assigned to the top tokens with masculine and feminine gender. If either a masculine or feminine form did not occur in the list of top 50 tokens, we record its probability as 0. We examine both the percentage of cases where either masculine or feminine genders were the winning ones (winning rate), and the average probabilities assigned to masculine and feminine forms.

5.3 Results and discussion

Table 6 shows the winning rate and the average probability for masculine and feminine forms appearing in the pronoun, verb or adjective slot.

	Winning rate		Avg. prob.	
	M	F	M	F
EN pronouns	50%	50%	0.268	0.296
RU pronouns	93%	7%	0.460	0.03
RU verbs	100%	0%	0.299	0.047
RU adjectives	100%	0%	0.091	0

Table 6: Winning rate of one gender over the other and average probabilities for genders in particular position.

As it can be seen from the table, in Russian there is a large skew towards masculine forms for all analysed parts of speech, while in English the gender labels for pronouns were distributed almost equally. It does not in any way imply the absence of bias: we observed the well-known phenomenon of assigning the masculine gender to both "manly" professions such as *mechanic* or *guard* and high-status jobs such as *CEO*, *manager* or *lawyer*, while the feminine gender was mainly assigned either to assisting roles such as *clerk* or *secretary* or to creative professions such as *editor* or *designer*. However, in Russian even such professions as *hairdresser* or *assistant*, which are more likely to be marked as feminine in English, had a higher probability of masculine forms than that of feminine ones. This is even more so for verbs and adjectives, all of which had masculine forms. Thus we can conclude that the strong gender bias in Russian which we observed is rather a grammatical phenomenon than encoded connotations of professions of particular type, as in English. In particular, though the words we studied are gender-neutral in terms of their applicability to people of both genders, grammatically they have a masculine form, and unlike native speakers who would choose feminine forms when referring to female professionals, the model is unable to do that and selects the most probable form based on the grammatical form only.

6 Conclusions and future work

In this study we used linguistic probes and masked language models to explore several aspects of morphology and syntax representation in Transformer-based models. In particular, we examined the ability of the model and its particular layers to encode the correct word order in languages with contrasting morphology and syntax, their ability to capture hierarchical structure represented by long-distance agreement, and the degree of bias encoding in languages with and without gender morphology. In doing so, we once again showed that the number of layers in the model roughly corresponds to the complexity of the encoded features, but also discovered that languages differ in layers where such encoding happens.

One of the most important takeaways of analysing the pre-trained models' performance layer by layer is that the best accuracy is not necessarily achieved at the last layer, which leads us to question the practice of using the complete model for all downstream tasks. Therefore, a potential extension of this work would be to explore the performance of such tasks as classification or generation when using only some layers of the pre-trained model. Another observation is that in general the Russian model needed more layers to achieve its optimal performance, while both Korean and English ones showed their best results at much earlier layers. It can be explained by more complicated morphology and syntax of Russian language which potentially can require more layers to be properly encoded. Thus it leads to a question whether adding more layers to pre-trained models for inflected languages with rich morphology and syntax (for example, Spanish or German) can help to improve performance of downstream tasks. That said, one of the limitation of the present study is that we focused only on one type of Transformer-based models and compared only two languages at a time; to ensure the general applicability of our experiments, they should be expanded to more languages with similar typological characteristics to those analysed above, and to attention-based models with different training approaches.

Acknowledgements

This initiative was funded by the Department of Defence and the Office of National Intelligence under the AI for Decision Making Program, delivered in partnership with the Defence Science Institute in Victoria, Australia.

References

Alexis Conneau, Germán Kruszewski, Guillaume Lample, Loïc Barrault, and Marco Baroni. 2018. What you can cram into a single vector: Probing sentence embeddings for linguistic properties. In *Proceedings of the 56th Annual Meeting of the Association for Computational Linguistics*.

Wietse de Vries, Andreas van Cranenburgh, and Malvina Nissim. 2020. What's so special about BERT's layers? A closer look at the NLP pipeline in monolingual and multilingual models. In *Proceedings of the 2020 Conference on Empirical Methods in Natural Language Processing: Findings*.

Jacob Devlin, Ming-Wei Chang, Kenton Lee, and Kristina Toutanova. 2019. BERT: Pre-training of deep bidirectional transformers for language understanding. In *Proceedings of the 2019 Conference of the North American Chapter of the Association for Computational Linguistics: Human Language Technologies, Volume 1 (Long and Short Papers)*, pages 4171–4186, Minneapolis, Minnesota. Association for Computational Linguistics.

Yoav Goldberg. 2019. Assessing BERT's syntactic abilities. *arXiv preprint arXiv:1901.05287*.

Kristina Gulordava, Piotr Bojanowski, Edouard Grave, Tal Linzen, and Marco Baroni. 2018. Colorless green recurrent networks dream hierarchically. *arXiv preprint arXiv:1803.11138*.

Hubert Haider. 2015. Head directionality. *Contemporary Linguistic Parameters: Contemporary Studies in Linguistics*, pages 73–97.

Diederik P Kingma and Jimmy Ba. 2014. ADAM: A method for stochastic optimization. *arXiv preprint arXiv:1412.6980*.

Natalia Klyueva and Ondřej Bojar. 2008. UMC 0.1: Czech-Russian-English multilingual corpus. In *Proceedings of International Conference in Corpus Linguistics*.

Mikhail Korobov. 2015. Morphological analyzer and generator for Russian and Ukrainian languages. In *International conference on analysis of images, social networks and texts*, pages 320–332. Springer.

Yuri Kuratov and Mikhail Arkhipov. 2019. Adaptation of deep bidirectional multilingual transformers for Russian language. *arXiv preprint arXiv:1905.07213*.

Winfred P Lehmann. 1973. A structural principle of language and its implications. *Language*, pages 47–66.

Tal Linzen, Emmanuel Dupoux, and Yoav Goldberg. 2016. Assessing the ability of LSTMs to learn syntax-sensitive dependencies. *Transactions of the Association for Computational Linguistics*, 4:521–535.

Rachel Rudinger, Jason Naradowsky, Brian Leonard, and Benjamin Van Durme. 2018. Gender bias in coreference resolution. *arXiv preprint arXiv:1804.09301*.

Gabriel Stanovsky, Noah A. Smith, and Luke Zettlemoyer. 2019. Evaluating gender bias in machine translation. In *ACL*, Florence, Italy. Association for Computational Linguistics.

Ian Tenney, Dipanjan Das, and Ellie Pavlick. 2019. BERT Rediscovers the Classical NLP Pipeline. In *Proceedings of the 57th Annual Meeting of the Association for Computational Linguistics*.

Ashish Vaswani, Noam Shazeer, Niki Parmar, Jakob Uszkoreit, Llion Jones, Aidan N Gomez, Łukasz Kaiser, and Illia Polosukhin. 2017. Attention is all you need. In *Proceedings of the 31st International Conference on Neural Information Processing Systems*.

A Selected triggers

For the gender bias experiments we selected the following English names of professions and their direct translations into Russian:

English: developer, mechanic, clerk, mover, analyst, assistant, salesperson, librarian, lawyer, hairdresser, cook, teacher, physician, baker, farmer, CEO, manager, guard, editor, auditor, secretary, designer, supervisor, cashier, driver, construction worker, counselor, carpenter, janitor

Russian: разработчик, механик, клерк, грузчик, аналитик, ассистент, продавец, библиотекарь, адвокат, парикмахер, повар, учитель, врач, пекарь, фермер, CEO, менеджер, охранник, редактор, аудитор, секретарь, дизайнер, супервизор, кассир, водитель, строитель, психолог, плотник, дворник

Tweaking UD annotations to investigate the placement of determiners, quantifiers and numerals in the noun phrase

Luigi Talamo
Language Science and Technology, Saarland University
luigi.talamo@uni-saarland.de

Abstract

We describe a methodology to extract with finer accuracy word order patterns from texts automatically annotated with Universal Dependency (UD) trained parsers. We use the methodology to quantify the word order entropy of determiners, quantifiers and numerals in ten Indo-European languages, using UD-parsed texts from a parallel corpus of prosaic texts. Our results suggest that the combinations of different UD annotation layers, such as UD Relations, Universal Parts of Speech and lemma, and the introduction of language-specific lists of closed-category lemmata has the two-fold effect of improving the quality of analysis and unveiling hidden areas of variability in word order patterns.

1 Introduction

Most of the work on word order variation using Universal Dependencies (UD: de Marneffe et al., 2021) is based on curated dependency treebanks, with only a few works using dependency corpora derived from raw texts. Although the accuracy rate of NLP systems trained on UD models is reportedly very high (Hajič and Zeman, 2017; Zeman and Hajič, 2018; Straka et al., 2019; Qi et al., 2020), a certain level of noise i.e., erroneous annotations is in fact present when working with automatically annotated texts (Levshina et al., to appear; Talamo and Verkerk, to appear); furthermore, different layers of UD annotations such as Universal Parts of Speech (UPOS) and UD Relations are not always used consistently across languages, often resulting in the cross-linguistic comparison of different categories.

We discuss a methodology to tweak the UD annotations in order to achieve a better representation of word order entropy; the methodology is exemplified on three categories that are particularly difficult to analyze with automatic methods and from a cross-linguistic perspective. Determiners, quantifiers and numerals are often treated in descriptive grammars as heterogeneous categories; the lexical category of determiners includes articles and demonstratives, while the category of quantifiers often includes elements of other closed categories, such as pronouns and gradation markers, and sometimes members of open categories, such as adjectives and adverbs; finally, numerals are often not restricted to cardinal, ordinal and distributive numbers, but overlap with quantifiers.

This heterogeneity is reflected by the UD implementation of these categories, both at the Relation and the UPOS annotation layer. Numerals are treated as a separate category and represented at the syntactic level by the `nummod` UD Relation and at word category level by the NUM UPOS; by contrast, the UD framework conflates articles, demonstratives and quantifiers into one UPOS tag (DET) and into one UD Relation (`det`), resulting in the 'Determiners & Quantifiers' macro-category. At the language-specific level several individual POS tags and UD Relation subtypes are used; for instance, in Slavic languages quantifiers get two specific subtypes, `det:numgov` and `det:numposs`, and morpho-syntactic features of numerals can be specified using additional UD Relation subtypes.

Our methodology combines two layers of UD annotations, UPOS and UD Relations, with manually-compiled and language-specific lists of lemmata. We test the methodology against a parallel corpus of fiction texts and their translations in 10 Indo-European languages; given their particular genre, these texts are quite challenging for parsers that are mostly trained on non-fiction data such as Wiki and News. Following previous studies, we employ here Shannon's entropy as a metric for word order variation.

2 Related work

Since its inception in 2015 (Nivre et al., 2015), UD has been widely used in corpus-based studies on word order variability. However, as earlier

Proceedings of the 4th Workshop on Computational Typology and Multilingual NLP (SIGTYP 2022), pages 36 - 41
July 14, 2022

mentioned, corpora used in previous studies are "dependency corpora of the HamleDT 2.0 and Universal Dependencies 1.00" (Futrell et al., 2015), "the Universal Dependencies Treebank version 2.2" (Naranjo and Becker, 2018), "a selection of 55 treebanks from Universal Dependencies v2.4" (Yu et al., 2019), "Surface-Syntactic Universal Dependencies (SUD) [treebanks]" (Gerdes et al., 2019) and the "Universal Dependencies project, release 2.1" (Futrell et al., 2020). UD Treebanks can be considered de-facto gold standards, as large parts of them are manually compiled or at least semi-automatically checked for wrong annotations, allowing scholars to work with high quality of data. However, as UD Treebanks wildly vary across languages with respect to size and text genres (Levshina et al., to appear), results from most of the previous works are biased against these factors. Exceptions are represented by works using the LISCA parse assessment algorithm (Dell'Orletta et al., 2013), whose models have been trained on UD-parsed Wikipedia corpora (Alzetta et al., 2018) and tested on the so-called 'reference corpora', which consist "of a monolingual corpus of texts from the news and Wikipedia domains [...] morpho-syntactically annotated and dependency parsed by the UDPipe pipeline trained on the Universal Dependency treebanks, version 2.2" (Alzetta et al., 2020); automatically annotated texts are also partially employed in Levshina (2019), who uses eleven UD-parsed corpora from the Leipzig Corpora Collection for one of her case-studies on word order entropy. Finally, Talamo and Verkerk (to appear) is a study on word order variation in the nominal phrase and is entirely based on parallel texts that are parsed by the UDPipe pipeline trained on UD treebanks v.~2.5. To the best of our knowledge, Levshina (2019) and Talamo and Verkerk (to appear) are the only studies on word order variation combining UD Relations with other annotation layers; although her methodology is not fully disclosed, Levshina (2019) applies the UPOS annotation layer to the head in her first case study, where word order variability is taken from a syntactic perspective, and the wordform annotation layer to the dependent in her second case-study, where word order variability is investigated with respect to the lexically specific level; Talamo and Verkerk (to appear) take a step further and operationalize this methodology by introducing several combinations of UD Relation and UPOS annotation layer to restrict either the head, the dependent or both, and introducing language-specific list of lemmata to match modifiers at the lexical level.

3 Data and Methods

3.1 Corpus

We use the Parallel Corpus of Indo-European Prose and more (CIEP+: Talamo and Verkerk, to appear), which features prosaic texts and their translations in more than 30 languages; we select a sample of 10 Indo-European languages, belonging to the following branches: Balto-Slavic (Lithuanian, Polish), Celtic (Irish), Germanic (Danish, Dutch and German), Greek (Modern Greek), Romance (French, Portuguese and Spanish). All languages feature 18 books (approximately 120K of sentences for each language), with the exception of Irish that features 5 books (approximately 13K of sentences).

The corpus has been parsed using Stanford Stanza[1] with pre-trained UD Models[2] for the 10 languages. The resulting CoNLL-U files are processed with a Python script using the pyconll library[3]. The script extracts the occurrences of the specific UD Relations (see below) and determines the relative position of head and dependent; for each occurrence, we collect the following annotation fields for both the head and the dependent: UD Relations, UPOS tag and lemma.

Scripts and dataset, with the exception of the parsed corpus containing copyrighted texts, are available in the Supplementary Material[4].

3.2 Tweaking the UD annotations

Working with a dependency grammar, the most important annotation layer is represented by the UD Relations, which identifies the head and the dependent within the phrase; for our case study, we deal with various dependents (Table 1) and one type of head, the noun. This basic layer of annotation is then combined with other layers of annotation. By formulating the categories in Table 1 as comparative concepts (Haspelmath, 2010), we seek to integrate cross-linguistic definitions with the different layers of annotation (see 'Comparative Concepts

[1] Version 1.3.0 `https://stanfordnlp.github.io/stanza/`

[2] Version 2.8 `https://stanfordnlp.github.io/stanza/available_models.html`

[3] `https://pyconll.readthedocs.io/en/stable/`

[4] `https://doi.org/10.5281/zenodo.6580701`

Category	UPOS	UD Relation
nominal head	NOUN, PROPN	-
article	DET	`det`
demonstrative	DET *PRON*	`det`
quantifier	DET *ADJ ADV PRON*	`det det:nummod det:numgov`
numeral	NUM	`nummod nummod:entity nummod:gov nummod:flat`

Table 1: Values used to capture the categories of nominal heads, articles, demonstratives, quantifiers and numerals. Non-specific values are given in italics.

and Universal Dependencies' in the Supplementary Material).

Elaborating on Talamo and Verkerk (to appear), we propose three combinations, with each combination building on top of the previous one. The first combination, `rel`, uses the specific UD relation for the dependent, thus corresponding to most of the approaches taken in previous works; the second combination, `rel+upos`, adds the UPOS layers, using specific UPOS tags for the nominal head, and specific and non-specific UPOS tags for the dependent; the third combination, `rel+pos+lemma`, introduces language-specific list of lemmata for the dependent.

With 'specific' UPOS tags we refer to the values that are described by the UD Annotation Guidelines[5] as relevant for the investigated categories; we additionally add non-specific UPOS tags, which are based on the consultation of descriptive grammars and on the comparison of UD-parsed texts across the ten languages of the sample. See Table 1 for a detailed list of these values. Finally, language-specific lists of lemmata are aimed to capture the three components of the 'Determiners & Quantifiers' macro-category, namely, articles, demonstratives and quantifiers; we use these lists of lemmata, which are compiled using descriptive grammars and with the aid of native speakers, in intersective queries (positive match) on the lemma field for articles, demonstratives and quantifiers, and in non-intersective queries (negative match) on the lemma field for numerals.

3.3 Metrics

Word order variability is assessed using Shannon's entropy:

$$H(X) = -\sum_{i=1}^{n} P(x_i) \log_2 P(x_i)$$

where the upper bound of summation, n, is set to 2, indicating that there are two possible word order patterns i.e., the modifier is either prenominal or postnominal, and P represents the probability of the two order patterns; the resulting value of entropy is given in bits and ranges from 0 (only one of the two word order patterns is attested) to 1 (both word order patterns are attested with the same probability). For instance, we find in the Danish part of CIEP+ 5089 occurences of postnominal `nummod` (and subtypes) and 1392 of prenominal `nummod` (and subtypes), with a resulting entropy of .75.

4 Results

As shown in the left panel of Figure 1, entropy values captured by the second combination, `rel+upos`, are significantly lower than values captured by the `rel` combination. This is particularly clear for numerals, which display a substantial drop in entropy in half of the languages; furthermore, in some languages the entropy of numerals is reduced to near-zero values (German: .02, French and Irish: .04, Polish: .06). As for determiners & quantifiers, the introduction of the UPOS layer is overall less significant; a significant reduction of entropy is observed only for three languages (Greek, Lithuanian and Spanish). This is partly due to the low value of entropy already captured by the `rel` combination, but it also reflects the biunivocal relation between the DET UPOS tag `det` and the UD Relation and its subtypes; by contrast, the `nummod` UD relation and its subtypes are not in biunivocal relation with the NUM UPOS tag, since, as already mentioned above, this UD Relation is often used with quantifiers as well. The third combination, which adds language-specific lists of lemmata to the UPOS and UD Relation layers and is plotted in the right panel of Figure 1, allows us to zoom in on the entropy of determiners & quantifiers, disentangling the category into articles, demonstratives

[5]`https://universaldependencies.org/guidelines.html`

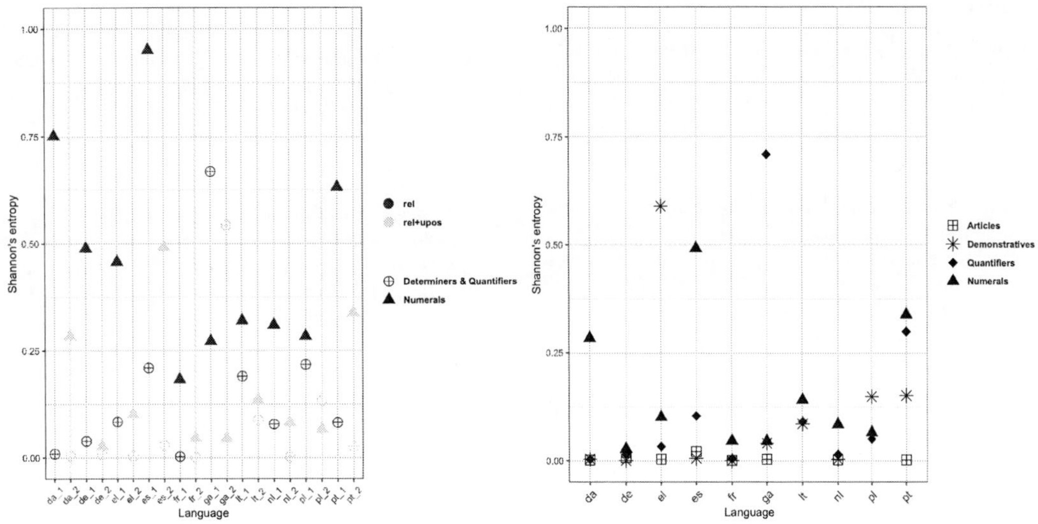

Figure 1: Left: entropy values for the categories of determiners & quantifiers and numerals, as captured by the `rel` combination and the `rel+upos` combination. Right: entropy values for the categories of articles, demonstratives, quantifiers and numerals, as captured by `rel+pos+lemma` combination.

and quantifiers; although the entropy of determiners & quantifiers is extremely low for all languages of the sample, two languages have moderate values of entropy for demonstratives or quantifiers. More specifically, Irish has the highest value of entropy for quantifiers (.71), while Greek the highest value for demonstratives (.59). According to Stenson (2020, 189-192), the position of quantifiers in Irish is lexically determined; most Irish quantifiers precede the noun, while few follow it; postnominal quantifiers include the high-frequency lexeme *uilig* 'all', which explains the high entropy of Irish quantifiers. As for Greek, the high value of entropy for demonstratives can be accounted on a pragmatic and semantic basis, as postnominal demonstratives have an emphatic reading (Lascaratou, 1998, 164). Furthermore, low-to-moderate values of entropy are observed for quantifiers in Portuguese (.30) and Spanish (.10) and for demonstratives in Portuguese (.15). As for numerals, we use language-specific lists of quantifiers as negative matches against the lemma field; this approach is however of little use, as entropy values captured by the third combination are the same of the second combination. Thanks to the introduction of language-specific list of lemmata, the third combination is suitable for closed categories such as articles, demonstratives and quantifiers, while the second combination is already effective for capturing open categories such as numerals.

5 Conclusion

We have discussed a methodology to extract with better accuracy word order patterns from CoNLL-U files obtained from the automatic parsing of raw texts; the methodology, which exploits different UD annotation layers and language-specific list of lemmata, is exemplified on the heterogenous lexical categories of determiners and numerals, whose word order patterns are analyzed in a parallel corpus of 10 Indo-European languages. We have shown that the methodology is able to correct some of the errors introduced by the automatic parsing and inconsistent use of UPOS tags and UD Relations, thus improving the quality of the analysis, as shown with the category of numerals. Furthermore, the methodology sheds light on areas of variability, which were previously hidden by the UD lumping of articles, demonstratives and quantifiers into a unitary category. Given the very high frequency of articles, whose variability is close to zero, this unitary category displays very low values of entropy across languages; once this unitary category is split into its three components, some languages show moderate-to-high levels of entropy with respect to demonstratives (Greek) and quantifiers (Irish and Portuguese).

References

Chiara Alzetta, Felice Dell'Orletta, Simonetta Montemagni, Petya Osenova, Kiril Simov, and Giulia Venturi. 2020. Quantitative linguistic investigations across universal dependencies treebanks. In *CLiC-it*.

Chiara Alzetta, Felice Dell'Orletta, Simonetta Montemagni, and Giulia Venturi. 2018. Universal Dependencies and quantitative typological trends. a case study on word order. In *Proceedings of the Eleventh International Conference on Language Resources and Evaluation (LREC 2018)*, Miyazaki, Japan. European Language Resources Association (ELRA).

Marie-Catherine de Marneffe, Christopher D. Manning, Joakim Nivre, and Daniel Zeman. 2021. Universal Dependencies. *Computational Linguistics*, 47(2):255–308.

Felice Dell'Orletta, Giulia Venturi, and Simonetta Montemagni. 2013. Linguistically-driven Selection of Correct Arcs for Dependency Parsing. *Computación y Sistemas*, 17:125 – 136.

Richard Futrell, Roger P. Levy, and Edward Gibson. 2020. Dependency locality as an explanatory principle for word order. *Language*, 96(2):371–412.

Richard Futrell, Kyle Mahowald, and Edward Gibson. 2015. Quantifying word order freedom in dependency corpora. In *Proceedings of the Third International Conference on Dependency Linguistics (Depling 2015)*, pages 91–100, Uppsala, Sweden. Uppsala University, Uppsala, Sweden.

Kim Gerdes, Sylvain Kahane, and Xinying Chen. 2019. Rediscovering greenberg's word order universals in UD. In *Proceedings of the Third Workshop on Universal Dependencies (UDW, SyntaxFest 2019)*, pages 124–131, Paris, France. Association for Computational Linguistics.

Jan Hajič and Dan Zeman, editors. 2017. *Proceedings of the CoNLL 2017 Shared Task: Multilingual Parsing from Raw Text to Universal Dependencies*. Association for Computational Linguistics, Vancouver, Canada.

Martin Haspelmath. 2010. Comparative concepts and descriptive categories in cross-linguistic studies. *Language*, 86(4).

Chryssoula Lascaratou. 1998. Basic characteristics of modern greek word order. In Anna Siewierska, editor, *Constituent Order in the Language of Europe*, pages 151–171. Mouton de Gruyter, Berlin.

Natalia Levshina. 2019. Token-based typology and word order entropy: A study based on universal dependencies. *Linguistic Typology*, 23(3):533–572.

Natalia Levshina, Savithry Namboodiripad, Alex Kramer, Annemarie Verkerk, Luigi Talamo, Marc Tang, Gabriela Garrido Rodriguez, Timothy Michael Gupton, Evan Kidd, Gabriela Garrido Rodriguez, Chiara Naccarato, Rachel Nordlinger, Anastasia Panova, Natalya Stoynova, Liu Ying, and Sasha Wilmoth. to appear. Why we need a gradient approach to word order. *Linguistics*.

Matias-Guzmán Naranjo and Laura Becker. 2018. Quantitative word order typology with UD. In *Proceedings of the 17th International Workshop on Treebanks and Linguistic Theories (TLT 2018)*, pages 91–104, Oslo, Norway. Linköping Electronic Conference Proceedings 155:10.

Joakim Nivre, Željko Agić, Maria Jesus Aranzabe, Masayuki Asahara, Aitziber Atutxa, Miguel Ballesteros, John Bauer, Kepa Bengoetxea, Riyaz Ahmad Bhat, Cristina Bosco, Sam Bowman, Giuseppe G. A. Celano, Miriam Connor, Marie-Catherine de Marneffe, Arantza Diaz de Ilarraza, Kaja Dobrovoljc, Timothy Dozat, Tomaž Erjavec, Richárd Farkas, Jennifer Foster, Daniel Galbraith, Filip Ginter, Iakes Goenaga, Koldo Gojenola, Yoav Goldberg, Berta Gonzales, Bruno Guillaume, Jan Hajič, Dag Haug, Radu Ion, Elena Irimia, Anders Johannsen, Hiroshi Kanayama, Jenna Kanerva, Simon Krek, Veronika Laippala, Alessandro Lenci, Nikola Ljubešić, Teresa Lynn, Christopher Manning, Cătălina Mărănduc, David Mareček, Héctor Martínez Alonso, Jan Mašek, Yuji Matsumoto, Ryan McDonald, Anna Missilä, Verginica Mititelu, Yusuke Miyao, Simonetta Montemagni, Shunsuke Mori, Hanna Nurmi, Petya Osenova, Lilja Øvrelid, Elena Pascual, Marco Passarotti, Cenel-Augusto Perez, Slav Petrov, Jussi Piitulainen, Barbara Plank, Martin Popel, Prokopis Prokopidis, Sampo Pyysalo, Loganathan Ramasamy, Rudolf Rosa, Shadi Saleh, Sebastian Schuster, Wolfgang Seeker, Mojgan Seraji, Natalia Silveira, Maria Simi, Radu Simionescu, Katalin Simkó, Kiril Simov, Aaron Smith, Jan Štěpánek, Alane Suhr, Zsolt Szántó, Takaaki Tanaka, Reut Tsarfaty, Sumire Uematsu, Larraitz Uria, Viktor Varga, Veronika Vincze, Zdeněk Žabokrtský, Daniel Zeman, and Hanzhi Zhu. 2015. Universal dependencies 1.2. LINDAT/CLARIAH-CZ digital library at the Institute of Formal and Applied Linguistics (ÚFAL), Faculty of Mathematics and Physics, Charles University.

Peng Qi, Yuhao Zhang, Yuhui Zhang, Jason Bolton, and Christopher D. Manning. 2020. Stanza: A Python natural language processing toolkit for many human languages. In *Proceedings of the 58th Annual Meeting of the Association for Computational Linguistics: System Demonstrations*.

Nancy Stenson. 2020. *Modern Irish: A Comprehensive Grammar*. Comprehensive grammars. London & New York: Routledge.

Milan Straka, Jana Straková, and Jan Hajic. 2019. Evaluating contextualized embeddings on 54 languages in POS tagging, lemmatization and dependency parsing. *CoRR*, abs/1908.07448.

Luigi Talamo and Annemarie Verkerk. to appear. A new methodology for an old problem: a corpus-based typology of adnominal word order in European languages. *Italian Journal of Linguistics*.

Xiang Yu, Agnieszka Falenska, and Jonas Kuhn. 2019. Dependency length minimization vs. word order constraints: An empirical study on 55 treebanks. In *Proceedings of the First Workshop on Quantitative Syntax (Quasy, SyntaxFest 2019)*, pages 89–97, Paris, France. Association for Computational Linguistics.

Daniel Zeman and Jan Hajič, editors. 2018. *Proceedings of the CoNLL 2018 Shared Task: Multilingual Parsing from Raw Text to Universal Dependencies*. Association for Computational Linguistics, Brussels, Belgium.

A Database for Modal Semantic Typology

Qingxia Guo and **Nathaniel Imel** and **Shane Steinert-Threlkeld**
Department of Linguistics, University of Washington
Box 354340, Seattle, WA, 98195-4340
{qg07,nimel,shanest}@uw.edu

Abstract

This paper introduces a database for crosslinguistic modal semantics. The purpose of this database is to (1) enable ongoing consolidation of modal semantic typological knowledge into a repository according to uniform data standards and to (2) provide data for investigations in crosslinguistic modal semantic theory and experiments explaining such theories. We describe the kind of semantic variation that the database aims to record, the format of the data, and a current snapshot of the database, emphasizing access and contribution to the database in light of the goals above. We release the database at `https://clmbr.shane.st/modal-typology`.

1 Introduction

Modals—expressions used to talk about situations other than the actual one—are ubiquitous in natural language and have been the focus of intense study in the semantics thereof (Kratzer, 1981; Portner, 2009; Matthewson, 2019). An increasingly large body of work has gathered data on the crosslinguistic variation in this domain, i.e. the ways in which languages agree and differ in their mechanisms for expressing modality (Rullmann et al., 2008a; Vander Klok, 2013b; Cable, 2017, i.a.).

This paper introduces and describes a *Modal Typology Database*: a repository that consolidates much of this crosslinguistic knowledge in a format that is uniform and easy both to consume and to produce. Such a resource can play several enabling roles in semantic typology research. For example, it can enable the verification of robust semantic universals (Nauze, 2008; Vander Klok, 2013b; Steinert-Threlkeld et al., 2022) and possibly trigger the formulation of new ones. Similarly, these data and their format can be used in comparison to artificial languages to attempt to *explain* what pressures have shaped semantic typology in the domain of modality, as has been done in several other domains (Kemp and Regier, 2012; Zaslavsky et al., 2018; Steinert-Threlkeld and Szymanik, 2019, 2020; Steinert-Threlkeld, 2021; Denić et al., 2022; Mollica et al., 2021; Uegaki, 2022, i.a.).

After describing some of what is known about the variation in modals (Section 2), we describe a data schema for representing particular axes of variation (namely: force and flavor) in modals crosslinguistically in a relatively theory-netural manner (Section 3.1). We then (Section 4) describe how to access this data, which we make available in two distinct formats: a 'basic' format, and one that conforms to the Cross-Linguistic Data Formats (CLDF; Forkel et al. 2018) schema. We illustrate how to use these data to verify a semantic universal in Section 4.3, before explaining how researchers can contribute their own data (Section 5) and providing a snapshot of what data the database currently has (Section 6). We provide a discussion around future directions in Section 7 before summarizing the present work in Section 8.

2 Modal Typology

Modals are expressions that are used to talk about alternative ways the world could be, over and above the way the world actually is. Languages utilize various syntactic forms to express modality. For example, English uses auxiliary verbs like *may* and *must* as modals, in addition to adjectives like *possible*; Javanese makes use of auxiliaries, a main verb, and several adverbs (Vander Klok, 2013a). Since at least Kratzer (1981), the semantics of modals have been explicated in terms of two axes of variation: force and flavor. These axes can be illustrated with the examples listed in table 1.

The *must* examples exhibit strong (i.e. universal) force, but differ in flavor. For example, (1) in the table 1 can be glossed as saying: all of the worlds compatible with my evidence are worlds in which it is raining. The universal quantification represents

Proceedings of the 4th Workshop on Computational Typology and Multilingual NLP (SIGTYP 2022), pages 42 - 51
July 14, 2022

	Context	Expression	Axes Values
(1)	A friend walks in and shakes off a wet umbrella. You say:	It must be raining.	strong epistemic
(2)	You are reading the specifications of a homework assignment. It partially reads:	You *must* upload your homework as a PDF.	strong deontic
(3)	A friend is leaving and grabs an umbrella on the way out, saying:	It *may* be raining	weak epistemic
(4)	A mother offers a treat to a child for finishing an assignment, saying:	You *may* have a cookie	weak deontic

Table 1: Examples of force and flavors in English.

the force, and the domain of worlds (those compatible with my evidence) the flavor, in this case epistemic. (2) exhibits universal force with deontic flavor, roughly saying that all the worlds in which you follow the rules are ones in which you upload a PDF. The examples with *may* in (3) and (4) exhibit weak (i.e. possibility) force: their meaning says that some world satisfies the prejacent. (3) and (4) again differ in flavor, with the former being epistemic and the latter being deontic. In addition to epistemic and deontic flavors, many others have been identified: bouletic (worlds in which desire are fulfilled), teleological (worlds in which goals are satisfied), *et cetera*. Similarly, there are arguably more forces than just weak and strong: for instance, there are weak necessity modals (e.g. *should*, *ought*) which intuitively express universal quantification over a smaller domain of worlds (von Fintel and Iatridou, 2008). See Matthewson 2019 and references therein for further discussion of these two axes. The examples above show that English modals lexically specify modal force (each modal has a fixed quantificational force) but exhibit variability across flavors (the modals can express more than one flavor). We note that such variability does not require that all modals in English can express multiple flavors: for instance, *might* arguably can only be used epistemically. Kratzerian semantics for modals capture this by hard-coding quantificational force into the meaning of a modal but relying on context to determine the flavor.[1]

Not all languages are like English: some exhibit so-called *variable force modals*, which specify flavor but not force. This has been found at least in St'át'icmets (Rullmann et al., 2008a), Nez Perce (Deal, 2011), Old English (Yanovich, 2016), and Pintupi-Luritja (Gray, 2021). We illustrate the phenomenon with elicited examples of St'át'icmets *k'a*:[2]

(5) [Context: You have a headache that won't go away, so you go to the doctor. All the tests show negative. There is nothing wrong, so it must just be tension.]

nilh *k'a*
FOC INFER
lh(el)-(t)-en-s-wá(7)-(a)
from-DET-1SG.POSS-NOM-IMPF-DET
ptinus-em-sút
think-MID-OOC

'It *must* be from my worrying.'

(6) [Context: His car isn't there.]

plan k'a qwatsáts
already INFER leave

'Maybe he's already gone.'

Example (5) shows *k'a* being used with strong force and epistemic flavor. Example (6) shows *k'a* being used with weak force and epistemic flavor. Further analysis in Rullmann et al. (2008a) shows that *k'a* can only be used with epistemic flavor, so it is an example with lexically specified flavor but variable force. Finally, some languages have modals which exhibit variability along *both* the force and flavor axes. Bochnak (2015b,a) has argued that the modal verb *-eʔ* in Washo can be used in both possibility and necessity contexts with

[1]Typical implementations determine the flavor as the product of two parameters: a modal base and an ordering source. We set aside this distinction for present purposes and focus only on flavor.

[2]These are examples (5c) and and (5e) from Rullmann et al. 2008a, p. 321. See their footnote 5 on p. 320 for the abbreviations.

a range of modal flavors. Similarly, Močnik and Abramovitz (2019) demonstrate that the Koryak attitude verb *ivək* can be used to express both necessity and possibility. For the doxastic flavor, this means that *ivək* can be used to mean roughly 'believe' (necessity) as well as 'allow for the possibility that' (possibility). They also argue that the expression can be used to express both doxastic and assertive flavors, thus demonstrating variability on both axes.[3]

3 Representing Modal Semantics in a Database

A database for cross-linguistic modal semantics should be theory-neutral while still capturing the basic parameters of variation and facts upon which linguists agree. A natural way to proceed is to simply record the flavors and forces a particular modal can be used to express. We elaborate on this analysis in the following subsections.

3.1 General Framework

We assume that force and flavor are fundamentally properties of contexts of use. This reflects current practice in semantic fieldwork as applied to modality (Matthewson, 2004; Bochnak and Matthewson, 2020; Vander Klok, 2021).[4] For example, the modal questionnaire of Vander Klok 2021 consists exactly of discourse contexts designed to isolate a single force-flavor pair. These contexts can be used at least for elicitation, translation, and acceptability tasks. Specifically, we will say that a modal M *can express* a force-flavor pair just in case a bare positive sentence of the form Mp is judged felicitous in a context with that pair.[5] For example, English *must* can express the pair (universal, deontic) because there is a reading for that pair under the context in 1 in table 1. Here we identify a modal as the set of (force, flavor) pairs that it can express. We intend this level of modeling to apply to the expression of modality by diverse syntactic means (as mentioned in the Introduction), and not to be specific to any one syntactic category. A language is (generously) identified as a list of modals.

We adopt this level of generality because it avoids commitment on the exact formal semantics of these expressions, which is often still being debated. For example, we can say that a *variable force modal* is one that can express more than one pair with the same force. This is useful because there are two broad approaches to the semantics of such variable force modals: they actually encode existential quantification but lack a universal scalemate (Deal, 2011) or they encode universal quantification but rely on some mechanism of domain restriction (Rullmann et al., 2008a; Bochnak, 2015a; Močnik and Abramovitz, 2019). On such analyses, the underlying semantics contains one specific quantifier; in the present setting, they will still be considered variable force since bare positive sentences are used in contexts with multiple forces.

This approach to encoding the semantics of modals allows straightforward evalutation of universals, such as proposed by Nauze (2008), Vander Klok (2013b), and Steinert-Threlkeld et al. (2022) which are testable hypotheses and potential targets of explanation. All of these modal semantic universals are formulated constraints on the kinds of sets of (force, flavor) pairs found in any human language. For example, Steinert-Threlkeld et al. (2022) propose the INDEPENDENCE OF FORCE AND FLAVOR (IFF) universal: All modals in natural language satisfy the independence of force and flavor property: if a modal can express the pairs (fo_1, fl_1) and (fo_2, fl_2), then it can also express (fo_1, fl_2) and (fo_2, fl_1). A database that catalogs which force-flavor pairs are expressed by various modals cross-linguistically can thus be used to empirically verify whether this universal holds unrestrictedly or at least very robustly. In Section 4.3 we show how our database can be used in exactly this way.

3.2 Concrete Schema

We can implement the above framework according to the principles of tidy data (Wickham, 2014). Such tabular data has the following properties: every column is a variable, every row an observation, and every cell a value. According to the framework just described, a basic observation in cross-linguistic modal semantics says that a particular modal expression can or cannot express a particular (force, flavor) pair.

[3] There are also apparently bouletic uses of *ivək*, but Močnik and Abramovitz (2019) argues that this flavor does not come from *ivək* alone but from interaction with material in the embedded clause.

[4] In addition to the particular studies already mentioned, see Matthewson 2013; Cable 2017 for more examples of the application of these methods.

[5] We intend 'judged felicitous' to also include the case where such sentences are produced naturally in elicitation tasks, as well as when such sentences are found in naturally-occuring contexts which have a clear force-flavor pair.

Our basic data schema, accordingly, will be a table with four columns (we also record metadata about the language of an expression, in a way detailed in the next section):

1. expression: the name of the particular expression
2. force
3. flavor
4. can_express: a binary variable, with 1 meaning that the expression can express the pair of values in the force and flavor columns, and a 0 meaning that it cannot.[6]

with each row being one observation. For example, we can represent the fact that English *may* can only be used to express weak epistemic and weak deontic combinations as follows:

expression	force	flavor	can_express
may	weak	epistemic	1
may	weak	deontic	1
may	strong	epistemic	0
may	strong	deontic	0

Table 2: Example of our basic data format for English *may*.

A note about possible values of force and flavor: while these are generally thought to be shared cross-linguistically, our data format does not commit to a pre-specified ontology of either. In particular, in order to capture the fact that certain languages make different / finer distinctions than others, we aim to be as liberal as possible in recording featural diversity. The consequences of balancing these goals are that during data collection the list of modal forces or flavors might not be completely exhaustive and disjoint. Later on, features can be collapsed or renamed as necessary, as the database grows, or as particular analysis needs require. For example, the English possibility modal *can* expresses deontic and circumstantial flavors, and so may be considered a "root" modal, but we aim for precision by recording deontic and circumstantial flavors rather than a higher-level grouping. Similarly, it is possible that when recording data from a descriptive grammar, one will find a unique or nonstandard name for a possible flavor. One can record that flavor as given in that grammar, and in a later analysis step, attempt to map that flavor value onto ones that are used in other resources.

On the force side, we are primarily intended in capturing weak, strong, and weak necessity modals, setting aside for the time being the full range of possibilities of graded modality, including probabilistic expressions (Kratzer, 1981; Portner, 2009; Klecha, 2014; Lassiter, 2017). At the present state of theorizing, there is not enough concensus about their typology. That being said, on some approaches to graded modality, the database as currently structured could be easily modified or extended to include some aspects of them: if graded modals are genuinely scalar terms (Klecha, 2014; Lassiter, 2017; Bowler and Gluckman, 2021), then features from the semantics of gradable expressions such as scale-type and the minimum/maximum/relative distinction could be recorded (Kennedy and McNally, 2005; Kennedy, 2007).

4 Accessing the Database

The database may be found at `https://clmbr.shane.st/modal-typology`. This landing page—which will contain more information in the future—will point the reader to a repository containing the data. It is made publicly available in two formats. First, we have a 'raw' format: this is oriented around individual languages and is designed to make it easy for linguists to contribute new data. We describe this format in the next subsection (4.1) and how to contribute in Section 5. Secondly, we have a script to convert the raw format into a Cross-Linguistic Data Formats (CLDF; Forkel et al. 2018) format, which has several benefits of its own that are described in more detail in Section 4.2. We then demonstrate one of these benefits, by showing how to verify the IFF universal using the data in the database (in either format) in Section 4.3.

4.1 Basic Format

The basic format, found in the `basic-format/` sub-directory, contains information both at the language-level and then aggregated across languages. We explain these types of data in turn.

[6] We also will sometimes use a '?' in this column to indicate that it is unclear. As an example, in Tlingit (Cable, 2017), there are some cases where the author writes that it is implausible that an expression can express a particular force-flavor pair, but that there has not been concrete negative evidence to support that judgment. We record cases such as those with a '?'.

To see the data for one language, we will look at Tlingit. The data for this language comes from the fieldwork reported in Cable 2017. To access it, go to the sub-folder named `Tlingit`. There, you will find two files:

1. `metadata.yml`: this contains information about the language and the source(s) from which the modals data was compiled. In particular:
    - Glotto code: this is an ID for the language from Glottlog[7] (Hammarström et al., 2021)
    - Reference: a citation for the source
    - Reference_key: a BibTeX key to a shared bib file (described below)
    - URL: a URL to find the reference
    - Reference_type: the type of source that the reference is
      We note that this will be especially useful in distinguishing languages where the information derives from targeted semantic fieldwork (as in the present case of Tlingit) and from descriptive grammars. The latter tends to lack explicitly *negative* evidence, upon which some analyses may depend, and so those languages may need to be excluded.At present, the values for this field that exist in our database are 'paper_journal' and 'reference_grammar'.
    - Complete_language: whether the reference purports to describe the complete modal system of the language or not.
      Many sources only provide data for some, but not all, modals. Such expression-level data is still very useful, but researchers may wish to exclude incomplete languages from analyses at the language level.

2. `modals.csv`: this is a comma-separated-value (CSV) file, containing the core data in the format described in the previous section

Popping back out to the main `basic-format/` directory, there are several aggregated data files that are generated automatically from the language-specific data:

- `all_observations.csv`: this effectively concatenates `modals.csv` from each language, while also adding columns identifying which language the relevant modal in the observation comes from.
- `all_metadata.csv`: this aggregates the metadata from each language and puts it into one CSV table.
- `all_modals.csv`: this presents a new view of the aggregated data *at the level of indidivudal modals*. In particular, each row corresponds to one expression in one language. In this table, there are columns for each (force, flavor) pair, with the corresponding value from the `can_express` column from the relevant `modals.csv` file in that cell. This allows researchers to see the set of force-flavor pairs that each modal expresses in one place, and may assist analyses that depend on that set.
  Note: If a particular (force, flavor) pair was not annotated for a given modal in a given language, there will be an "NA" as the value in that column in this file. This should be viewed as a distinct value from either 1, 0, or ?.

All of these files are generated by running the R script `combine_data.R`, which also exists in this directory. There are three more files present in this directory: one for forces, one for flavors, and a BibTeX file containing all of the reference material. We will mention these in more detail in Section 5, when explaining how to contribute to the database.

4.2 CLDF Format

While the raw format described above is the easiest for human consumption and for contribution by field linguists (see 5), we have also implemented a script that converts the raw data into a database in the Cross-linguistic Dataset Format (CLDF; Forkel et al. 2018). This dataset format—which underlies resources such as the World Atlas of Language Structures (WALS; Dryer and Haspelmath 2013) and Glottolog (Hammarström et al., 2021)—was designed to make the myriad cross-linguistic data being collected "FAIR": Findable, Accessible, Interoperable, and Reusable. While the raw dataset formats are also based on a set of tables in CSV format, it comes with tools (e.g. the Python library pycldf[8]) for converting those into other formats such as an SQLite database, which can enable

[7] See `https://glottolog.org`

[8] `https://github.com/cldf/pycldf`

researchers to asked detailed questions in a full-powered query language.

Similarly, data in CLDF format can be consumed by the tools from the Cross-Linguistic Linked Data project[9], which can be used for instance to develop interactive web applications to interact with the data. Such an application could for example, provide a graphical interface for research to explore which (force, flavor) pairs are most frequently expressed across the recorded languages, which sets of pairs tend to be expressed by the same morphemes, which languages satisfy certain semantic universals (as they are proposed), and so on. Compared to reading each cited descriptive resource for a given language, these data tools could provide quick initial answers to questions about modal typology that may otherwise take significant time to explore at the same level of detail.

While we refer the reader to the aforementioned reference and their webpage[10] for more information and motivation about this format, we here outline some of its properties in order to highlight novel changes that were necessary for our database. CLDF defines specifications for two types of dataset at the highest level: Wordlist and StructureDataset. A Wordlist is intended to capture lexicon-level information, associating concepts with lexical items in a language (often linking to external resources for the available concepts). The World Loanword Database (WOLD; Haspelmath and Tadmor 2009) is a paradigm example. A StructureDataset primarily captures grammatical features at the language level: a basic entry says that a particular language has a paritcular value for a particular parameter. The World Atlas of Language Structures (WALS; Dryer and Haspelmath 2013) is a paradigm example.

Our data, however, can be seen as a mix of these two types of data: we are recording feature values (e.g. *can_express*), but at the lexical level, not the language level. We have implemented this in the following way: in addition to language-level parameter and value tables (which record which modals exist in which languages), we have also added *unit parameter* and *unit value* tables, which record the exact observations about which modals can express which force-flavor pairs as recorded in the basic-format. We refer the reader to the `README.md` file in the `cldf-format` subdirectory for more information on the exact tables in this dataset. We also note that CLDF was designed with extensbility in mind; it is possible that this dataset format will get added to the standard in the future if more datasets are released with the use of it.[11]

The CLDF Format of the data is automatically generated from the basic format by running the script `./build.sh` in the root directory. This script moves basic format data to the appropriate locations and then executes a CLDFBench (Forkel and List, 2020) script for converting raw data into the relevant CLDF tables. We, the maintainers of the dataset, will run this script whenever a new contribution to the basic format is made, so that the CLDF format stays up-to-date. Future work will explore implementing this via continuous integration, so that the CLDF format is automatically built whenever the basic format is updated, without human intervention.

4.3 Case Study: Verifying the IFF Universal

We here provide a small proof-of-concept of the kind of cross-linguistic semantic research that can be benefited from and enabled by the kind of database that we are releasing here. In particular, we show how to query the data to check whether the IFF universal described in Section 3.1 holds. As more data gets added to the database, we can easily and continuously search for counterexamples to this proposed universal. We provide examples of doing this in both data formats.

4.3.1 Basic Format

Running the file `iff.py` in the `basic-format` directory performs a simple check of `all_observations.csv` for expressions that do not satisfy IFF as stated, and outputs the language, expression, and its corresponding observations for inspection. At the time of writing, there are no counterexamples to the universal in our database.

4.3.2 CLDF Format

One other advantage of the CLDF format and toolkit is that it enables researchers to define custom commands that can be run on the command-line to either manipulate the data or verify certain properties thereof. We have illustrated this functionality by implementing a small command

[9] `https://clld.org/`

[10] `https://cldf.clld.org/`

[11] See discussion here about this dataset format: `https://github.com/cldf/cldf/issues/117`. We are grateful to Robert Forkel for his assistance here.

that checks whether the data supports the IFF Universal described above in Section 3.1. In particular, running `cldfbench modals.iff` from the `cldf-format/` directory will execute a Python script for verifying whether every modal in the database satisfies the IFF universal. (The actual implementation can be found in `cldf-format/modalscommands/iff.py`.)

5 Contributing to the Database

We have designed the database—and the basic format in particular—to be structured in a way that makes it easy for linguists to contribute new data from languages that they are studying. As the primary data resides in a GitHub repository, contributing relies heavily on the mechanism of forking and submitting a pull request; for more information on those specific mechanics, we refer to their documentation.[12] The basic process for contributing data from a new language goes as follows (with further details provided in the file `CONTRIBUTING.md` in the repository):

1. Fork the GitHub repository and edit or create a new folder for your language in the `basic-format` directory of the repository.

2. Add a `metadata.yml` file with the information as described in Section 4.1. You can start by copying an existing such file if desired.

3. Edit `basic-format/sources.bib` with the BibTeX information of the descriptive source of your data. Note that the key used in this entry should exactly match the value for 'Reference_key' in the metadata file.

4. Add a `modals.csv` file to your folder, with the corresponding observations. Columns should be: expression, force, flavor, can_express, notes.

5. Optional: run the combine_data.R script to combine this new data with the existing aggregate data files. (If a contributor does not want to do this step, we are happy to do this upon merging the new data into the main repository.)

6. Submit a pull request to the main repository from your fork.

We will use the pull request interface to note any minor formatting issues and have any necessary discussions of the new data. After that quick process, we will merge your new data into the main database, and run the relevant scripts to join it with the rest of the data, including in the CLDF format version.

6 Snapshot

At the time of writing, we have added data from 17 languages to the database. Some information about these languages, including the reference (and its type) that we used to gather this data, may be found in Table 3. Five of the 17 languages have data coming from detailed semantic fieldwork (the ones with 'paper_journal' as their type), with the rest of the data coming from descriptive grammars. There are at present 435 unique observations in our aggregate data file `all_observations.csv`, each one corresponding to one judgment that a particular modal in a language can or cannot express a particular force-flavor pair.

7 Discussion

Most langauges (12 out of 17) in Table 3 are gathered from descriptive sources, i.e. reference grammars that provide general descriptions of the languages. While these languages add diversity to our typology database, the data often lack negative judgements for the relation between expression forms and force-flavor pairs. In other words, it is very often difficult to tell whether an expression *cannot* express a force-flavor pair (i.e. to categorize any expression form and force-flavor pair with a can_express value being 0) from a reference grammar. Researchers conducting analyses with languages with data from reference grammars should beware of this lack of negative data when proceeding. The data stemming from controlled semantic fieldwork tends to provide more negative and more complete data.

While those data tend to come from understudied languages, the methodologies used could be deployed to generate more conistent data for many 'high-resource' languages by eliciting data through crowdsourcing, which has been shown to produce high-quality semantic typology data (Beekhuizen and Stevenson, 2015). The questionnaire of Vander Klok 2021 provides a template for

[12]In particular, the "Working with forks" and "Creating a pull request from a fork" sub-pages of `https://docs.github.com/en/pull-requests/collaborating-with-pull-requests`.

Language	Glotto.code	Reference.key	Reference.type	Complete.language
Donmari	doma1258	(Matras, 2012)	reference-grammar	True
Gitksan	gitx1241	(Matthewson, 2013)	paper-journal	True
Goemai	goem1240	(Hellwig, 2011)	reference-grammar	True
Hinuq	hinu1240	(Forker, 2013)	reference-grammar	True
Hup	hupd1244	(Epps, 2005)	reference-grammar	True
Jamul-Tipay	kumi1248	(Miller, 2001)	reference-grammar	True
Javanese-Paciran	java1254	(Vander Klok, 2013a)	paper-journal	True
Kwaza	kwaz1243	(Voort, 2004)	reference-grammar	True
Lillooet-Salish	lill1248	(Rullmann et al., 2008b)	paper-journal	True
Logoori	logo1258	(Gluckman and Bowler, 2020)	paper-journal	True
Mani	bull1247	(Childs, 2011)	reference-grammar	True
Mian	mian1256	(Fedden, 2011)	reference-grammar	True
Nuosu	sich1238	(Gerner et al., 2013)	reference-grammar	True
Qiang	nort2722	(LaPolla and Huang, 2003)	reference-grammar	True
Tlingit	tlin1245	(Cable, 2017)	paper-journal	True
Tundra-Nenets	nene1249	(Nikolaeva, 2014)	reference-grammar	True
Vaeakau-Taumako	pile1238	(Næss, 2011)	reference-grammar	True

Table 3: Snapshot of current metadata in the Modal Typology Database. Note: we have replaced the 'Reference.key' column with actual references using those keys.

the desired crowdsourcing elicitation process. The questionnaire establishes discourse contexts to retreive modal expressions for various force-flavor pairs. It underspecifies the form of targeted tasks to preserve its adaptablity. Future work could investigate applicable crowdsourcing procedures and how to adapt the questionnaire to elicit the expected form of data. This should enable the production of more complete data with negative examples for many languages.

8 Conclusion

This paper introduced the *Modal Typology Database*, a public repository for typological data on the semantics of modals across langauges. It is intended to be a living database for consolidating cross-linguistic knowledge about modal semantic variation and evaluating and explaining modal semantic universals, among other possible uses. As an example, a recent efficient communication analysis of modal typology by Imel and Steinert-Threlkeld (2022) compared artificial languages based on how many modals therein satisfy particular universals; this analysis could be supplemented with the data presented here to directly compare natural and artificial languages. We have presented a simple model for expressing parameters of variation of the semantics of modals in a theory-neutral manner and outlined how the data are structured as well as how anyone (theoretical linguists, fieldworkers, etc.) may contribute new data. We encourage others to both consume and produce these data, and to reach out to discuss any issues that arise therein.

In addition to expanding the core database with more data and encouraging other uses thereof, future work will focus on building visualization and other tools for interacting with the data in a more user-friendly way. (The CLDF format of the data may be especially well-suited to these goals.) The data schema may also be extended to include more information about the syntactic forms of the expression of modality (possibly using elements of the CLDF schema for forms), in addition to the phenomena of gradable modals and other expressions that often partially contribute modality as well (e.g. tense, evidentiality).

References

Barend Beekhuizen and Suzanne Stevenson. 2015. Crowdsourcing elicitation data for semantic typologies. In *Proceedings of the 37th Annual Meeting of the Cognitive Science Society, CogSci 2015, Pasadena, California, USA, July 22-25, 2015*. cognitivesciencesociety.org.

M Ryan Bochnak. 2015a. Underspecified modality in Washo. In *Proceedings of the Workshop on Structure and Constituency in Languages of the Americas 18 & 19*, volume 39 of *University of Britisch Columbia Working Papers in Linguistics*, pages 3–17.

M Ryan Bochnak. 2015b. Variable force modality in Washo. In *Proceedings of North-East Linguistic Society (NELS) 45*, pages 105–114.

M. Ryan Bochnak and Lisa Matthewson. 2020. Techniques in Complex Semantic Fieldwork. *Annual Review of Linguistics*, 6(1):261–283.

Margit Bowler and John Gluckman. 2021. Cross-categorial gradability in Logoori. *Semantics and Linguistic Theory*, 30(0):273–293.

Seth Cable. 2017. The expression of modality in tlingit: A paucity of grammatical devices1. *International Journal of American Linguistics*, 83:619 – 678.

George Tucker Childs. 2011. *A grammar of Mani*. Mouton grammar library ; 54. De Gruyter Mouton, Berlin ; Boston.

Amy Rose Deal. 2011. Modals Without Scales. *Language*, 87(3):559–585.

Milica Denić, Shane Steinert-Threlkeld, and Jakub Szymanik. 2022. Indefinite Pronouns Optimize the Simplicity/Informativeness Trade-Off. *Cognitive Science*, 46(5):e13142.

Matthew S. Dryer and Martin Haspelmath, editors. 2013. *WALS Online*. Max Planck Institute for Evolutionary Anthropology, Leipzig.

Patience Epps. 2005. *A grammar of Hup*. Ph.D. thesis, University of Virginia.

Sebastian Fedden. 2011. *A grammar of Mian*. Mouton grammar library ; 55. De Gruyter Mouton, Berlin.

Robert Forkel and Johann-Mattis List. 2020. CLDFBench: Give your cross-linguistic data a lift. In *Proceedings of the 12th Language Resources and Evaluation Conference*, pages 6995–7002, Marseille, France. European Language Resources Association.

Robert Forkel, Johann-Mattis List, Simon J. Greenhill, Christoph Rzymski, Sebastian Bank, Michael Cysouw, Harald Hammarström, Martin Haspelmath, Gereon A. Kaiping, and Russell D. Gray. 2018. Cross-linguistic data formats, advancing data sharing and re-use in comparative linguistics. *Scientific Data*, 5(1):180205.

Diana Forker. 2013. *A grammar of Hinuq*. Mouton grammar library, 63. De Gruyter Mouton, Berlin ; Boston.

Matthias Gerner, Georg Bossong, and Matthew Dryer. 2013. *A Grammar of Nuosu*, volume 64 of *Mouton Grammar Library [MGL]*. De Gruyter, Inc, Berlin/Boston.

John Gluckman and Margit Bowler. 2020. The expression of modality in logoori. *Journal of African Languages and Linguistics*, 41(2):195–238.

James Gray. 2021. Variable Modality in Pintupi-Luritja Purposive Clauses. *Languages*, 6(1):52.

Harald Hammarström, Robert Forkel, Martin Haspelmath, and Sebastian Bank. 2021. glottolog/glottolog: Glottolog database 4.5.

Martin Haspelmath and Uri Tadmor, editors. 2009. *WOLD*. Max Planck Institute for Evolutionary Anthropology, Leipzig.

Birgit Hellwig. 2011. *A grammar of Goemai*. Mouton grammar library ; 51. De Gruyter Mouton, Berlin ; Boston.

Nathaniel Imel and Shane Steinert-Threlkeld. 2022. Modals in natural language optimize the simplicity/informativeness trade-off. In *Proceedings of Semantics and Linguistic Theory (SALT 32)*.

Charles Kemp and Terry Regier. 2012. Kinship categories across languages reflect general communicative principles. *Science*, 336(6084):1049–1054.

Christopher Kennedy. 2007. Vagueness and grammar: The semantics of relative and absolute gradable adjectives. *Linguistics and Philosophy*, 30:1–45.

Christopher Kennedy and Louise McNally. 2005. Scale Structure, Degree Modification, and the Semantics of Gradable Predicates. *Language*, 81(2):345–381.

Peter Klecha. 2014. *Bridging the Divide: Scalarity and Modality*. Ph.D. thesis, University of Chicago.

Angelika Kratzer. 1981. The Notional Category of Modality. In Hans-Jürgen Eikmeyer and Hannes Rieser, editors, *Words, Worlds, and Context*, pages 38–74. Walter de Gruyter.

Randy J LaPolla and Chenglong Huang. 2003. *A Grammar of Qiang: With annotated texts and glossary*, 1. aufl. edition, volume 31 of *Mouton Grammar Library [MGL]*. Mouton de Gruyter, Berlin/Boston.

Daniel Lassiter. 2017. *Graded Modality: Qualitative and Quantitative Perspectives*. Oxford University Press.

Yaron Matras. 2012. *A Grammar of Domari*, 1. aufl. edition, volume 59 of *Mouton Grammar Library [MGL]*. Mouton de Gruyter, Berlin/Boston.

Lisa Matthewson. 2004. On the Methodology of Semantic Fieldwork. *International Journal of American Linguistics*, 70(4):369–415.

Lisa Matthewson. 2013. Gitksan modals. *International Journal of American Linguistics*, 79(3):349–394.

Lisa Matthewson. 2019. Modality. In Maria Aloni and Paul Dekker, editors, *The Cambridge Handbook of Formal Semantics*, pages 525–559. Cambridge University Press.

Amy Miller. 2001. *A grammar of Jamul Tiipay: Amy Miller*, volume 23 of *Mouton grammar library*. De Gruyter Mouton.

Francis Mollica, Geoff Bacon, Noga Zaslavsky, Yang Xu, Terry Regier, and Charles Kemp. 2021. The forms and meanings of grammatical markers support efficient communication. *Proceedings of the National Academy of Sciences*, 118(49).

Maša Močnik and Rafael Abramovitz. 2019. A Variable-Force Variable-Flavor Attitude Verb in Koryak. In *Proceedings of the 22nd Amsterdam Colloquium*, pages 494–503.

Fabrice Dominique Nauze. 2008. *Modality in Typological Perspective*. Ph.D. thesis, Universiteit van Amsterdam.

Irina Nikolaeva. 2014. *A grammar of Tundra Nenets*. Mouton grammar library ; Volume 65. De Gruyter Mouton, Berlin, [Germany] ; Boston, [Massachusetts].

Ashild Næss. 2011. *A grammar of Vaeakau-Taumako*. Mouton grammar library ; 52. De Gruyter Mouton, Berlin ; New York.

Paul Portner. 2009. *Modality*. Oxford University Press.

Hotze Rullmann, Lisa Matthewson, and Henry Davis. 2008a. Modals as distributive indefinites. *Natural Language Semantics*, 16(4):317–357.

Hotze Rullmann, Lisa Matthewson, and Henry Davis. 2008b. Modals as distributive indefinites. *Natural Language Semantics*, 16(4):317–357.

Shane Steinert-Threlkeld. 2021. Quantifiers in Natural Language: Efficient Communication and Degrees of Semantic Universals. *Entropy*, 23(10):1335.

Shane Steinert-Threlkeld, Nathaniel Imel, and Qingxia Guo. 2022. A Semantic Universal for Modality. Submitted to Semantics and Pragmatics.

Shane Steinert-Threlkeld and Jakub Szymanik. 2019. Learnability and Semantic Universals. *Semantics & Pragmatics*, 12(4).

Shane Steinert-Threlkeld and Jakub Szymanik. 2020. Ease of Learning Explains Semantic Universals. *Cognition*, 195.

Wataru Uegaki. 2022. The informativeness / complexity trade-off in the domain of Boolean connectives. *Linguistic Inquiry*.

Jozina Vander Klok. 2013a. Pure possibility and pure necessity modals in pariran javanese. *Oceanic Linguistics*, 52(2):341–374.

Jozina Vander Klok. 2013b. Restrictions on semantic variation: A case study on modal system types. In *Workshop on Semantic Variation*.

Jozina Vander Klok. 2021. Revised Modal Questionnaire for Cross-Linguistic Use. Unpublished.

Kai von Fintel and Sabine Iatridou. 2008. How to Say Ought in Foreign: The Composition of Weak Necessity Modals. In Jacqueline Guéron and Jacqueline Lecarme, editors, *Time and Modality*, volume 75 of *Studies in Natural Language and Linguistic Theory*, pages 115–141. Springer Netherlands.

Hein van der Voort. 2004. *A Grammar of Kwaza*, 1. aufl. edition, volume 29 of *Mouton Grammar Library [MGL]*. Mouton de Gruyter, Berlin/Boston.

Hadley Wickham. 2014. Tidy data. *The Journal of Statistical Software*, 59.

Igor Yanovich. 2016. Old English *motan, variable-force modality, and the presupposition of inevitable actualization. *Language*, 92(3):489–521.

Noga Zaslavsky, Charles Kemp, Terry Regier, and Naftali Tishby. 2018. Efficient compression in color naming and its evolution. *Proceedings of the National Academy of Sciences*, 115(31):7937–7942.

The SIGTYP 2022 Shared Task on the Prediction of Cognate Reflexes

Johann-Mattis List[ɯ] **Ekaterina Vylomova**[ɘ] **Robert Forkel**[ɯ]
Nathan W. Hill[ʌ] **Ryan D. Cotterell**[ð]

[ɯ]MPI-EVA Leipzig [ɘ]University of Melbourne [ʌ]University of Dublin [ð]ETH Zürich
mattis_list@eva.mpg.de

Abstract

This study describes the structure and the results of the SIGTYP 2022 shared task on the prediction of cognate reflexes from multilingual wordlists. We asked participants to submit systems that would predict words in individual languages with the help of cognate words from related languages. Training and surprise data were based on standardized multilingual wordlists from several language families. Four teams submitted a total of eight systems, including both neural and non-neural systems, as well as systems adjusted to the task and systems using more general settings. While all systems showed a rather promising performance, reflecting the overwhelming regularity of sound change, the best performance throughout was achieved by a system based on convolutional networks originally designed for image restoration.

1 Introduction

In historical-comparative linguistics, scholars typically assemble words from related languages into *cognate sets*. In contrast to the notion of cognacy in language teaching and synchronic NLP applications, cognate sets are understood as sets of words that share a common origin regardless of their meaning in historical-comparative linguistics and that should not contain borrowed words. The individual members of a cognate set are typically called *cognate reflexes* or simply *reflexes* (Trask, 2000, 278). Cognate reflexes typically show regular sound correspondences. This means that one can define a mapping across the individual phoneme systems of the individual languages. Thus, English *t* typically corresponds to a German *ts* (compare *ten* vs. *zehn*), and English *d* corresponds to German *t* (compare *dove* vs. *Taube*). The mappings often depend on certain contextual conditions and may differ, depending on the position in which they occur in a word. With the help of regular sound correspondences, linguists can often predict fairly well how the cognate counterpart of a word in one language might sound in another language. However, prediction by linguists rarely takes only one language pair into account. The more reflexes a cognate set has in different languages, the easier it is to predict reflexes in individual languages.

1.1 The Reflex Prediction Task

In its simplest form, the data we need for the task of reflex prediction is a table in which each column represents a different language and each row a different cognate set. We also assume that word forms (or "reflexes" of a cognate set) are represented in standardized phonetic transcriptions (such as the International Phonetic Alphabet). Whenever a reflex in a specific language is missing, this reflex can in theory be predicted with the help of the remaining reflexes. As an example, consider Table 2, showing reflexes of cognate sets in German, English, and Dutch. Since the reflex for the BELLY cognate sets is missing in English, we could try and predict it from known correspondences to German and Dutch. The correct prediction would be *bouk*. This form has been still preserved for some time in English in the meaning of "torso", going back to Old English *būk* "belly" (Pfeifer, 1993), although it has nowadays come out of use. When provided with more data of this kind, one can build a model that would be able to predict an English form given a German and a Dutch form, as well as a German form, given a Dutch and an English form, and so on. Note that not all cognate sets in real-life data will have reflexes for all words. Thus, we know about English *bouk* from dialect records, but without dialects or written sources from Middle English, we could only rely on prediction itself in order to guess how the word would sound if it would have been retained.

Since predictions for words that have been completely lost cannot be evaluated directly, we will base our task on the prediction of artificially ex-

Proceedings of the 4th Workshop on Computational Typology and Multilingual NLP (SIGTYP 2022), pages 52 - 62
July 14, 2022 ©2022 Association for Computational Linguistics

Training Data

Dataset	Source	Version	Family	Languages	Words	Cognates
⋆abrahammonpa	Abraham (2005)	v3.0	Tshanglic	8	2063	403
⋆allenbai	Allen (2007)	v4.0	Bai	9	5773	969
⋆backstromnorthernpakistan	Backstrom and Radloff (1992)	v1.0	Sino-Tibetan	7	1426	248
⋆castrosui	Castro and Pan (2015)	v3.0.1	Sui	16	10139	1048
davletshinaztecan	Davletshin (2012)	v1.0	Uto-Aztecan	9	771	118
felekesemitic	Feleke (2021)	v1.0	Afro-Asiatic	19	2583	340
⋆hantganbangime	Hantgan and List (2018)	v1.0	Dogon	16	4405	971
hattorijaponic	Hattori (1973)	v1.0	Japonic	10	1802	278
listsamplesize	List (2014)	v1.0	Indo-European	4	1320	512
mannburmish	Mann (1998)	v1.2	Sino-Tibetan	7	2501	576

Surprise Data

Dataset	Source	Version	Family	Languages	Words	Cognates
bantubvd	Greenhill and Gray (2015)	v4.0	Atlantic-Congo	10	1218	388
beidazihui	Běijīng Dàxué (1962)	v1.1	Sino-Tibetan	19	9750	518
birchallchapacuran	Birchall et al. (2016)	v1.1.0	Chapacuran	10	939	187
bodtkhobwa	Bodt and List (2022)	v3.1.0	Western Kho-Bwa	8	5214	915
⋆bremerberta	Bremer (2016)	v1.1	Berta	4	600	204
⋆deepadungpalaung	Deepadung et al. (2015)	v1.1	Palaung	16	1911	196
hillburmish	Gong and Hill (2020)	v0.2	Sino-Tibetan	9	2202	467
kesslersignificance	Kessler (2001)	v1.0	Indo-European	5	565	212
luangthongkumkaren	Luangthongkum (2019)	v0.2	Sino-Tibetan	8	2363	379
⋆wangbai	Wang and Wang (2004)	v1.0	Sino-Tibetan	10	4356	658

Table 1: Training and surprise data data used in our study. Datasets with identifiers preceded by an asterisk are those in which we automatically searched for cognates. The remaining datasets all provided expert cognates, which we used for the shared task. All datasets are archived with Zenodo, and the supplementary material provides a direct reference to their Zenodo DOI and their GitHub repository URLs.

cluded word forms. Thus, we first take a dataset with cognates in a few related languages, and then artificially delete some of the words in the datasets, using varying proportions. When training a model to predict the missing word forms, we can then compare the predicted words directly with the words we have deleted automatically (List, 2019a).

A special case of the reflex prediction task, *supervised phonological reconstruction*, focuses on the prediction of words in ancestral languages, thus mimicking the process of *phonological reconstruction* as one of the key aspects of the traditional *comparative method* (Weiss, 2015). While we predict reflexes in any language in the generic reflex prediction task, in automated phonological reconstruction we predict one specific reflex of a cognate set, viz. the form in the ancestral language. Apart from the restriction in scope, however, the two tasks do not differ much, and most methods which solve the one task could also be used to solve the other.

Cognate Set	German	English	Dutch
ASH	a ʃ ɛ	æʃ	ɑ s
BITE	b ai s ə n	b ai t	b ɛi t ə
BELLY	b au x	-	b œi k

Table 2: Exemplary cognate reflexes in German, English, and Dutch.

1.2 Background on Reflex Prediction

Quite a few studies on cognate reflex prediction have been published during the past years. Beinborn et al. (2013) uses character-based machine translation approaches to predict cognate candidates in a bilingual setting. Bodt and List (2022) use a method for cognate reflex prediction originally tested by List (2019a) to predict cognate reflexes in so far unobserved data, which was later verified in fieldwork. The method by List (2019a) uses automatically identified *sound correspondence patterns* and phonetic alignment analyses in order to predict for a given set of cognate words how reflexes in languages missing in the cognate set would sound. Meloni et al. (2021) make use of an encoder-decoder model in order to reconstruct Latin words from cognate sets in Romance languages. Fourrier et al. (2021) model cognate reflex prediction as a low-resource machine translation task, building several translation models for Romance languages and using these to evaluate word prediction accuracy. Dekker and Zuidema (2021) use recurrent neural networks for cognate reflex prediction and illustrate how word prediction can be used to solve additional tasks in computational historical linguistics, such as phylogenetic reconstruction or sound correspondence detection.

List et al. (2022a) build on the framework for sound correspondence pattern detection by List (2019a) in order to propose a new framework for supervised phonological reconstruction and cognate reflex prediction which they expand by *enriching* phonetic alignment analyses in such a way that contextual information can be taken account.

1.3 Difficulties of Reflex Prediction

For traditional as well as modern approaches to reflex prediction, there are a couple of challenges that algorithmic solutions need to account for. The first challenge consists in the prediction of sounds which have no corresponding counterpart in the source languages from which one predicts a word in the target language. As an example, consider Dutch *tand* [t ɑ n d] "tooth" and English *tooth* [t ʊː θ]. It is easy to see that the [t] in Dutch corresponds to a [t] in English, such as [aː] corresponds to [ʊː] and [θ] corresponds to [d]. However, the [n] in Dutch has no counterpart in English, since English [n] was lost when followed by a [θ]. Since there is no one-to-one sound match between the sound in English and the sound in Dutch, the prediction has to be based on the *conditioning context*, which is notoriously difficult to handle in computational approaches.

A further difficulty consists in the *sparsity* and the *patchiness* of the data. Data are *sparse* with respect to the number of cognate sets which we can use to train computers or humans. Even for well-established language groups, etymological dictionaries, which list more than 1000 reconstructed items are quite rare. Apart from being *sparse*, data are also *patchy*. Only a very small amount of the proto-forms listed in etymological dictionaries is reflected in the majority of the branches, and an even smaller amount has survived without notable irregularities in the sound changes or the morphology of the word forms. Thus, even if one works with datasets consisting of large numbers of related words, there will always be situations in which important reflexes are missing and at times only one witness may be left that we can use for the prediction of the cognate reflex in question.

2 Materials and Methods

2.1 Materials

Data for the shared task were taken from the Lexibank repository, which offers wordlists from 100 standardized datasets (List et al. 2022a, `https://github.com/lexibank/lexibank-analysed`). In this repository, a large collection of datasets with cognate sets provided by experts and phonetic transcriptions added by the Lexibank team are provided. An even larger number of datasets has only standardized phonetic transcriptions but no cognate judgments. Since cognate detection methods work well by now, we can determine the cognates specifically for shallower language families with quite some confidence; this enabled us to assemble a larger amount of datasets from different language families and either use cognate sets provided by experts or inferring cognates ourselves, using state-of-the-art methods for automated cognate detection implemented in the LingPy software library (List and Forkel, 2021).

For each the training and the surprise phase, 10 datasets were selected. Following the Lexibank workflow for the curation of lexical wordlists, all datasets were curated on GitHub and additionally archived with Zenodo. Standardization of the data included mapping the language names to Glottolog (Hammarström et al., 2021), linking the concept elicitation glosses to the Concepticon reference catalog (`https://concepticon.clld.org`, List et al. 2022c), and adding standardized phonetic transcriptions, following the B(road)IPA system of the Cross-Linguistic Transcription Systems reference catalog (`https://clts.clld.org`, Anderson et al. 2018), with the help of orthography profiles (Moran and Cysouw, 2018). Since only a smaller number of the datasets came along with suitable cognate judgments needed for the cognate reflex prediction task, cognates were automatically inferred with standard settings, using a variant of the LexStat algorithm for automatic cognate detection (List, 2012a) that searches for partial rather than full-word cognates (List et al., 2016). Searching for partial cognates is justified, since both the identification of regular sound correspondences and the prediction of cognate reflexes can only be carried out on material that is entirely cognate (Schweikhard and List, 2020). Since full-word cognates may often contain non-cognate material, the prediction of full cognates would unnecessarily exacerbate the reflex prediction task, adding a random component that cannot be handled algorithmically in a principled way. In all cases, we excluded all singleton cognate sets (cognate sets that occur only in one language), since these cannot be used in our prediction experiments. Table 1 lists all datasets for the test and training phase along with some basic statistics.

The datasets were used as the basis for the data used for test and training during our shared task. For this purpose, each dataset was split into five training and test partitions in which the data retained for testing was varied, starting from a proportion of 10% retained for testing (proportion 0.1), followed by 20% (proportion 0.2), 30% (proportion 0.3), 40% (proportion 0.4), and finally 50% (proportion 0.5). The training data was not modified further and used as primary input for the training phase of all systems. The test data, however, was artificially constructed from the test partition. We first iterated over all cognate sets and then created individual test sets from each cognate set iterating over all words in a cognate set and deleting each word in a row. For a cognate set of n words, this would result in n test cases, in which each word in each language would have to be predicted one time.

2.2 Methods

2.2.1 Evaluation

Among the most commonly used evaluation measures for the word prediction task is the edit distance, which computes the number of operations needed in order to convert the predicted word into the attested word (Levenshtein, 1965). In its primary form, the edit distance is an integer. In order to normalize the measure, correcting for a bias resulting from the length of the compared strings, scholars have proposed to divide the distance by the length of the largest string (Holman et al., 2008), or by the mean length of both strings being compared (Nerbonne et al., 1999). A further possibility closer to notions of distance in bioinformatics, which we used in our shared task, is to divide the edit distance by the length of the alignment of both strings. The normalized edit distance then corresponds to the normalized Hamming distance between two aligned sequences (Hamming, 1950), or – when subtracting from 1 – to the notion of *percentage identity* in evolutionary biology (Raghava and Barton, 2006). It is, however, important to note that actual differences in these normalization procedures are usually small.

The edit distance, both normalized and unnormalized, has been employed in many word prediction and phonological reconstruction experiments as the basic evaluation measure for the prediction accuracy (Meloni et al., 2021; Bouchard-Côté et al., 2013). Its clearest shortcoming lies in the fact that it only accounts for *surface* differences between prediction and attested words (also called 'phenotypic differences' by Lass 1997), while structural aspects (called 'genotypic differences' by Lass 1997) are ignored. Thus, if a method mistakenly maps a certain sound x to a certain sound y in all cases in which the x occurs, the edit distance will treat each occurrence of the error independently and may therefore provide drastically lowered results. It would, therefore, be good to account for the relative *regularity* of the co-occurrence of x and y. List (2019b) proposes to compute B-Cubed F-scores (Amigó et al., 2009) from the aligned predicted and attested words. B-cubed F-scores only check for the regularity of occurrences. This results in scores of 1 (indicating complete identity) for sequence pairs like `abbc` compared with `1223`. Indeed, both sequences are structurally completely identical since a simple mapping between the symbols in both sequences can convert one string into the other and vice versa. If a method has systematic errors but otherwise does a good job in prediction, B-Cubed F-Scores penalize results less strongly than edit distance. As a final evaluation score, we followed Fourrier et al. (2021) in providing BLEU scores (Papineni et al., 2002). These scores are usually used to investigate how well an automated translation corresponds to the translated target test. BLEU scores and B-Cubed F-Scores range from 0 to 1, with 1 indicating perfect agreement, the normalized edit distance ranges between 1 (maximal difference) and 0 (string identity).

2.2.2 Baselines

Our baselines were taken from the reflex prediction framework by List et al. (2022b). This framework consists of four major stages. In stage (1), cognate sets are aligned with the help of standard methods for multiple phonetic alignment analyses (List, 2012b). In stage (2), alignments are *trimmed* by merging all columns in the alignment in which the attested languages all show a gap with their preceding column. As a result, a word like Latin *cenāre* [k eː n aː r ɛ] would be rendered as [k eː n aː r.ɛ], when being aligned with Spanish *cenar* [θ e n a ɾ], since the final [ɛ] in Latin corresponds to a gap in Spanish and could therefore not be predicted (see List et al. 2022b for details on this procedure). In stage (3), alignments are *enriched* by coding for potentially conditioning context, which is added to the alignments in the form of additional rows. In stage (4), the individual alignment columns are converted to a matrix from which a classifier can be trained. During prediction, cognate sets fed to the algorithm are again being aligned and enriched, but the trimming procedure is not needed, since it only relates to the target language that one wants to predict.

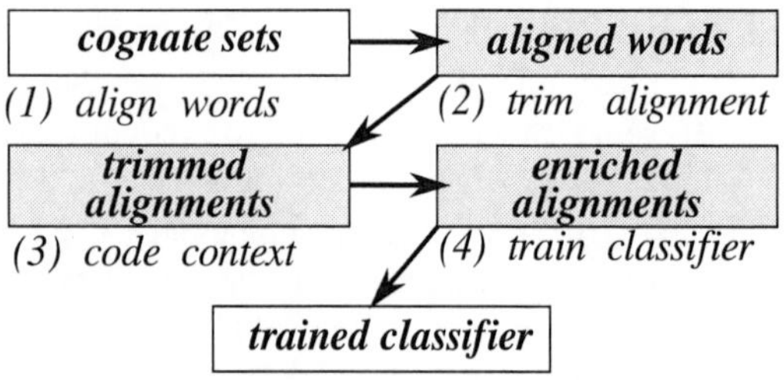

Figure 1: Major steps of the reflex prediction framework underlying the baseline.

Based on this general framework, we created two baselines, one primary baseline that uses the correspondence pattern recognition (**CorPaR**) method by List (2019a) as a classifier, and one extended baseline which predicts words with the help of a support vector machine (**SVM**, see List et al. 2022b for details on both systems). From previous studies on supervised phonological reconstruction we know that the **SVM** variant of the framework outperforms the **CorPaR** classifier clearly, although differences are not extremely high (ibid.).

2.2.3 Implementation

We created specific software package that allows to (1) automatically download the data in the particular versions of the individual CLDF datasets which we used, (2) create the test and training data, (3) apply the baseline methods to the data, and (4) carry out the evaluation. The software package is written in Python and can be accessed both using the commandline and from within Python scripts. It is curated on GitHub and archived with Zenodo (see Section Supplementary Material for details). Different versions were created in order to first release the training data (version 1.1), followed by the release of the surprise data (version 1.2), and finally followed by the release of the official results of the evaluation (version 1.4, providing extended evaluations in contrast to the version 1.3 planned earlier).

Major dependencies of the software package are LingPy (List and Forkel, 2021), used for the computation of the edit distance and of phonetic alignments, Lingrex (List and Forkel, 2022), providing access to the baseline method for cognate reflex prediction, Scikit-learn (Pedregosa et al., 2011), providing access to support vector machines, and Matplotlib (Hunter, 2007), used for plotting.

3 Systems

Four teams submitted their systems for our shared task. Since these systems are described in individual papers (Kirov et al., 2022; Jäger, 2022; Tresoldi, 2022; Celano, 2022), we will only briefly present their main features here.

Team CrossLingference, represented by Gerhard Jäger (University Tübingen), provided a workflow Jäger 2022, implemented in the **Julia** programming language, that makes specifically use of Bayesian phylogenetic inference. In contrast to the remaining systems submitted to our shared task, Jäger's approach takes phylogenetic information into account, extending an earlier workflow for phonological reconstruction (Jäger, 2019).

Team Mockingbird, represented by Christo Kirov, Richard Sproat, and Alexander Gutkin (Google Research), provided two models for the prediction of cognate reflexes. The first model, the **NEIGHBOR TRANSFORMER MODEL**, was originally designed to find problems in the readings of Japanese place names spelled in kanji (Jones et al., 2022), and is based on the popular transformer architecture (Vaswani et al., 2017), which was specifically adjusted for the task. Since the training data would be too small for the transformer model, the authors augmented it with new instances generated by randomly sampling subsets of a corresponding cognate set. In addition to that, they also enriched each set with synthetic instances using n-gram language modelling. The second model, the **IMAGE INPAINTING MODEL**, compares the cognate reflex prediction task to the task of restoring corrupted parts of a 2D image, in which dimensions correspond to languages and cognate phonemic representations. The restoration is achieved with the help of convolutional neural networks (Liu et al., 2018). For this model, no data augmentation steps were undertaken. The authors provide four model configurations of the neighbor model, with the first three (**N1-A**, **N1-B**, and **N1-C**) differing in the number of training steps and not being publicly released, while the last one (**N2**), which was only applied to the 0.1 proportion of the data, being publicly released. For the image inpainting model, one configuration was provided (**I1**).

Team Leipzig, represented by Giuseppe G. A. Celano (University Leipzig), provided a TRANSFORMER-based architecture with character and position embeddings for the prediction of cognate reflexes (Vaswani et al., 2017), in which language information was one-hot encoded and the model was trained on individual reflex pairs on each language independently. In order to predict a word from several reflexes in different languages, the system first predicts individual target tensors of probabilities for each attested reflex and then averages them to produce the prediction.

Team CEoT, represented by Tiago Tresoldi (Uppsala University), provided a workflow that predicts cognate reflexes based on phonetic alignments (Tresoldi, 2022), which is quite similar to the extended baselines of our shared task (List et al., 2022b). In contrast to our baseline approaches, their system **EXTALIGN-RF** skips the trimming procedure (stage 2), varies the techniques for alignment enrichment by taking preceding and following context into account (stage 3), and uses a random forests classifier rather than a support vector machine.

While all teams tried hard to provide results for all of their systems, some results could not be computed in time, to be included in the shared task. All teams were asked to share their data in such a way that users can easily replicate the results and also apply their methods to new data. Unfortunately, there was no time for the team organizing the shared task to individually check all systems with respect to replicability and transparency. The team checked, however, that all systems were properly archived with repositories offering long-term storage of data, such as Zenodo, and we communicated the importance of replication with all authors.

4 Results

Given that we measure system performance with four evaluation measures (edit distance, normalized edit distance, B-Cubed F-Scores, and BLEU scores adjusted for word prediction), one might expect that systems perform differently with respect to different evaluation measures. As can be seen from the results in Table 3, however, the results are rather clearly favoring the system **I1** by the team Mockingbird as the winner in almost all proportions. The only case where the Mockingbird **I1** system does not show the best performance is the test with 50% of the words being retained for test-

Proportion in Test: 0.1				
System	**ED**	**NED**	**B-Cubes**	**BLEU**
Baseline	1.2095	0.3119	0.7231	0.5716
Baseline-SVM	**1.0189**	**0.2625**	**0.7626**	0.6387
CEoT-Extalign-RF	1.0377	0.2763	0.7475	0.6243
CrossLingference-Julia	1.4804	0.3929	0.7251	0.4793
Leipzig-Transformer	1.3901	0.3687	0.6489	0.5114
Mockingbird-I1	0.9201	0.2431	0.7673	0.6633
Mockingbird-N1-A	1.0223	0.2568	0.7604	**0.6479**
Mockingbird-N1-B	1.0437	0.2625	0.7572	0.6398
Mockingbird-N1-C	1.1263	0.2867	0.7302	0.6115
Mockingbird-N2	1.2095	0.3135	0.7054	0.5744
Proportion in Test: 0.2				
System	**ED**	**NED**	**B-Cubes**	**BLEU**
Baseline	1.3253	0.3361	0.6680	0.5412
Baseline-SVM	1.1723	0.2928	**0.7067**	0.5985
CEoT-Extalign-RF	1.2208	0.3175	0.6798	0.5709
CrossLingference-Julia	1.4954	0.3912	0.6882	0.4760
Leipzig-Transformer	1.5787	0.4046	0.5683	0.4646
Mockingbird-I1	1.0413	0.2648	0.7120	0.6326
Mockingbird-N1-A	**1.1512**	**0.2825**	0.7011	**0.6138**
Mockingbird-N1-B	1.1726	0.2901	0.6910	0.6054
Mockingbird-N1-C	1.2196	0.3051	0.6669	0.5841
Proportion in Test: 0.3				
System	**ED**	**NED**	**B-Cubes**	**BLEU**
Baseline	1.4354	0.3556	0.6372	0.5195
Baseline-SVM	1.3713	0.3310	**0.6565**	0.5554
CEoT-Extalign-RF	1.4038	0.3525	0.6331	0.5286
CrossLingference-Julia	1.6116	0.4130	0.6508	0.4503
Leipzig-Transformer	1.7746	0.4467	0.5129	0.4207
Mockingbird-I1	1.1762	0.2899	0.6717	0.6059
Mockingbird-N1-A	**1.2565**	**0.3119**	0.6557	0.5779
Mockingbird-N1-B	1.2712	0.3103	0.6531	**0.5792**
Mockingbird-N1-C	1.3009	0.3215	0.6343	0.5636
Proportion in Test: 0.4				
System	**ED**	**NED**	**B-Cubes**	**BLEU**
Baseline	1.6821	0.4011	0.6001	0.4717
Baseline-SVM	1.6159	0.3891	0.5990	0.4903
CEoT-Extalign-RF	1.5695	0.3960	0.5805	0.4773
CrossLingference-Julia	1.6059	0.4112	**0.6411**	0.4473
Leipzig-Transformer	1.9221	0.4800	0.4736	0.3893
Mockingbird-I1	1.2725	0.3162	0.6428	0.5724
Mockingbird-N1-A	**1.4542**	**0.3521**	0.6294	0.5293
Mockingbird-N1-B	1.3618	0.3349	0.6212	**0.5466**
Mockingbird-N1-C	1.4353	0.3547	0.5999	0.5228
Proportion in Test: 0.5				
System	**ED**	**NED**	**B-Cubes**	**BLEU**
Baseline	1.8889	0.4445	0.5617	0.4265
Baseline-SVM	1.9330	0.4619	0.5371	0.4204
CEoT-Extalign-RF	1.8434	0.4576	0.5194	0.4128
CrossLingference-Julia	1.6794	0.4274	0.6193	0.4296
Leipzig-Transformer	2.1036	0.5257	0.4306	0.3438
Mockingbird-I1	1.4170	0.3518	**0.6050**	0.5337
Mockingbird-N1-A	1.5527	0.3800	0.5959	0.4934
Mockingbird-N1-B	**1.5066**	**0.3734**	0.5864	**0.4989**
Mockingbird-N1-C	1.5818	0.3950	0.5610	0.4749

Table 3: Results for the varying proportions and our four evaluation measures, edit distance (ED), normalized edit distance (NED), B-Cubed F-scores (B-Cubes) and BLEU Scores (BLEU) on the surprise data. Cells shaded in gray highlight the best score obtained for a given proportion, bold font marks the second best score.

System	Rank	NED	B-Cubes	BLEU	Aggregated
Mockingbird-I1	1	1	1.2	1	1.1 ± 0.3
Mockingbird-N1-A	2	2.6	3	2.6	2.7 ± 0.4
Mockingbird-N1-B	3	2.4	4	2.4	2.9 ± 0.9
Baseline-SVM	4	5.2	4	5	4.7 ± 1.9
Mockingbird-N1-C	5	4.6	6.6	4.6	5.3 ± 1.3
CEoT-Extalign-RF	6	6	7	6.2	6.4 ± 1.1
CrossLingference-Julia	7	7.6	4	7.6	6.4 ± 2.5
Baseline	8	6.8	6.2	6.8	6.6 ± 0.8
Leipzig-Transformer	9	8.8	9	8.8	8.9 ± 0.4

Table 4: Overview of the average ranks of all nine systems for the different dataset proportions along with aggregated ranks.

ing (proportion 0.5), where the **JULIA** system by the CrossLingference team shows the best performance with respect to the B-Cubed F-Scores. Since B-Cubed F-Scores emphasize the systematicity of the prediction quality rather than the accuracy in individual cases, we can see that the **JULIA** system copes better with systematic aspects of the word prediction tasks in those cases, where the data for the training of the system is limited. That the different scoring systems show at least some degree of independence can also be seen in Figure 2, which shows results for the 10% partition, where the **JULIA** system performs worst with respect to edit distances and BLEU scores, while showing a better performance than **N2**, **TRANSFORMER**, and the baseline in B-Cubed F-Scores.

While the **SVM** baseline shows a surprisingly good performance on the lowest proportion of data excluded and retained for testing (proportion 0.1), it looses ground with more data excluded for testing. Here, the **N1-A** and **N1-B** systems, again from the Mockingbird team, show the best performance.

Table 4 provides the aggregated ranks for the normalized edit distance, the B-Cubed F-Scores, and the BLEU scores for all systems obtained for all splits of the data. The classical edit distance was excluded in this overview, since it correlates highly with the normalized edit distance and would therefore artificially increase the overall ranks of systems performing well in this regard. Furthermore, the **N2** system by the Mockingbird team was excluded in this analysis, since results could only be provided for the smallest proportion of words retained for testing (proportion 0.1). For each of the five splits of the data and for each of the methods, we ranked the systems according to their performance and later calculated the average of all ranks for each system on each of the three evaluation methods. The aggregated ranks, in which all three evaluation measures are ranked equally, allow us to rank the overall performance of all systems. It shows the overall superiority of the **I1** system of the Mockingbird team, followed by the teams' **N1-A** and **N1-B** methods. The **SVM** baseline and the **N1-C** method by team Mockingbird follow on places four and five. At the end of these ranks are the **EXTALIGN-RF** system by team CeOT, the **JULIA** system by Team CrossLingference, followed by the simple baseline and the **TRANSFORMER** approach of team Leipzig.

Overall, all systems do quite a good job at recovering unknown words from their cognate sets, specifically in those cases, where only a small part of the test data was retained for the evaluation process. Judging from our practical experience and independently published results on word prediction experiments (List et al., 2022b; Bodt and List, 2022), B-Cubed F-Scores higher than 0.7 and average edit distances of about 1 provide a good starting point for computer-assisted approaches and can already provide active help in various practical annotation tasks in historical linguistics. Thus, scholars working on the reconstruction of certain language families could use predicted proto-forms and later manually correct them, or field workers could use automatically predicted words when trying to elicit specific lexical items to search for cognate words that might have shifted their meanings.

5 Discussion

It was one of the crucial insights made by historical linguists in the early 19th century (Grimm, 1822; Rask, 1818), that sound change proceeds in a surprisingly regular, systematic manner, affecting all sounds in the lexicon of a language that recur in similar phonotactic positions. Without the systematicity and regularity of sound change, it would not be possible to predict the pronunciation of words in one language based on the pronunciation of cognate words in related languages. While it has been known for a long time to linguists that these kinds of predictions can be made on the basis of historical language comparison, the task of cognate reflex prediction has only recently attracted the attention of scholars working in the field of Natural Language Processing and computational linguistics.

With our shared task on cognate reflex prediction, we hoped to achieve two major goals. On the one hand, we wanted to highlight the importance of classical scholarship for computational applications in historical linguistics and linguistic

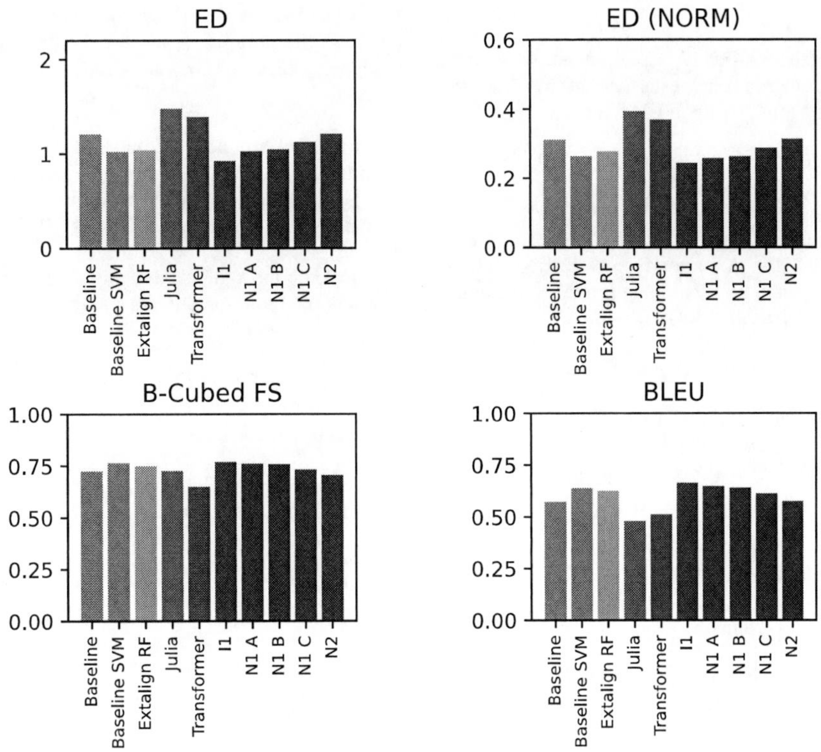

Figure 2: Results for the surprise dataset of the 0.1 proportion, with 10% of data retained for testing.

typology, showing that quite a few problems which are up to today exclusively solved manually might profit from computational treatment. On the other hand, we wanted to trigger the interest of scholars with diverse backgrounds in this task, assembling teams that address the problem with different strategies that might inspire each other and help to lead to largely improved methods in the future.

With the four teams that participated, we have seen an interesting and diverse assembly of systems that all deal with the cognate reflex prediction task. While two teams made use of state-of-the-art machine learning methods based on neural networks (team Mockingbird and team Leipzig), two teams represented systems based on workflows using classical approaches in the emerging discipline of computational historical linguistics (team CrossLingference and team CEoT), using phonetic alignments, and – in the case of team CrossLingference – even Bayesian methods for phylogenetic reconstruction. From the overall performance of the systems in our shared task, we can see that some of the neural approaches outperform the more targeted solutions. Given differences in the performance with respect to the evaluation methods, which highlight different aspects of prediction accuracy, however, we could also see that targeted methods like the Julia method by CrossLingference or the extended Baseline come very close to the best neural systems, and even outperform them at times.

Acknowledgements

This study was partially supported by the Max Planck Society Research Grant "Beyond CALC: Computer-Assisted Approaches to Human Prehistory, Linguistic Typology, and Human Cognition (CALC³)", awarded to Johann-Mattis List (2022-2024). We thank Clémentine Fourrier for comments and suggestions on the evaluation procedure, and we thank all participants for their feedback during the task.

Supplementary Material

Data and code for the shared task along with results for all systems are curated GitHub (`https://github.com/sigtyp/ST2022`, Version 1.4) and have been archived with Zenodo (`https://doi.org/10.5281/zenodo.6586772`).

References

Binny et al Abraham. 2005. A sociolinguistic research among selected groups in Western Arunachal Pradesh highlighting Monpa. Unpublished manuscript.

Bryan Allen. 2007. *Bai Dialect Survey*. SIL International, Dallas.

Enrique Amigó, Julio Gonzalo, Javier Artiles, and Felisa Verdejo. 2009. A comparison of extrinsic clustering evaluation metrics based on formal constraints. *Information Retrieval*, 12(4):461–486.

Cormac Anderson, Tiago Tresoldi, Thiago Costa Chacon, Anne-Maria Fehn, Mary Walworth, Robert Forkel, and Johann-Mattis List. 2018. A Cross-Linguistic Database of Phonetic Transcription Systems. *Yearbook of the Poznań Linguistic Meeting*, 4(1):21–53.

Peter C. Backstrom and Carla F. Radloff. 1992. *Languages of Northern Areas*, volume 2 of *Sociolinguistic Survey of Northern Pakistan*. National Institute of Pakistan Studies, Islamabad.

Lisa Beinborn, Torsten Zesch, and Iryna Gurevych. 2013. Cognate production using character-based machine translation. In *Proceedings of the Sixth International Joint Conference on Natural Language Processing*, pages 883–891.

Joshua Birchall, Michael Dunn, and Simon J. Greenhill. 2016. A Combined Comparative and Phylogenetic Analysis of the Chapacuran Language Family. *International Journal of American Linguistics*, 82(3):255–284.

Timotheus Adrianus Bodt and Johann-Mattis List. 2022. Reflex prediction. A case study of Western Kho-Bwa. *Diachronica*, 39(1):1–38.

Alexandre Bouchard-Côté, David Hall, Thomas L. Griffiths, and Dan Klein. 2013. Automated reconstruction of ancient languages using probabilistic models of sound change. *Proceedings of the National Academy of Sciences of the United States of America*, 110(11):4224–4229.

Nate D. Bremer. 2016. *A sociolinguistic survey of six Berta speech varieties in Ethiopia*. SIL International, Addis Ababa.

Beijing University Běijīng Dàxué. 1962. *Hànyǔ fāngyīn zìhuì 汉语方音字汇 [Chinese dialect character pronunciation list]*. Wénzì Gǎigé, Běijīng.

Andy Castro and Xingwen Pan, editors. 2015. *Sui dialect research*. SIL International, Guizhou.

Giuseppe G. A. Celano. 2022. A Transformer architecture for the prediction of cognate reflexes. In *The Fourth Workshop on Computational Typology and Multilingual NLP*, Online. Association for Computational Linguistics.

Albert Davletshin. 2012. Proto-uto-aztecans on their way to the proto-aztecan homeland: linguistic evidence. *Journal of Language Relationship*, 1(8):75–92.

Sujaritlak Deepadung, Supakit Buakaw, and Ampika Rattanapitak. 2015. A lexical comparison of the Palaung dialects spoken in China, Myanmar, and Thailand. *Mon-Khmer Studies*, 44:19–38.

Peter Dekker and Willem Zuidema. 2021. Word prediction in computational historical linguistics. *Journal of Language Modelling*, 8(2):295–336.

Tekabe Legesse Feleke. 2021. Ethiosemitic languages: Classifications and classification determinants. *Ampersand*, page 100074.

Clémentine Fourrier, Rachel Bawden, and Benoît Sagot. 2021. Can cognate prediction be modelled as a low-resource machine translation task? In *Findings of the Association for Computational Linguistics: ACL-IJCNLP 2021*, pages 847–861, Online. Association for Computational Linguistics.

Xun Gong and Nathan Hill. 2020. *Materials for an Etymological Dictionary of Burmish*. Zenodo, Geneva.

Simon J Greenhill and Russell D Gray. 2015. Bantu Basic Vocabulary Database.

Jacob Grimm. 1822. *Deutsche Grammatik*, 2 edition, volume 1. Dieterichsche Buchhandlung, Göttingen.

Harald Hammarström, Martin Haspelmath, Robert Forkel, and Sebastiaon Bank. 2021. *Glottolog [Dataset, Version 4.5]*. Max Planck Institute for Evolutionary Anthropology, Leipzig.

Richard W. Hamming. 1950. Error detection and error detection codes. *Bell System Technical Journal*, 29(2):147–160.

Abbie Hantgan and Johann-Mattis List. 2018. Bangime: Secret language, language isolate, or language island?

Shirō Hattori. 1973. Japanese dialects. In Henry M. Hoenigswald and Robert H. Langacre, editors, *Diachronic, areal and typological linguistics*, number 11 in Current Trends in Linguistics, pages 368–400. Mouton, The Hague and Paris.

Eric W. Holman, Søren Wichmann, Cecil H. Brown, Viveka Velupillai, André Müller, and Dik Bakker. 2008. Advances in automated language classification. In Antti Arppe, Kaius Sinnemäki, and Urpu Nikann, editors, *Quantitative Investigations in Theoretical Linguistics*, pages 40–43. University of Helsinki, Helsinki.

John D. Hunter. 2007. Matplotlib: A 2D graphics environment. *Computing In Science & Engineering*, 9(3):90–95.

Llion Jones, Richard Sproat, and Haruko Ishikawa. 2022. Helpful neighbors: Leveraging geographic neighbors to aid in placename pronunciation. In preparation.

Gerhard Jäger. 2019. Computational historical linguistics. *Theoretical Linguistics*, 45(3-4):151–182.

Gerhard Jäger. 2022. Bayesian phylogenetic cognate prediction. In *The Fourth Workshop on Computational Typology and Multilingual NLP*, Online. Association for Computational Linguistics.

Brett Kessler. 2001. *The significance of word lists*. CSLI Publications, Stanford.

Christo Kirov, Richard Sproat, and Alexander Gutkin. 2022. Mockingbird at the SIGTYP 2022 Shared Task: Two types of models for the prediction of cognate reflexes. In *The Fourth Workshop on Computational Typology and Multilingual NLP*, Online. Association for Computational Linguistics.

Roger Lass. 1997. *Historical linguistics and language change*. Cambridge University Press, Cambridge.

Vladimir. I. Levenshtein. 1965. Dvoičnye kody s ispravleniem vypadenij, vstavok i zameščenij simvolov [binary codes with correction of deletions, insertions and replacements]. *Doklady Akademii Nauk SSSR*, 163(4):845–848.

Johann-Mattis List. 2012a. LexStat. Automatic detection of cognates in multilingual wordlists. In *Proceedings of the EACL 2012 Joint Workshop of Visualization of Linguistic Patterns and Uncovering Language History from Multilingual Resources*, pages 117–125, Stroudsburg.

Johann-Mattis List. 2012b. SCA: Phonetic alignment based on sound classes. In Marija Slavkovik and Dan Lassiter, editors, *New directions in logic, language, and computation*, pages 32–51. Springer, Berlin and Heidelberg.

Johann-Mattis List. 2014. Investigating the impact of sample size on cognate detection. *Journal of Language Relationship*, 11:91–101.

Johann-Mattis List. 2019a. Automatic inference of sound correspondence patterns across multiple languages. *Computational Linguistics*, 45(1):137–161.

Johann-Mattis List. 2019b. Beyond Edit Distances: Comparing linguistic reconstruction systems. *Theoretical Linguistics*, 45(3-4):1–10.

Johann-Mattis List and Robert Forkel. 2021. *LingPy. A Python library for quantitative tasks in historical linguistics [Software Library, Version 2.6.9]*. Max Planck Institute for Evolutionary Anthropology, Leipzig.

Johann-Mattis List and Robert Forkel. 2022. *LingRex: Linguistic reconstruction with LingPy [Software Library, Version 1.2]*. Max Planck Institute for Evolutionary Anthropology, Leipzig.

Johann-Mattis List, Robert Forkel, Simon J. Greenhill, Christoph Rzymski, Johannes Englisch, and Russell D. Gray. 2022a. Lexibank, A public repository of standardized wordlists with computed phonological and lexical features. *Scientific Data*, pages 1–31.

Johann-Mattis List, Nathan W. Hill, and Robert Forkel. 2022b. A new framework for fast automated phonological reconstruction using trimmed alignments and sound correspondence patterns. In *Proceedings of the 3rd Workshop on Computational Approaches to Historical Language Change*, Dublin [Online]. Association for Computational Linguistics.

Johann-Mattis List, Philippe Lopez, and Eric Bapteste. 2016. Using sequence similarity networks to identify partial cognates in multilingual wordlists. In *Proceedings of the Association of Computational Linguistics 2016 (Volume 2: Short Papers)*, pages 599–605, Berlin. Association of Computational Linguistics.

Johann-Mattis List, Annika Tjuka, Christoph Rzymski, Simon J. Greenhill, Nathanael E. Schweikhard, and Robert Forkel. 2022c. *Concepticon. A resource for the linking of concept lists [Dataset, Version 2.6.0]*. Max Planck Institute for Evolutionary Anthropology, Leipzig.

Guilin Liu, Fitsum A. Reda, Kevin J. Shih, Ting-Chun Wang, Andrew Tao, and Bryan Catanzaro. 2018. Image inpainting for irregular holes using partial convolutions. In *Proceedings of the 15th European Conference on Computer Vision (ECCV 2018)*, pages 89–105, Munich, Germany. Springer International Publishing. Preprint.

Theraphan Luangthongkum. 2019. A view on Proto-Karen phonology and lexicon. *Journal of the Southeast Asian Linguistics Society*, 12(1):i–lii.

Noel Walter Mann. 1998. *A phonological reconstruction of Proto Northern Burmic*. Phd, The University of Texas, Arlington.

Carlo Meloni, Shauli Ravfogel, and Yoav Goldberg. 2021. Ab antiquo: Neural proto-language reconstruction. In *Proceedings of the 2021 Conference of the North American Chapter of the Association for Computational Linguistics: Human Language Technologies*, pages 4460–4473, Online. Association for Computational Linguistics.

Steven Moran and Michael Cysouw. 2018. *The Unicode Cookbook for Linguists: Managing writing systems using orthography profiles*. Language Science Press, Berlin.

John Nerbonne, Wilbert Heeringa, and Peter Kleiweg. 1999. Edit distance and dialect proximity. In David Sankoff and Joseph. B. Kruskal, editors, *Time warps, string edits, and macromolecules. The theory and practice of sequence comparison*, reprint edition, pages V–XV. CSLI Publications, Stanford.

Kishore Papineni, Salim Roukos, Todd Ward, and Wei-Jing Zhu. 2002. Bleu: a method for automatic evaluation of machine translation. In *Proceedings of the 40th Annual Meeting of the Association for Computational Linguistics*, pages 311–318, Philadelphia, Pennsylvania, USA. Association for Computational Linguistics.

F. Pedregosa, G. Varoquaux, A. Gramfort, V. Michel, B. Thirion, O. Grisel, M. Blondel, P. Prettenhofer, R. Weiss, V. Dubourg, J. Vanderplas, A. Passos, D. Cournapeau, M. Brucher, M. Perrot, and E. Duchesnay. 2011. Scikit-learn: Machine learning in Python. *Journal of Machine Learning Research*, 12:2825–2830.

Wolfgang Pfeifer. 1993. *Etymologisches Wörterbuch des Deutschen*, 2 edition. Akademie, Berlin.

G. P. S. Raghava and Geoffrey J. Barton. 2006. Quantification of the variation in percentage identity for protein sequence alignments. *BMC Bioinformatics*, 7(415).

Rasmus K. Rask. 1818. *Undersögelse om det gamle Nordiske eller Islandske sprogs oprindelse*. Gyldendalske Boghandlings Forlag, Copenhagen.

Nathanael E. Schweikhard and Johann-Mattis List. 2020. Developing an annotation framework for word formation processes in comparative linguistics. *SKASE Journal of Theoretical Linguistics*, 17(1):2–26.

Robert L. Trask. 2000. *The dictionary of historical and comparative linguistics*. Edinburgh University Press, Edinburgh.

Tiago Tresoldi. 2022. Approaching reflex predictions as a classification problem from extended phonological alignments. In *The Fourth Workshop on Computational Typology and Multilingual NLP*, Online. Association for Computational Linguistics.

Ashish Vaswani, Noam Shazeer, Niki Parmar, Jakob Uszkoreit, Llion Jones, Aidan N Gomez, Łukasz Kaiser, and Illia Polosukhin. 2017. Attention is all you need. In *Proceedings of the 31st Conference on Neural Information Processing Systems (NIPS 2017)*, pages 5998–6008, Long Beach, CA. Curran Associates Inc.

Feng Wang and William S.-Y. Wang. 2004. Basic words and language evolution. *Language and Linguistics*, 5(3):643–662.

Michael Weiss. 2015. The comparative method. In Claire Bowern and Nicholas Evans, editors, *The Routledge handbook of historical linguistics*, pages 127–145. Routledge, New York.

Bayesian Phylogenetic Cognate Prediction

Gerhard Jäger
University of Tübingen
Seminar für Sprachwissenschaft
gerhard.jaeger@uni-tuebingen.de

Abstract

In Jäger (2019) a computational framework was defined to start from parallel word lists of related languages and infer the corresponding vocabulary of the shared proto-language. The SIGTYP 2022 Shared Task is closely related. The main difference is that what is to be reconstructed is not the proto-form but an unknown word from an extant language. The system described here is a re-implementation of the tools used in the mentioned paper, adapted to the current task.

1 Introduction

In Jäger (2019) I presented a pilot study of a computational historical linguistics workflow. Starting from parallel word lists (taken from Wichmann et al. 2016) of 29 Romance languages and dialects, covering 40 core concepts, it produced reconstructions of the Proto-Romance words for the same concepts.

The intermediate steps of this workflow are

1. for each concept, cluster the corresponding sound strings into *cognate classes*,
2. infer a posterior distribution of phylogenies of the covered doculects using Bayesian inference,
3. apply Bayesian inference to identify the *maximum a posteriori* cognate class at the root of the tree for each concept (*ancestral state reconstruction*, ASR),
4. apply multiple sequence alignment (MSA) to the words of each cognate class,
5. apply ASR to each alignment column of the MSAs of the cognate classes identified in step 3; gaps are treated as regular characters, and
6. concatenate the reconstructions and removing gaps.

The result turned out to be an imperfect but reasonable approximations of the attested Latin wordlist.

The SIGTYP 2022 Shared Task on the Prediction of Cognate Reflexes (https://github.com/sigtyp/ST2022, List et al. 2022) is very similar in nature. The system described here is an adaptation of Jäger's (2019) workflow to this task.

2 Data

The authors of the Shared Task made parallel word lists for 20 language families available. For details of the provinence of the data and the pre-processing steps performed, see List et al. (2022). Each dataset comprises between four and 19 related languages, and between 500 and ca. 10,000 words. Words are classified according to cognate classes, which are based either on expert judgments or are inferred via automatic cognate detection. No information about the meanings of the words are available for training or inference. All words are transcribed in IPA and tokenized.

The data are arranged in a table with cognate classes as rows and languages as columns. In Table 1, a small part from the dataset kesslersignificance (based on Kessler 2001) is shown for illustration.

Each dataset was split into a training set and a test set. The proportion of test data was varied between 10%, 20%, 30%, 40% and 50%, leading to a total of 50 datasets, each consisting of a training and a test set. For the test data, one word per row was masked, using each attested word for masking in turn. The task is to predict the masked words from the other cognates in the same row.

Table 2 contains an example row from such a test set. The task is to infer the French word which is cognate to Albanian *piski*, English *fɪʃ*, German *fiʃ* and Latin *piski*. In a separate file which is only to be used for evaluation, the correct solution — *pʃ* in this case — is given.

Proceedings of the 4th Workshop on Computational Typology and Multilingual NLP (SIGTYP 2022), pages 63 - 69
July 14, 2022 ©2022 Association for Computational Linguistics

COGID	Albanian	English	French	German	Latin
920		h ɑ r t	k œ r	h e r ts ə n	k o r d
1083		h ɔ r n	k ɔ r n	h o r n	k o r n u:
1150	ʃ k u r t ə r	ʃ ɔ r t	k u r t	k u r ts	

Table 1: Example training data

COGID	Albanian	English	French	German	Latin
353-3	p e ʃ k	f ɪ ʃ	?	f i ʃ	p i s k i

Table 2: Example test data

For each of the 50 datasets, a system can be trained using the complete training set. For prediction, the trained system only "sees" one row of the test data and has to predict the masked word.

3 Methods

This task differs from the one described in (Jäger, 2019) mainly by the fact that not some ancestral word form has to be inferred but a word from an extant language. For the particular inference methods used, this difference is actually inessential, since it is based on a *time-reversible* model of language change.

The first step of the workflow by Jäger (2019), identifying cognate classes, has already been performed here. This led to the following workflow:

1. Train a pair-hidden Markov model (pHMM; see Durbin et al. 1989) for pairwise string alignment.[1]

2. Infer a preliminary phylogenetic tree via UPGMA (Sokal and Michener, 1958).

3. Perform MSA per cognate class using the T-Coffee algorithm (Notredame et al., 2000).

4. Join all MSA matrices and use this as character matrix for Bayesian phylogenetic inference.[2]

5. Infer the posterior distribution of the mutation rate of symbols within the columns of the MSAs.

6. Apply MSA to the non-masked entries in the test row using the model trained in steps 1 and 2.

7. Find the *maximum a-posteriori* state for each MSA column for the masked entry, using the posterior distributions inferred in steps 4 and 5 as priors. Concatenate the states inferred in the previous step and remove gap symbols.

Each of these steps will be briefly explained in the following subsections.

3.1 Training a Pair-Hidden Markov Model

A *pair-Hidden Markov Model* (pHMM) is a Hidden Markov model with two parallel output tapes. In each state, the model may emit a symbol on the first, the second or on both tapes. The architecture used here is taken from Durbin et al. (1989) and schematically displayed in Figure 1.

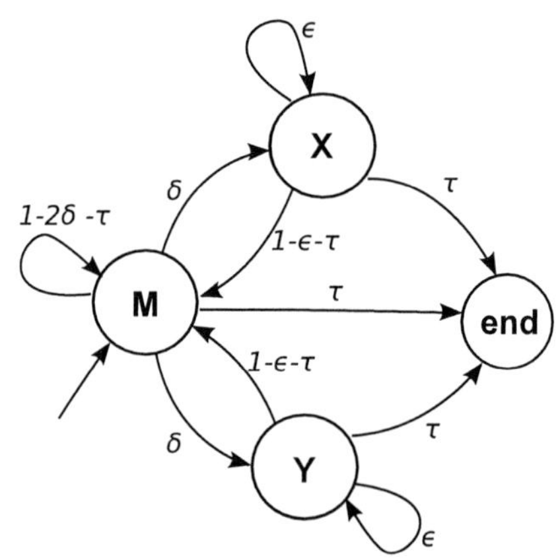

Figure 1: Pair Hidden Markov Model

The state **M** is the *match* state, where the model simultaneously emits one symbol on each tape. In

[1]In Jäger (2019), pairwise string alignment was performed using the Needleman-Wunsch algorithm (Needleman and Wunsch, 1970) with parameters trained on the entire ASJP database (Wichmann et al., 2016). Since the rules of the Shared Task precludes the use or external data for parameter training, I opted for a method here were parameters can be estimated from scratch using only the licit training data.

[2]In Jäger (2019) phylogenetic inference was performed using cognate data, but since the Shared Task does not make information about the meaning of the words available, this was not possible here.

state **X** only a symbol to the first tape is emitted, and likewise for state **Y** and the second tape. When the model reaches the **end** state (where no symbol is emitted), each tape contains a symbol sequence. The joint probability of this sequence and the simultaneous sequence of hidden states is determined by the product of the transition and emission probabilities used.

Crucially, the sequence of hidden states of one pass of the model determines a pairwise alignment of the strings produced. **M** identifies a match column, **X** a column with a gap in the second string, and **Y** a gap in the first string. If the parameters of the model are known, the maximum likelihood alignment between two strings can be found using the *Viterbi algorithm*.[3]

It is assumed that the alphabet from which the words are constructed are known in advance. The parameters of the model are the transition probabilities δ, ϵ and τ, and the emission probabilities for each state. For state **M**, this is a probability distribution over pairs of symbols from the alphabet. I assume the emission probabilites for states **X** and **Y** to be identical; both are a probability distribution over the alphabet.

Given a training set of pairs of strings, parameters of the model can be estimated using the *Baum-Welch algorithm*, an incarnation of the EM algorithm. If values for all parameters of the model are given, the frequency of all transitions and all emissions for a given set of string pairs are estimated (expectation step). The conditional relative frequencies for each transition and emission are then used as new parameter values (maximization step). This procedure is repeated many times, starting from an arbitrary initial state.

In the system described here, the pHMM was initialized with transition probabilities $\delta = \tau = 0.25, \epsilon = 0.375$. The initial emission probabilities at the gap states **X** and **Y** are uniform distributions. The emission probabilities in the match state **M** are

$$\begin{aligned} p(a,b) &\propto 1 && \text{if } a \neq b \\ p(a,a) &\propto |\text{alphabet}| + 1 \end{aligned}$$

These choices are motivated by the idea that Viterbi alignment in the initial state should approximate Levenshtein alignment.

[3]This inference step amounts to a notational variant of the Needleman-Wunsch algorithm, cf. Needleman and Wunsch (1970).

For training and MSA, all training strings (and later test strings) were converted into the ASJP alphabet (Brown et al., 2008), which comprises just 41 sound classes, to keep the number of parameters to be estimated manageable.[4] The conversion was performed using the software package *LingPy* (List and Forkel, 2021). Training word pairs, i.e., all pairs of cognate words from the training set, were arranged in random order and split into mini-batches of size 20. An EM step was performed for each mini-batch. This procedure was repeated for two epochs over all mini-batches.

3.2 UPGMA Tree

As preparation for multiple sequence alignment, a guide tree over the languages is required. For this purpose, the pairwise normalized Levenshtein distance (i.e., the edit distance divided by the length of the longer string) was computed between any pair of cognate words. The distance between two languages was then computed as the average word distance between any two cognate words from these languages.

The resulting pairwise language distances were used as input for the UPGMA algorithm to infer a language tree. E.g., for the dataset *kesslersignificance* with 10% test data, the resulting tree has the topology ((Latin, (French, Albanian)), (English, German)).

This topology is evidently not perfect (Albanian having the wrong location), but the next step, while requiring a guide tree, is not very sensitive to the specific tree topology.

3.3 Multiple Sequence Alignment

The alignment method described in Subsection 3.1 above is only capable of performing pairwise sequence alignment. Modifying it to multiple strings would require to increase the number of states, and concommittantly computation time, exponentially in the number of sequences. The T-Coffee method of multiple sequence alignment (Notredame et al., 2000) represents a compromise combining good results with computational efficiency.

To compute an MSA for a group of words, first all pairs of words are aligned pairwise. For this step, I used Viterbi alignment with the pHMM parameters described in Subsection 3.1. During the next step of T-Coffee, all threefold alignments are

[4]Here and elsewhere, symbols indicating morpheme boundaries were ignored.

computed simply by combining two pairwise alignments from the previous step. The alignment scores between any pair of symbol *tokens* are obtained by counting all threefold alignments where these symbols occur in the first and last column, weighted by the Hamming similarity between the entire first and last row.

Using these scores, *progressive alignment* (Feng and Doolittle, 1987) is performed using a guide tree.

To continue the example mentioned above, the MSA covering the first row of Table 1 comes out as in Table 3.

Albanian	-	-	-	-	-	-
English	h	o	r	t	-	-
French	k	E	r	-	-	-
German	h	e	r	C	I	n
Latin	k	o	r	d	-	-

Table 3: Example MSA

3.4 Bayesian Phylogenetic Inference

The MSAs for the training data thus obtained were used to perform more sophisticated, Bayesian phylogenetic inference. For this purpose each symbol in the MSA is replaced by the corresponding Dolgopolsky class (Dolgopolsky, 1986). This conversion was performed using LingPy (List and Forkel, 2021) as well.

For each alignment column, the symbols in this column are conveived of as states of a continuous time Markov process. The specific type of Markov process used is due to Jukes and Cantor (1969).

Let a phylogeny — i.e., a tree with branch lengths — over the languages in question be given. It is assumed that the types of symbols within an alignment colum are the states of a continuous time Markov process. A complete model is one where each node is assigned exactly one state. For the leaf nodes, these are the entries of the MSA column. Let u and l be the states at the top and at the bottom of a branch of the phylogenetic tree, and let t be the length of the branch.

The likelihood of this branch is

$$P(l|u) = \begin{cases} \frac{1}{n} + \frac{n-1}{n}e^{-rt} & \text{if } u = l \\ \frac{1}{n} - \frac{1}{n}e^{-rt} & \text{else,} \end{cases}$$

where n is the number of distinct symbols occurring in the MSA column. The rate r is a model paramter and is always positive.

The total likelihood of an assignment of states to the nodes of the tree is the product of all branch likelihood, times the likelihood of the state at the root. For this I assumed a uniform distribution.

The marginal likelhood of the states at the leaves, given a phylogeny $\mathcal{T}$ and rate r is the sum of the likelihoods of all assignments of states to non-leaf nodes. The likelihood of a complete character matrix, given a phylogeny and an assignment of a rate value for each character (i.e., MSA column), is the product of the likelihoods of the individual characters. When a character state for a language is unknown — either because it is a gap in the MSA, or the language does not have a reflex for the corresponding cognate class — the marginal likelihood is computed as the sum of the likelihoods for all possible character states.

Given suitable priors for the phylogeny and the rates, the posterior distribution over trees can be estimated via Bayesian inference for the collection of MSAs as data.

This step was carried out using the software *MrBayes* (Ronquist and Huelsenbeck, 2003). Rates were allowed to vary between characters, but are drawn from a discretized Gamma distribution with equal mean and variance. The mean of this hyperprior distribution is drawn from a standard exponential distribution. A uniform prior distribution over tree topologies was assumed, paired with a standard exponential prior distribution over the tree age and a uniform prior distribution over the branch lengths.

The posterior tree distribution for the running example is visualized in Figure 2 (produced with the software *densitree*, Bouckaert and Heled 2014). It can be seen that there is considerable uncertainty regarding the position of French and Albanian in the tree, as well as regarding the height of the tree.

3.5 Inferring Mutation Rates

While I used Dolgopolsky sound classes for phylogenetic inference, cognate inference has to operate on IPA characters. For this purpose, I used the posterior tree distribution from the previous step as prior distribution. Data are MSAs of IPA strings. For the running example, this looks as in Table 4. (Note that the MSA is computed on the basis of ASJP strings, and ASJP symbols are replaced by the corresponding IPA symbols afterwards.)

As a further deviation from the previous step, gaps (indicated by "-") are treated as normal char-

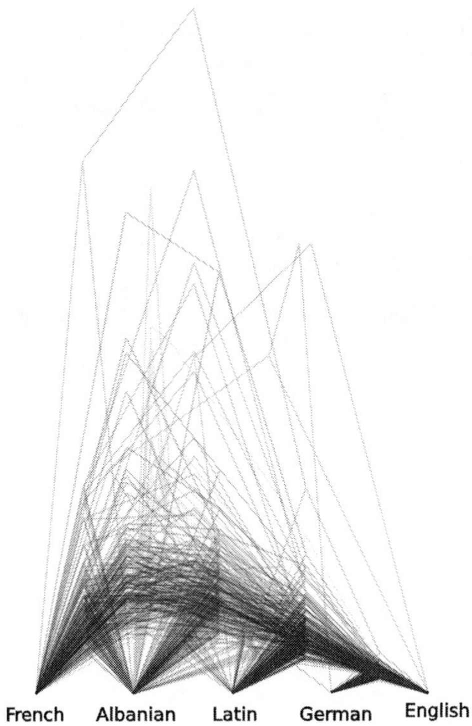

Figure 2: Posterior tree distribution

Albanian	.	.	.	.	.	.
English	h	ɑ	r	t	–	–
French	k	œ	r	–	–	–
German	h	e	r	ts	ə	n
Latin	k	o	r	d	–	–

Table 4: Example MSA with IPA characters

acter states, while missing data (indicated by ".") are marginalized out.

For this step I assumed a constant rate over all characters. Inference was performed using the *Julia* package *MCPhylo.jl* (Wahle 2021; `https://juliapackages.com/p/mcphylo`), leading to a sample from the posterior distribution over rates.

3.6 Multiple Sequence Alignment of Test Data

For cognate prediction, the attested entries of the cognate class in question are aligned using the procedure and the model described in Subsection 3.3. If the test data contain symbols not occurring in the training data, their emission probabilities are set to the minimal emission probability of any symbol from the training data, and emission probabilities are re-normalized in the trained pHMM.

For the running example, the MSA is shown in Table 5. The entries for French (shown in boldface)

Albanian	p	e	ʃ	k	–
English	f	ɪ	ʃ	–	–
French	**p**	**i**	**ʃ**	**k**	**–**
German	f	i	ʃ	–	–
Latin	p	i	s	k	i

Table 5: MSA for cognate prediction

are unknown and have to be inferred in the final step.

3.7 Cognate Prediction

Missing-value imputation is done column-wise. Using the posterior distribution over trees and rates described in Subsections 3.4 and 3.5, for each slot the posterior probability distribution over the symbols occurring elsewhere in the column was computed. This was practically implemented by separately computing the posterior probabilities for all candidate symbols separately and normalizing them.

As prediction, the symbol with the highest posterior probability was chosen. The final cognate prediction is the result of removing all gap symbols — *piʃk* in the example.

4 Discussion

Let me close with a brief reflection on what kind of information this system extracts from the training set to perform cognate prediction. There are mainly two patterns the system pays attention to. The first is the regularity of sound correspondences which are encapsulated in the emission probabilites of the trained pHMM, especially its **M** state. The system does not pay attention to the specific languages the words to be aligned come from, so it is unaware of language-specific sound correspondences. Therefore the prediction step does not make use of specific sound laws in any way.

Second, the system employs phylogenetic information. This amounts to a weighing of the importance of the cognates from other languages when deciding on the choice of the missing value imputation.

Also, since the missing value imputation is performed column-wise for the alignment matrix, no syntagmatic information is being used. It is not checked which candidate predictions are phonotactically or morphologically most similar to the training words from the same languages.

In future research, it is worth considering to extend the system towards the usage of language-specific sound correspondences and syntagmatic information.

Supplementary Material

The source code and instructions how to run the system are publicly available at `https://github.com/gerhardJaeger/gerhardSigtyp2022` (also archived on Zenodo under the doi 10.5281/zenodo.6559085). Most of the workflow was implemented in the *Julia* language (`https://julialang.org/`), a relatively new language combining the convenient syntax and interactive functionality of languages such as *Python* with execution speed of optimized code close to *C* or *Java*. Essential *Julia* packages used are Johannes Wahle's *MCPhylo.jl* (which is based on Brian J. Smith' *Mamba.jl* package; `https://mambajl.readthedocs.io/en/latest/`) for phylogenetic Bayesian inference and my own package *SequenceAlignment.jl* (`https://github.com/gerhardJaeger/SequenceAlignment.jl`, v0.9.1) for sequence alignment.

For conversions between different sound class systems, the *Python* package *LingPy* (List and Forkel, 2021) was used. Besides *MCPhylo.jl*, I used *MrBayes* (Ronquist and Huelsenbeck, 2003) for phylogenetic inference. Postprocessing of the output of *MrBayes* was done with the *R* package *ape* (Paradis et al., 2004).

Acknowledgements

I am grateful to Johannes Wahle for technical support during the implementation.

This research was supported by the DFG Centre for Advanced Studies in the Humanities Words, Bones, Genes, Tools (DFG-KFG 2237) and by the European Research Council (ERC) under the European Union's Horizon 2020 research and innovation programme (Grant agreement 834050).

References

Remco R. Bouckaert and Joseph Heled. 2014. Densitree 2: Seeing trees through the forest. *BioRxiv*. `doi.org/10.1101/012401`.

Cecil H. Brown, Eric W. Holman, Søren Wichmann, and Viveka Velupillai. 2008. Automated classification of the world's languages: A description of the method and preliminary results. *STUF — Language Typology and Universals*, 4:285–308.

Aaron B. Dolgopolsky. 1986. A probabilistic hypothesis concerning the oldest relationships among the language families of Northern Eurasia. In V. V. Shevoroshkin, editor, *Typology, Relationship and Time: A collection of papers on language change and relationship by Soviet linguists*, pages 27–50. Karoma Publisher, Ann Arbor.

Richard Durbin, Sean R. Eddy, Anders Krogh, and Graeme Mitchison. 1989. *Biological Sequence Analysis*. Cambridge University Press, Cambridge, UK.

Da-Fei Feng and Russell F. Doolittle. 1987. Progressive sequence alignment as a prerequisitetto correct phylogenetic trees. *Journal of Molecular Evolution*, 25(4):351–360.

Gerhard Jäger. 2019. Computational historical linguistics. *Theoretical Linguistics*, 45(3-4):151–182.

Thomas H. Jukes and Charles R. Cantor. 1969. Evolution of protein molecules. In H. N. Munro, editor, *Mammalian protein metabolisum*, pages 21–132. Academic Press, New York and London.

Brett Kessler. 2001. *The significance of word lists*. CSLI Publications, Stanford.

Johann-Mattis List and Robert Forkel. 2021. Lingpy. A Python library for historical linguistics. version 2.6.9. URL: https://lingpy.org, DOI: https://zenodo.org/badge/latestdoi/5137/lingpy/lingpy. With contributions by Greenhill, Simon, Tresoldi, Tiago, Christoph Rzymski, Gereon Kaiping, Steven Moran, Peter Bouda, Johannes Dellert, Taraka Rama, Frank Nagel. Leizpig: Max Planck Institute for Evolutionary Anthropology.

Johann-Mattis List, Ekaterina Vylomova, Robert Forkel, Nathan W. Hill, and Ryan Cotterell. 2022. The SIGTYP 2022 shared task on the prediction of cognate reflexes. In *The Fourth Workshop on Computational Typology and Multilingual NLP*, Online. Association for Computational Linguistics.

Saul B. Needleman and Christian D. Wunsch. 1970. A general method applicable to the search for similarities in the amino acid sequence of two proteins. *Journal of Molecular Biology*, 48:443–453.

Cédric Notredame, Desmond G Higgins, and Jaap Heringa. 2000. T-Coffee: A novel method for fast and accurate multiple sequence alignment. *Journal of Molecular Biology*, 302(1):205–217.

Emmanuel Paradis, Julien Claude, and Korbinian Strimmer. 2004. APE: analyses of phylogenetics and evolution in R language. *Bioinformatics*, 20(2):289–290.

Frederik Ronquist and John P. Huelsenbeck. 2003. MrBayes 3: Bayesian phylogenetic inference under mixed models. *Bioinformatics*, 19(12):1572–1574.

Robert R. Sokal and Charles D. Michener. 1958. A statistical method for evaluating systematic relationships. *University of Kansas Science Bulletin*, 38:1409–1438.

Johannes Wahle. 2021. No-U-Turn sampling for phylogenetic trees. *bioRxiv*. doi.org/10.1101/2021.03.16.435623.

Søren Wichmann, Eric W. Holman, and Cecil H. Brown. 2016. The ASJP database (version 17). http://asjp.clld.org/.

Mockingbird at the SIGTYP 2022 Shared Task: Two Types of Models for the Prediction of Cognate Reflexes

Christo Kirov
Google Research, US
ckirov@google.com

Richard Sproat
Google Research, Japan
rws@google.com

Alexander Gutkin
Google Research, UK
agutkin@google.com

Abstract

The SIGTYP 2022 shared task concerns the problem of word reflex generation in a target language, given cognate words from a subset of related languages. We present two systems to tackle this problem, covering two very different modeling approaches. The first model extends transformer-based encoder-decoder sequence-to-sequence modeling, by encoding all available input cognates in parallel, and having the decoder attend to the resulting joint representation during inference. The second approach takes inspiration from the field of image restoration, where models are tasked with recovering pixels in an image that have been masked out. For reflex generation, the missing reflexes are treated as "masked pixels" in an "image" which is a representation of an entire cognate set across a language family. As in the image restoration case, cognate restoration is performed with a convolutional network.

1 Introduction

The cognate reflex prediction task can be understood by considering a simple example. English *dream* is *droom* in Dutch and *Traum* in German. English *stream* is *stroom* in Dutch and *Strom* in German (so we can see that there is a bit of variation in how the cognate forms are realized). But now consider English *tree*, which is *boom* in Dutch and *Baum* in German. If there were a cognate in English, what would it look like? On analogy in particular with the *dream* example, one would expect the form to be *beam*—which is in fact cognate with the Dutch and German forms, though the meaning has shifted.

This study describes the two particular approaches to cognate reflex prediction code-named Mockingbird.[1] Both approaches use popular machine learning techniques adapted to the cognate reflex prediction task.

The *transformer-based* approach popularized by Vaswani et al. (2017) is a particular instance of sequence-to-sequence (Seq2Seq) recurrent neural bipartite encoder-decoder architecture (Cho et al., 2014; Sutskever et al., 2014) equipped with multi-head attention mechanism. It has the advantages inherent to Seq2Seq models. In particular it can represent arbitrarily long-distance contextual dependencies both within and across words. This rich representational capacity comes at the cost of high model complexity and need for computational resources (Strubell et al., 2019; Liu et al., 2019; Brown et al., 2020). Our particular transformer-based model was originally developed for place name pronunciation (Jones et al., 2022), and models cognate sets as a *neighborhood* where we are trying to predict the pronunciation of a target feature given its neighbors.

The *image inpainting model* (Liu et al., 2018) relies on a simple convolutional neural network, or CNN (O'Shea and Nash, 2015), which trains fairly quickly even on CPU. It treats cognate sets as holistic objects ("images"), with individual convolution filters representing partial joint alignments between all languages at once. Unlike transformers or RNN-based models, however, convolutional models with finite kernel sizes cannot capture arbitrary amount of context. As an extreme example, it would be difficult for a convolutional model to learn that the first character in one language cognate should always be aligned with the last character in another language's cognate, especially if long words are possible.

2 Related Work

The establishment of cognate correspondences and the prediction of cognate forms has a long and venerable history that dates at least to the original work of William Jones that established the Indo-

[1] The open-source implementation of both models: https://github.com/google-research/google-research/tree/master/cognate_inpaint_neighbors

Proceedings of the 4th Workshop on Computational Typology and Multilingual NLP (SIGTYP 2022), pages 70 - 79
July 14, 2022 ©2022 Association for Computational Linguistics

European language family (Jones, 1786), and later the work of the Neo-Grammarians (Paul, 1880).

Prior computational work related to this problem includes early work by Covington (1996) and Kondrak (2000) on methods for aligning cognate pairs at the segment level, and more recently work specifically on the prediction of cognate forms (List, 2019a; Meloni et al., 2021). The work of Meloni et al. (2021) in particular is most similar to the current proposed methods in that they use a neural character-level encoder-decoder sequence-to-sequence model, and demonstrate that this shows good performance on the task of proto-form reconstruction for a fairly large dataset of Romance languages.

3 Neighbors Transformer Model

3.1 General architecture

The "neighbors" transformer model was originally developed for detecting inconsistencies in the readings of Japanese place names in an industrial-scale maps database (Jones et al., 2022). Japanese place names are notoriously difficult to read even for native speakers, since two different place names that happen to be written with the same kanji sequence may have quite different pronunciations. A famous example is 日本橋, which in Tokyo is read as *Nihonbashi*, but where the identically written name in Osaka is read as *Nipponbashi*. While the place names themselves are unlikely to be wrong in the data, there are many named features in the data set—buildings, establishments, and so forth—which are named after the area—e.g. an apartment building named *Mezon (= Maison) Nipponbashi*, where the reading may be in error. The neighbors model is designed to detect such errors by considering the reading of features in the area and detecting if there is an apparent inconsistency. In training the model is provided with the target feature's written form and its reading (in *hiragana*), and the written forms and readings of features that are neighbors within a small geographic distance from the target feature. Since inconsistencies in such neighborhoods involve the minority of cases, the model learns that the same spelled name within a neighborhood usually agrees in terms of the reading. The general architecture of the model as applied to Japanese place names is shown in Figure 1.

The cognate reconstruction problem is similar in spirit to the place name problem just described. In this case the "neighbor pronunciations" are replaced with the cognates in the set, with the "main feature" being the cognate form to be predicted. The spellings on the other hand are replaced by a string representing the name of the language associated with the target and each of the neighboring cognates. This could be simply the language name itself, but it is better to encode the name as a unique identifier (e.g. a short sequence of arbitrary symbols, such as emoji), so that the model does not learn spurious associations between the name of the language and cognate forms.[2]

The model used here slightly differs from the version used for geographic names in that the language identifiers and cognate forms are interleaved and then concatenated together into a single one dimensional tensor, interleaved with ids for each cognate in the set. This allows the model to better attend to the individual cognate and to copy the cognate as needed.

For the transformer model, the provided data sets are far too small for the model to learn anything. We therefore augmented the data in two ways. First, since one cannot assume that in the test set one will find cognate forms for all neighbor languages for a given target language, we also augmented the data by randomly removing neighbors, thus making new neighborhoods for the same cognate set, which lacked one or more of the neighbor cognate examples. In our experiments we generated 500 such random subsets for each original neighborhood, of which about half were randomly copies of the original neighborhood.

Second, in addition to the actual provided cognate groups, we synthesized similar cognates for each of the "neighbor" languages and the target. Two methods were used, the first being a simple pair unigram model and the second a bigram model that we will briefly mention in Section 5. For the unigram model, a Levenshtein-distance alignment was computed between each pair of cognates for all language pairs, and correspondences between IPA symbols were counted. These unigram counts were then used to randomly generate new pairs of "cognates". We generated ten random neighborhoods of this kind for each real or subset neighborhood as described above. For example, for the English set in the LISTSAMPLESIZE

[2]For example, in the Northern Pakistan set, there are number of variants of Balti in the set, and we wish to avoid the model learning to depend on the string *Balti* in making its predictions. See Table 4 in Appendix A for an example.

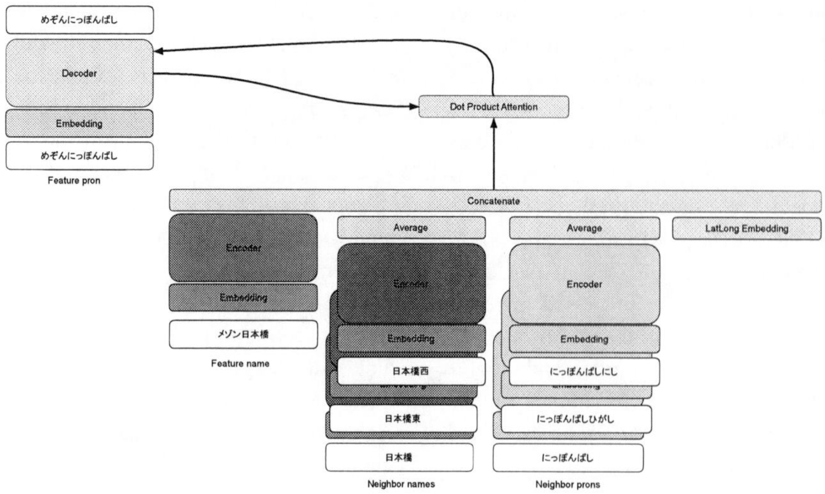

Figure 1: The transformer neighbors model, showing how the main feature and neighbor features are encoded. Colors for the embeddings reflect the shared embedding structure for the Transformer model. Example shown is メゾン日本橋 *mezon nipponbashi*, and some neighboring features 日本橋 *nipponbashi*, 日本橋西 *nipponbashi nishi* and 日本橋東 *nipponbashi higashi*.

data set, the original approximately 300 neighborhoods was expanded into about 4.2 million neighborhoods.

3.2 Model Details

The neighbors model is implemented using Lingvo (Shen et al., 2019), which is a framework for building neural networks in TensorFlow (Abadi et al., 2016), particularly sequence models. The core architecture of our transformer model derives from the Lingvo implementation of the neural machine translation system by Chen et al. (2018).[3]

We use the compact transformer configuration because the amount of data available for this task even after data augmentation is small. In our configuration, the encoders and decoders in Figure 1 use multi-head attention mechanism with two attention heads (Vaswani et al., 2017). There are three transformer layers, and the dimension of the feed-forward layer as well as the embedding dimension are set to 32. Dropout is applied during training with probability of 0.1 to residual layers, attention weights, and each feed-forward layer of the Transformer. Finally, we employ label smoothing to the decoder outputs, where the probability for correct class labels is reduced by the uncertainty factor $\epsilon = 0.2$ and for all other cases increased by ϵ/K, where K is the size of the vocabulary (Szegedy et al., 2016).

For training, we optimize sparse categorical cross-entropy loss using Adam procedure with initial learning rate $\alpha = 0.001$ and the parameters $\beta_1 = 0.9$, $\beta_2 = 0.98$ and $\epsilon = 10^{-9}$ (Kingma and Ba, 2015). We optimize the word error error (WER) between the sequences of ground truth and the predicted phonemes. The batch size is set to 32 examples. No development set was set aside from the training data because we did not perform any parameter tuning. The latest and not necessarily best (according to the test set) checkpoints were chosen after the training ran for a specified number of steps. We employ beam search with the beam width of 8 during inference.

3.3 Open-Source Implementation Notes

The code publicly released for the shared task is mostly identical to our internal version used to produce the shared task results, but with some notable differences. First, in the open-source verson we do not encode the language names using unique emojis. Second, we used the development versions of TensorFlow and Lingvo integrated with XManager,[4] a platform for managing distributed machine learning experiments, for our internal experiments. This implies that our main results may

[3] `https://github.com/tensorflow/lingvo/tree/master/lingvo/tasks/mt`

[4] `https://github.com/deepmind/xmanager`

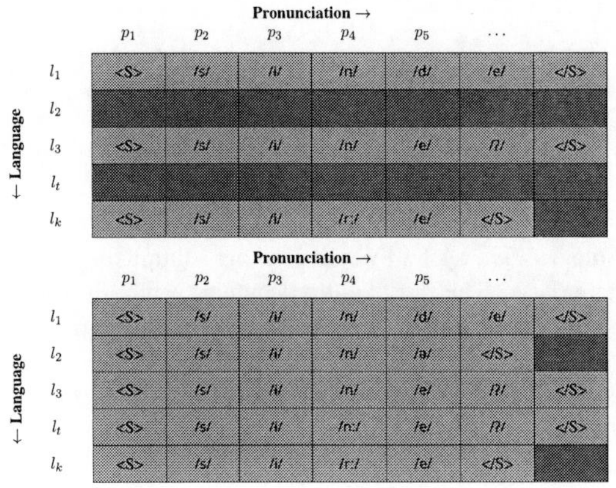

Figure 2: (Top) Cognate set input represented as an "image". The individual pixel coordinates (x, y) correspond to (l, p), where l_i is a language and p_j is a phoneme. The pronunciations in this example are taken from FELEKESEMITIC cognate set for cognate ID 638. Short cognates are marked with padding. One or more cognates may be masked out entirely. (Bottom) Equivalent output image. Missing cognate "pixels" have been restored.

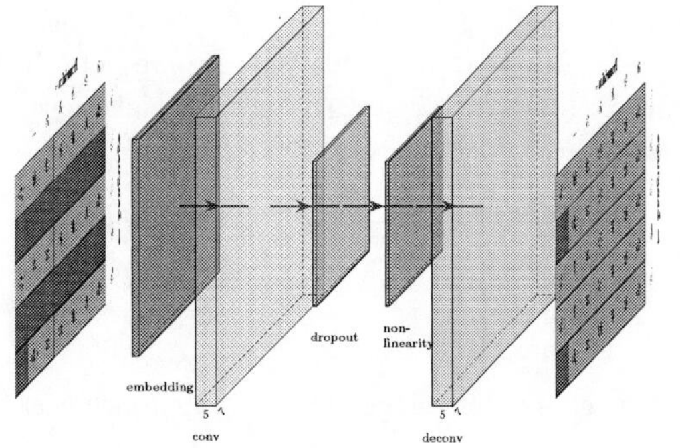

Figure 3: Simplified inpainting CNN architecture.

not be exactly reproducible with the open-source system, something that we discuss further in Section 5.

4 Cognate Reconstruction as Image Inpainting

The neighborhood model presented above casts the reflex generation task as a straightforward extension of Seq2Seq modeling. Here, we take a different tack, noting that if we treat the entire set of cognates as a unit (an "image"), then the task of generating unknown cognates is analogous to recovering missing/masked/corrupted parts of that image. In the field of image reconstruction, this is sometimes referred to as image inpainting (Qin et al., 2021; Jam et al., 2021; Peng et al., 2021). One of the popular state-of-the art methods employs convolutional neural networks (CNNs) to recover missing pixel values. In this work we apply one such architecture by Liu et al. (2018) from NVIDIA to cognate generation. As we see below, cognate set "images" contain relatively few "pixels", so we can get away with small networks with a single pair or convolution and deconvolution layers that are fast to train and evaluate, even on CPU.

4.1 Model Details

The model's input and output structure are shown in Figure 2. Input cognates are book-ended with start and end symbols, padded to a fixed length (20 in all our experiments), and stacked to form a grid. Crucially some cognates may be masked out when forming an input image, resulting in rows of nothing but padding. Each symbol is embedded, resulting in a data structure with n embedding dimensions per symbol, corresponding to the "channels" in an image[5]. Optionally, this image may be scaled by a constant factor equivalent to the total number of languages divided by the number of languages present. This ensures constant total "brightness" no matter how many cognates are masked out.

The image is then processed by a 2D convolution layer, with kernel height fixed to the number of languages in the cognate set, and kernel width determined by a hyperparameter. Convolution is followed by dropout and a nonlinearity, after which a deconvolution layer recovers logits at each pixel position for the available character set. The logits, in turn, can be used to predict the most likely character at each position, or to calculate a sparse categorical cross-entropy loss during training, given a target symbol. The simplified diagram of the model is shown in Figure 3.

The convolution operation for a given kernel with weights W is shown below, and mirrors that used in NVIDIA's paper (Liu et al., 2018). Here X is the set of input pixels, which are multiplied pointwise with a binary mask M, where missing cognate positions are set to 0. The result is scaled

[5]If the input was a standard RGB image, these would be values for red, green, and blue color intensity. Here, embedding dimensions don't necessarily correspond to any real-world scale.

by a factor equivalent to the sum of what the mask would look like if all languages were present (all values set to 1) divided by the sum of actual binary mask:

$$x' = \begin{cases} W^T(X \odot M)\frac{\text{sum}(1)}{\text{sum}(M)}, & \text{if sum}(M) \geq 1 \\ 0, & \text{otherwise} \end{cases}$$

4.2 Training Regime

As one goal of the image inpainting approach was to keep it as simple as possible, no synthetic data augmentation was used during training — just the base training data made available for the SIGTYP shared task.

For each language family, the available training data was further broken down by a random 80%/20% split into a base cognate training set, and a development set used for tuning. For the development set, each group of cognates was broken down into multiple dev samples by setting each available cognate as the reconstruction target in turn (replacing it with '?'). As the overall datasets available are small, each dev set held out in this way will only cover a few cognate groups, introducing significant model bias when used for parameter tuning. To counteract this, we generate ten different train/dev splits at random, which were used for ensembling as described below.

Given a train/dev split, actual training proceeded as follows. For S training steps per epoch, a random cognate group was drawn from the available training set, and a random subset of the cognates present was masked out (at least one cognate always remained present so the model would have some information to work with). This masked sample was fed as an image to the inpainting model, whose task was to recover the entire cognate group. For backpropagation, cross-entropy loss was calculated only for rows of the image where a cognate was present in the original cognate group — all other positions contributed zero loss since there was no target information available.

For each training step, parameter updates were performed using the Adam procedure (Kingma and Ba, 2015) with default TensorFlow parameters. Training was run for a total of 150 epochs consisting of 500 steps each. After each epoch, the exact-match word error rate (WER) was calculated for each sample in the dev set for each language, and a macro average across of the per-language WER values was taken. Checkpoints were saved only in cases where macro-WER performance on the dev set improved.

Name	Type	Alias
Mockingbird-I1	Inpainting	I1
Mockingbird-N1-A	Neighbors	N1-A
Mockingbird-N1-B	Neighbors	N1-B
Mockingbird-N1-C	Neighbors	N1-C
Mockingbird-N2	Neighbors	N2

Table 1: Five system configurations submitted to the shared task. The third column contains a shorthand of the full configuration name that we use in this paper.

For each train/dev split, a separate model was prepared with its own set of tuned hyperparameters. Hyperparameter tuning was done using Google's Vizier smart grid search procedure (Golovin et al., 2017),[6] which optimized macro-WER on the dev set for 100 total Vizier trials, with at most 10 trials running in parallel at any one time. The list of tunable model hyperparameters is provided in Appendix B.

4.3 Open-Source Implementation Notes

The core CNN model implementation in Tensorflow (Abadi et al., 2016) has been released as is and can be used for training and inference. We are not releasing the scaffolding required for integration with Vizier hyperparameter tuning because our internal implementation is quite different from the publicly available version. However, the tuned set of hyperparameters (residing in `hparams.json`) for each model have been released together with the results. These hyperparameters can be used to train models that should perform similarly to those described here.[7] It is also possible to implement an alternative smart grid search procedure using Keras Tuner (Shawki et al., 2021)[8] or any other framework for hyper-parameter optimization and neural architecture search that supports Tensorflow (Menghani, 2021).

5 Results and Discussion

The SIGTYP 2022 Shared Task was evaluated over 20 language-family specific datasets taken from the LexiBank repository (List et al., 2021).

[6] https://cloud.google.com/ai-platform/optimizer/docs/overview

[7] Trained model checkpoints are also available upon request — they were not included in the results package due to file size considerations.

[8] https://keras.io/keras_tuner/

Each dataset consisted of a series of cognate groups presented in CLDF (Forkel et al., 2018) format, with each cognate form stored as an IPA phonetic transcription. 10 datasets were provided for system development, and 10 "surprise" language families were held aside for final evaluation. Furthermore, each dataset was provided in five sparsity conditions (dropping 10%, 20%, 30%, 40%, and 50% of the available cognate forms). For brevity, we only discuss the 10% ("dense") and 50% ("sparse") conditions in this paper.[9]

We submitted five system configurations, shown in Table 1, to the shared task.[10] The first configuration `i1` is the inpainting CNN approach described in Section 4, while the rest of configurations are the Neighbors Transformer models introduced in Section 3.

There are four Neighbors Transformer configurations. The first three configurations (`N1-A`, `N1-B` and `N1-C`) correspond to the models built using our internal pipeline. The only difference between these configurations is the number of training steps: 25,000 (`N1-A`), 35,000 (`N1-B`), and 100,000 (`N1-C`). For these configurations we mapped the language names to unique emojis during training and inference.

The final Transformer configuration `N2` corresponds to the model trained using the released open-source pipeline. The training regime has some notable differences with the other Transformer configurations. First, as noted above, no language name-to-emoji mapping was performed. Second, when generating each random example $\{(p_t, l_t), (p_n, l_n)\}$ consisting of target t and neighbor n pronunciation/language pairs, the neighbor pronunciation p_n is randomly generated using a first-order Markov chain trained from all the bigrams constructed from the pronunciations available for language l_n, as opposed to unigrams used by the `N1` systems. Also, the target pronunciation p_t is generated from p_n by sampling from the distribution obtained using sound class-based pairwise alignment algorithm implementation from (List and Forkel, 2021) described in (List et al., 2018). Finally, the stopping criterion for the training process was rather ad-hoc: training for each language group was stopped after eyeballing the training set loss. Unlike the rest of the submitted systems, the `N2` configuration was only trained in the 10% ("dense") sparsity condition.

For the inpainting model, results were produced via a majority ensemble. For each language family, ten models were trained using the procedure described above corresponding to ten random 80%/20% train/dev splits of the available training data. Predictions for each test sample were obtained from each of the models, and the most common prediction across the set was retained.

Model results were evaluated according to four metrics selected by the shared task organizers. The first two are raw and normalized (divided by the number of characters in the target form) Levenshtein edit distances (Levenshtein, 1966) between the predicted and expected test cognate forms. For these metrics, lower is better as it indicates a closer match. The third metric, B-Cubed F-Scores, is designed to avoid overly penalizing systematic errors a system might make, discounting errors that occur across multiple trials (List, 2019b). The metric derives from the B-Cubed measure (Amigó et al., 2009) frequently used in historical linguistics to evaluate automatic cognate detection techniques (Hauer and Kondrak, 2011). For this metric, higher is better. Finally, standard BLEU scores (Papineni et al., 2002) as used when evaluating machine translation (again, higher is better) were included.

Tables 2 and 3 summarize the evaluation in the dense and sparse data conditions. Overall, both the Inpainting and Neighbor `N1` models match or improve upon the baseline method provided by the Shared Task organizers. The Inpainting model shows an overall advantage – its simplicity might mitigate against overfitting in such small datasets, but this isn't universal across all language families, and wanes as the task becomes more difficult moving from the dense to the sparse condition. In particular, the Neighbor models are very effective in the FELEKESEMITIC language family in the sparse data condition, while the Inpainting model behaves at baseline level. This could be due to the unique morphology of Semitic languages, and the ability of the N1 models to use contextual cues that the simpler model architectures aren't able to represent, but which compensate for data sparsity to an extent. The condition may also benefit more than most from the data augmentation strategy used in training the Neighbor models.

In terms of overall results on the "surprise"

[9]Please see `https://github.com/sigtyp/ST2022/tree/main/results` for all the available results.

[10]`https://github.com/sigtyp/ST2022/tree/main/systems`

	BL	I1	N1-A	N1-B	N1-C	N2
dev total	1.34 0.28 0.72 0.61	1.05 0.23 0.74 0.68	1.25 0.27 0.72 0.63	1.31 0.28 0.70 0.61	1.29 0.28 0.69 0.62	1.37 0.29 0.68 0.60
davletshinaztecan	2.07 0.33 0.64 0.52	1.87 0.30 0.66 0.56	2.04 0.33 0.63 0.53	2.20 0.36 0.62 0.49	1.94 0.32 0.64 0.56	2.28 0.38 0.59 0.45
felekesemitic	1.46 0.27 0.69 0.59	1.29 0.24 0.72 0.65	1.68 0.31 0.64 0.55	1.76 0.33 0.63 0.52	1.92 0.36 0.60 0.48	1.88 0.36 0.59 0.49
hantganbangime	1.31 0.33 0.62 0.54	1.12 0.29 0.64 0.58	1.28 0.33 0.61 0.54	1.32 0.34 0.60 0.53	1.47 0.37 0.56 0.49	1.57 0.38 0.54 0.47
hattorijaponic	0.91 0.19 0.80 0.73	0.71 0.16 0.83 0.78	0.94 0.20 0.80 0.72	0.92 0.20 0.78 0.74	0.88 0.19 0.79 0.75	1.12 0.21 0.75 0.72
listsamplesize	3.34 0.62 0.41 0.22	2.35 0.46 0.50 0.40	2.80 0.54 0.50 0.33	2.79 0.55 0.49 0.32	2.54 0.52 0.49 0.34	2.59 0.50 0.48 0.37
backstromnorthernpakistan	0.89 0.18 0.86 0.72	0.60 0.12 0.87 0.80	0.83 0.17 0.82 0.72	0.83 0.18 0.83 0.72	0.81 0.17 0.82 0.73	0.79 0.16 0.83 0.76
mannburmish	1.98 0.52 0.51 0.32	1.55 0.42 0.57 0.43	1.74 0.47 0.53 0.39	1.89 0.50 0.52 0.36	1.93 0.50 0.52 0.35	1.95 0.52 0.51 0.31
castrosui	0.16 0.04 0.95 0.94	0.14 0.03 0.95 0.95	0.16 0.04 0.95 0.94	0.15 0.03 0.95 0.95	0.20 0.05 0.93 0.92	0.29 0.07 0.91 0.89
allenbai	0.72 0.23 0.77 0.68	0.55 0.18 0.80 0.75	0.58 0.19 0.79 0.74	0.64 0.21 0.78 0.71	0.70 0.23 0.73 0.69	0.67 0.22 0.77 0.70
abrahammonpa	0.55 0.12 0.90 0.81	0.34 0.06 0.91 0.90	0.47 0.09 0.87 0.86	0.55 0.11 0.84 0.83	0.51 0.09 0.86 0.85	0.53 0.10 0.86 0.84
surprise total	1.21 0.31 0.72 0.57	0.92 0.24 0.77 0.66	1.02 0.26 0.76 0.65	1.04 0.26 0.76 0.64	1.13 0.29 0.73 0.61	1.21 0.31 0.71 0.57
beidazihui	1.10 0.30 0.73 0.58	0.50 0.14 0.84 0.80	0.48 0.13 0.86 0.81	0.40 0.11 0.87 0.84	0.45 0.12 0.86 0.83	1.13 0.29 0.70 0.60
hillburmish	1.18 0.32 0.66 0.57	1.06 0.29 0.68 0.61	1.13 0.30 0.66 0.60	1.13 0.30 0.66 0.60	1.37 0.37 0.62 0.53	1.50 0.39 0.59 0.48
bodtkhobwa	0.49 0.20 0.76 0.72	0.39 0.16 0.80 0.78	0.25 0.11 0.88 0.85	0.26 0.11 0.87 0.85	0.42 0.18 0.77 0.77	0.68 0.28 0.67 0.62
bantubvd	1.12 0.26 0.79 0.62	0.89 0.22 0.80 0.68	1.01 0.25 0.82 0.63	1.03 0.26 0.82 0.62	0.98 0.25 0.81 0.63	1.10 0.27 0.77 0.60
bremerberta	1.72 0.32 0.71 0.51	1.16 0.21 0.77 0.66	1.35 0.25 0.74 0.61	1.35 0.25 0.74 0.61	1.47 0.27 0.71 0.58	1.26 0.23 0.75 0.66
deepadungpalaung	1.07 0.42 0.76 0.44	0.55 0.22 0.89 0.70	0.73 0.27 0.85 0.63	0.88 0.32 0.82 0.57	0.92 0.34 0.80 0.54	0.86 0.31 0.83 0.58
luangthongkumkaren	0.38 0.10 0.91 0.84	0.36 0.09 0.90 0.86	0.26 0.07 0.92 0.89	0.29 0.08 0.91 0.88	0.33 0.09 0.89 0.87	0.35 0.10 0.90 0.85
birchallchapacuran	1.63 0.31 0.65 0.54	1.57 0.30 0.65 0.56	2.04 0.37 0.57 0.47	2.01 0.36 0.58 0.48	2.01 0.37 0.58 0.48	2.01 0.39 0.57 0.45
wangbai	0.62 0.18 0.80 0.73	0.49 0.14 0.83 0.79	0.48 0.14 0.83 0.80	0.53 0.16 0.81 0.77	0.61 0.18 0.78 0.74	0.62 0.18 0.80 0.74
kesslersignificance	2.77 0.70 0.47 0.17	2.23 0.67 0.51 0.20	2.49 0.67 0.49 0.18	2.55 0.68 0.50 0.18	2.69 0.69 0.47 0.17	2.60 0.71 0.47 0.16

Table 2: Results by model for the 0.10 data condition (BL=Baseline, I1=Inpainting, N*=Neighborhood model), averaged by language group. The four values per entry cover the four metrics used in the shared task (black=edit distance, olive=normalized edit distance, red=B-Cubed F-Score, blue=BLEU).

	BL	I1	N1-A	N1-B	N1-C
dev total	1.75 0.37 0.60 0.50	1.40 0.31 0.63 0.58	1.60 0.34 0.59 0.54	1.61 0.34 0.58 0.53	1.63 0.35 0.57 0.52
davletshinaztecan	2.09 0.36 0.59 0.48	1.69 0.30 0.63 0.56	2.29 0.38 0.54 0.46	2.44 0.40 0.51 0.44	2.21 0.37 0.54 0.48
felekesemitic	2.90 0.53 0.45 0.28	2.85 0.53 0.41 0.31	2.33 0.41 0.49 0.42	2.27 0.41 0.49 0.42	2.19 0.40 0.50 0.44
hantganbangime	1.98 0.48 0.44 0.36	1.38 0.36 0.53 0.50	1.65 0.42 0.48 0.43	1.65 0.42 0.47 0.43	1.86 0.47 0.44 0.37
hattorijaponic	1.50 0.30 0.65 0.58	1.33 0.27 0.69 0.63	1.66 0.32 0.60 0.57	1.57 0.31 0.61 0.59	1.50 0.30 0.63 0.60
listsamplesize	3.68 0.69 0.37 0.17	2.43 0.51 0.42 0.35	2.72 0.53 0.41 0.31	2.71 0.54 0.41 0.30	2.81 0.54 0.40 0.30
backstromnorthernpakistan	0.97 0.22 0.77 0.66	0.73 0.17 0.79 0.74	1.00 0.21 0.72 0.67	1.03 0.22 0.71 0.65	0.93 0.21 0.73 0.68
mannburmish	2.33 0.60 0.36 0.25	2.02 0.55 0.39 0.30	2.41 0.62 0.34 0.24	2.32 0.62 0.34 0.25	2.38 0.62 0.33 0.25
castrosui	0.39 0.10 0.88 0.84	0.29 0.07 0.90 0.88	0.32 0.08 0.89 0.87	0.34 0.08 0.88 0.87	0.41 0.10 0.85 0.84
allenbai	0.76 0.25 0.71 0.66	0.64 0.21 0.75 0.71	0.78 0.25 0.68 0.65	0.84 0.27 0.66 0.64	0.99 0.32 0.59 0.57
abrahammonpa	0.94 0.18 0.76 0.72	0.66 0.12 0.80 0.80	0.87 0.16 0.74 0.74	0.95 0.18 0.72 0.72	1.03 0.20 0.70 0.70
surprise total	1.89 0.44 0.56 0.43	1.42 0.35 0.61 0.53	1.55 0.38 0.60 0.49	1.51 0.37 0.59 0.50	1.58 0.40 0.56 0.47
bremerberta	2.49 0.46 0.53 0.35	1.58 0.30 0.62 0.56	1.99 0.38 0.56 0.46	1.85 0.35 0.58 0.49	2.05 0.39 0.55 0.44
wangbai	1.02 0.29 0.66 0.58	0.97 0.28 0.66 0.60	1.05 0.31 0.63 0.58	1.06 0.31 0.62 0.57	1.15 0.34 0.59 0.54
luangthongkumkaren	0.66 0.17 0.81 0.73	0.55 0.15 0.80 0.78	0.56 0.15 0.80 0.77	0.62 0.17 0.78 0.75	0.77 0.21 0.73 0.69
hillburmish	2.10 0.54 0.47 0.34	1.64 0.44 0.51 0.45	2.66 0.68 0.44 0.17	1.87 0.49 0.48 0.38	1.80 0.47 0.46 0.39
birchallchapacuran	3.17 0.47 0.48 0.32	2.81 0.47 0.44 0.35	2.80 0.47 0.44 0.34	2.80 0.47 0.45 0.33	2.83 0.48 0.44 0.33
bantubvd	1.99 0.45 0.56 0.39	1.53 0.36 0.61 0.50	1.29 0.31 0.69 0.55	1.43 0.34 0.65 0.51	1.45 0.35 0.64 0.50
kesslersignificance	4.06 0.89 0.29 0.04	2.85 0.73 0.30 0.15	2.77 0.67 0.34 0.17	2.81 0.68 0.34 0.16	2.95 0.71 0.33 0.14
bodtkhobwa	0.63 0.27 0.66 0.65	0.53 0.22 0.70 0.71	0.56 0.23 0.68 0.69	0.66 0.27 0.63 0.64	0.77 0.32 0.57 0.59
beidazihui	1.15 0.32 0.67 0.56	0.48 0.13 0.80 0.80	0.45 0.13 0.82 0.82	0.48 0.13 0.80 0.81	0.57 0.16 0.77 0.77
deepadungpalaung	1.63 0.58 0.50 0.30	1.23 0.44 0.60 0.43	1.39 0.48 0.57 0.39	1.49 0.52 0.54 0.36	1.47 0.52 0.53 0.35

Table 3: Results by model for the 0.50 data condition (BL=Baseline, I1=Inpainting, N*=Neighborhood model), averaged by language group. The four values per entry cover the four metrics used in the shared task (black=edit distance, olive=normalized edit distance, red=B-Cubed F-Scores, blue=BLEU).

sets, the worst performing configuration is the N2 model. It performs significantly worse than the N1 Neighbor and the Inpainting configurations using the edit distance-based metrics and decidely worse than the Inpainting method using B-Cubed F-Scores and BLEU. We hypothesize the existence of two confounding factors that may be affecting the model's performance. First, we trained it using significantly smaller (compared to N1 systems) amounts of augmented data. In addition, stopping the training process after a random number of steps may have resulted in under-training. Analysis of N2 model's results on individual language groups displays the uneven performance of this model. On the BREMERBERTA and DEEPADUNG-PALAUNG sets, the model strongly outperforms the baseline and improves upon one of the N1 configurations, while at the same time being significantly worse than the baseline on the HILLBURMISH set.

6 Conclusions

We presented two approaches to the problem of cognate reflex prediction, one based on the transformer Seq2Seq architecture, and one based on convolutional networks. Both approaches stem from natural, intuitive interpretations of the problem. The "neighbors" transformer approach treats the problem as one of reconstructing the phonetic form of a cognate by considering all the other cognates in the set, on analogy to the problem of reconstructing the reading of a geographical feature on the basis of the pronunciation of names of geographic neighbors. The inpainting approach treats the problem as being similar to filling in missing pixels in an image on the basis of the surrounding context pixels. We submitted 5 system variants (1 convolutional model and 4 transformer models) to the SIGTYP 2022 Shared Task, where they performed well relative to the provided baseline and other submissions.

Supplementary Material

The implementation of the Inpainting CNN and the Neighbors transformer models described in this work is available in Google Research repository on GitHub (`https://github.com/google-research/google-research/tree/59f02a3cb447f381a7450c89f37dda042819216e/cognate_inpaint_neighbors`). The results for these systems are curated on GitHub (`https://github.com/sigtyp/ST2022`) along with the results of the other systems submitted to the shared task, and have been archived with Zenodo (`https://doi.org/10.5281/zenodo.6538626`).

Acknowledgements

We would like to thank Llion Jones who developed the Transformer version of the neighbors model for the geographic names task described in Section 3.1. We also thank Brian Roark for useful feedback on an earlier version of this paper.

References

Martín Abadi, Paul Barham, Jianmin Chen, Zhifeng Chen, Andy Davis, Jeffrey Dean, Matthieu Devin, Sanjay Ghemawat, Geoffrey Irving, Michael Isard, Manjunath Kudlur, Josh Levenberg, Rajat Monga, Sherry Moore, Derek G. Murray, Benoit Steiner, Paul Tucker, Vijay Vasudevan, Pete Warden, Martin Wicke, Yuan Yu, Xiaoqiang Zheng, et al. 2016. TensorFlow: A system for large-scale machine learning. In *Proceedings of the 12th USENIX Symposium on Operating Systems Design and Implementation (OSDI 16)*, pages 265–283, Savannah, GA, USA.

Enrique Amigó, Julio Gonzalo, Javier Artiles, and Felisa Verdejo. 2009. A comparison of extrinsic clustering evaluation metrics based on formal constraints. *Information retrieval*, 12(4):461–486.

Tom Brown, Benjamin Mann, Nick Ryder, Melanie Subbiah, Jared D Kaplan, Prafulla Dhariwal, Arvind Neelakantan, Pranav Shyam, Girish Sastry, Amanda Askell, Sandhini Agarwal, Ariel Herbert-Voss, Gretchen Krueger, Tom Henighan, Rewon Child, Aditya Ramesh, Daniel Ziegler, Jeffrey Wu, Clemens Winter, Chris Hesse, Mark Chen, Eric Sigler, Mateusz Litwin, Scott Gray, Benjamin Chess, Jack Clark, Christopher Berner, Sam McCandlish, Alec Radford, Ilya Sutskever, and Dario Amodei. 2020. Language models are few-shot learners. In *Advances in Neural Information Processing Systems*, volume 33, pages 1877–1901. Curran Associates, Inc.

Mia Xu Chen, Orhan Firat, Ankur Bapna, Melvin Johnson, Wolfgang Macherey, George Foster, Llion Jones, Mike Schuster, Noam Shazeer, Niki Parmar, Ashish Vaswani, Jakob Uszkoreit, Lukasz Kaiser, Zhifeng Chen, Yonghui Wu, and Macduff Hughes. 2018. The best of both worlds: Combining recent advances in neural machine translation. In *Proceedings of the 56th Annual Meeting of the Association for Computational Linguistics (Volume 1: Long Papers)*, pages 76–86, Melbourne, Australia. Association for Computational Linguistics.

Kyunghyun Cho, Bart van Merriënboer, Caglar Gulcehre, Dzmitry Bahdanau, Fethi Bougares, Holger Schwenk, and Yoshua Bengio. 2014. Learning phrase representations using RNN encoder–decoder for statistical machine translation. In *Proceedings of the 2014 Conference on Empirical Methods in Natural Language Processing (EMNLP)*, pages 1724–1734, Doha, Qatar. Association for Computational Linguistics.

Michael Covington. 1996. An algorithm to align words for historical comparison. *Computational Linguistics*, 22(4):481–496.

Robert Forkel, Johann-Mattis List, Simon J Greenhill, Christoph Rzymski, Sebastian Bank, Michael Cysouw, Harald Hammarström, Martin Haspelmath, Gereon A Kaiping, and Russell D Gray. 2018. Cross-linguistic data formats, advancing data sharing and re-use in comparative linguistics. *Scientific data*, 5(1):1–10.

Daniel Golovin, Benjamin Solnik, Subhodeep Moitra, Greg Kochanski, John Karro, and David Sculley. 2017. Google Vizier: A service for black-box optimization. In *Proceedings of the 23rd ACM SIGKDD International Conference on Knowledge Discovery and Data Mining (KDD '17)*, pages 1487–1495, Halifax, NS, Canada.

Bradley Hauer and Grzegorz Kondrak. 2011. Clustering semantically equivalent words into cognate sets in multilingual lists. In *Proceedings of 5th International Joint Conference on Natural Language Processing*, pages 865–873, Chiang Mai, Thailand. Asian Federation of Natural Language Processing.

Geoffrey E. Hinton, Nitish Srivastava, Alex Krizhevsky, Ilya Sutskever, and Ruslan R. Salakhutdinov. 2012. Improving neural networks by preventing co-adaptation of feature detectors. *arXiv preprint arXiv:1207.0580*.

Jireh Jam, Connah Kendrick, Kevin Walker, Vincent Drouard, Jison Gee-Sern Hsu, and Moi Hoon Yap. 2021. A comprehensive review of past and present image inpainting methods. *Computer Vision and Image Understanding*, 203:103147.

Llion Jones, Richard Sproat, and Haruko Ishikawa. 2022. Helpful neighbors: Leveraging geographic neighbors to aid in placename pronunciation. In preparation.

William Jones. 1786. Third anniversary discourse to the Asiatic Society, Calcutta.

Diederik P. Kingma and Jimmy Ba. 2015. Adam: A method for stochastic optimization. In *3rd International Conference on Learning Representations (ICLR)*, San Diego, CA, USA.

Grzegorz Kondrak. 2000. A new algorithm for the alignment of phonetic sequences. In *Proceedings of the North American Chapter of the Association for Computational Linguistics*, pages 288–295, San Francisco, CA. ACL, Morgan Kaufmann.

Vladimir I. Levenshtein. 1966. Binary codes capable of correcting deletions, insertions, and reversals. *Soviet Physics — Doklady*, 10(8):707–710.

Johann-Mattis List. 2019a. Automatic inference of sound correspondence patterns across multiple languages. *Computational Linguistics*, 45(1):137–161.

Johann-Mattis List. 2019b. Beyond edit distances: Comparing linguistic reconstruction systems. *Theoretical Linguistics*, 45(3-4):247–258.

Johann-Mattis List and Robert Forkel. 2021. LingPy. A Python library for historical linguistics. July, version 2.6.8, `https://github.com/lingpy/lingpy`.

Johann-Mattis List, Robert Forkel, Simon J Greenhill, Christoph Rzymski, Johannes Englisch, and Russell D Gray. 2021. Lexibank: A public repository of standardized wordlists with computed phonological and lexical features. *Scientific Data*. To appear.

Johann-Mattis List, Mary Walworth, Simon J. Greenhill, Tiago Tresoldi, and Robert Forkel. 2018. Sequence comparison in computational historical linguistics. *Journal of Language Evolution*, 3(2):130–144.

Guilin Liu, Fitsum A. Reda, Kevin J. Shih, Ting-Chun Wang, Andrew Tao, and Bryan Catanzaro. 2018. Image inpainting for irregular holes using partial convolutions. In *Proceedings of the 15th European Conference on Computer Vision (ECCV 2018)*, pages 89–105, Munich, Germany. Springer International Publishing. Preprint.

Yinhan Liu, Myle Ott, Naman Goyal, Jingfei Du, Mandar Joshi, Danqi Chen, Omer Levy, Mike Lewis, Luke Zettlemoyer, and Veselin Stoyanov. 2019. RoBERTa: A robustly optimized BERT pretraining approach. *arXiv preprint arXiv:1907.11692*.

Andrew L. Maas, Awni Y. Hannun, and Andrew Y. Ng. 2013. Rectifier nonlinearities improve neural network acoustic models. In *Proceedings of the 30th International Conference on Machine Learning (ICML)*, volume 28, Atlanta, Georgia, USA.

Carlo Meloni, Shauli Ravfogel, and Yoav Goldberg. 2021. Ab antiquo: Neural proto-language reconstruction. In *Proceedings of the 2021 Conference of the North American Chapter of the Association for Computational Linguistics: Human Language Technologies*, pages 4460–4473, Online. Association for Computational Linguistics.

Gaurav Menghani. 2021. Efficient deep learning: A survey on making deep learning models smaller, faster, and better. *arXiv preprint arXiv:2106.08962*.

Vinod Nair and Geoffrey E. Hinton. 2010. Rectified linear units improve restricted Boltzmann machines. In *Proceedings of the 27th International Conference on Machine Learning (ICML)*, pages 807–814, Haifa, Israel. Association for Computing Machinery (ACM).

Keiron O'Shea and Ryan Nash. 2015. An introduction to convolutional neural networks. *arXiv preprint arXiv:1511.08458*.

Kishore Papineni, Salim Roukos, Todd Ward, and Wei-Jing Zhu. 2002. Bleu: a method for automatic evaluation of machine translation. In *Proceedings of the 40th Annual Meeting of the Association for Computational Linguistics*, pages 311–318, Philadelphia, Pennsylvania, USA. Association for Computational Linguistics.

Hermann Paul. 1880. *Prinzipien der Sprachgeschichte*. Max Niemeyer, Halle.

Jialun Peng, Dong Liu, Songcen Xu, and Houqiang Li. 2021. Generating diverse structure for image inpainting with hierarchical VQ-VAE. In *Proceedings of the IEEE/CVF Conference on Computer Vision and Pattern Recognition (CVPR)*, pages 10775–10784, Nashville, TN, USA. IEEE.

Zhen Qin, Qingliang Zeng, Yixin Zong, and Fan Xu. 2021. Image inpainting based on deep learning: A review. *Displays*, 69:102028.

N. Shawki, R. Rodriguez Nunez, I. Obeid, and J. Picone. 2021. On automating hyperparameter optimization for deep learning applications. In *Proceedings of 2021 IEEE Signal Processing in Medicine and Biology Symposium (SPMB)*, pages 1–7, Philadelphia, PA, USA. IEEE.

Jonathan Shen, Patrick Nguyen, Yonghui Wu, Zhifeng Chen, Mia X. Chen, Ye Jia, Anjuli Kannan, Tara Sainath, Yuan Cao, Chung-Cheng Chiu, Yanzhang He, Jan Chorowski, Smit Hinsu, Stella Laurenzo, James Qin, Orhan Firat, Wolfgang Macherey, Suyog Gupta, Ankur Bapna, Shuyuan Zhang, Ruoming Pang, Ron J. Weiss, Rohit Prabhavalkar, Qiao Liang, Benoit Jacob, Bowen Liang, HyoukJoong Lee, Ciprian Chelba, et al. 2019. LINGVO: A modular and scalable framework for sequence-to-sequence modeling. *arXiv preprint arXiv:1902.08295*.

Emma Strubell, Ananya Ganesh, and Andrew McCallum. 2019. Energy and policy considerations for deep learning in NLP. In *Proceedings of the 57th Annual Meeting of the Association for Computational Linguistics*, pages 3645–3650, Florence, Italy. Association for Computational Linguistics.

Ilya Sutskever, Oriol Vinyals, and Quoc V Le. 2014. Sequence to sequence learning with neural networks. In *Proceedings of the 27th International Conference on Neural Information Processing Systems (NIPS'14)*, pages 3104–3112. MIT Press.

Christian Szegedy, Vincent Vanhoucke, Sergey Ioffe, Jon Shlens, and Zbigniew Wojna. 2016. Rethinking the Inception architecture for computer vision. In *Proceedings of the 2016 IEEE Conference on Computer Vision and Pattern Recognition (CVPR)*, pages 2818–2826, Las Vegas, USA. IEEE.

Language Name	Emoji
`ChorbatBalti`	[illegible]
`KhapaluBalti`	👂
`KharmangBalti`	👃
`RonduBalti`	🧠
`ShigarBalti`	👅
`SkarduBalti`	👄
`SkarduPurki`	[illegible]

Table 4: The one-to-one mapping between the names of languages in BACKSTROMNORTHERNPAKISTAN language group and the corresponding Unicode emojis.

Ashish Vaswani, Noam Shazeer, Niki Parmar, Jakob Uszkoreit, Llion Jones, Aidan N Gomez, Łukasz Kaiser, and Illia Polosukhin. 2017. Attention is all you need. In *Proceedings of the 31st Conference on Neural Information Processing Systems (NIPS 2017)*, pages 5998–6008, Long Beach, CA. Curran Associates Inc.

A Language Name Emoji Mapping

The mapping between names of the Northern Pakistan languages as encoded in the shared task data for the BACKSTROMNORTHERNPAKISTAN language group and the emojis is shown in Table 4. The mapping takes place during the generation of the training data. The inverse mapping is applied during decoding at the inference stage to map the emojis back to language names.

B Tuning the Inpainting Model

For the cognate inpainting model there are six tunable hyperparameters:

- The symbol embedding dimension.
- The width w of the 2D convolution kernel (h, w), where h is the number of languages and w corresponds window of characters processed processed by each convolution and deconvolution operation.
- The number of convolution filters for the 2D convolution layer.
- Probability for the dropout layer that follows the convolution layer (Hinton et al., 2012).
- The nonlinearity activation applied to the convolved inputs after the dropout. This choice is between rectified linear units (ReLU) (Nair and Hinton, 2010), Leaky ReLU (Maas et al., 2013) and the hyperbolic tangent function.
- Whether to scale the embeddings, the outputs of the convolution layer or not to apply the scaling at all.

A Transformer Architecture for the Prediction of Cognate Reflexes

Giuseppe G. A. Celano
Leipzig University
Faculty of Mathematics and Computer Science
Institute of Computer Science
celano@informatik.uni-leipzig.de

Abstract

This paper presents the transformer model built to participate in the SIGTYP 2022 Shared Task on the Prediction of Cognate Reflexes. It consists of an encoder-decoder architecture with multi-head attention mechanism. Its output is concatenated with the one hot encoding of the language label of an input character sequence to predict a target character sequence. The results show that the transformer outperforms the baseline rule-based system only partially.

1 Introduction

The SIGTYP 2022 Shared Task on the Prediction of Cognate Reflexes investigates[1] the research question of to what extend machine learning can be employed to predict cognate reflexes, i.e., word forms assumed to derive from a common attested or reconstructed word form.

Such words prototypically present phonological features that are in part common to different languages and in part specific to each given language: consistent comparison between different words allows detection of structural similarities and recurrent change patterns, which can be explained by positing the existence of sets of cognate reflexes, i.e., sets of words belonging to different languages but deriving from a common form that has over time undergone consistent—and therefore to a large extent predictable—phonological/structural change according to the rules of each given language.

The study of cognate reflexes, which is at the heart of modern historical-comparative linguistics, was first applied successfully to the Indo-European languages, which have been argued, with ample and compelling evidence, to derive from a common ancestor, the Proto-Indo-European (e.g. see Lehmann, 1952). In this respect, the comparative method has even allowed reconstruction of parallel grammars, with description of detailed phonological and morphosyntactic correspondences between languages (e.g., see Sihler, 1995 for Ancient Greek and Latin).

The cognate-related computational research has been characterized by various tasks and approaches. Some are rule-based: for example, Dinu and Ciobanu (2014) automatically identify cognates by linking word etymologies; List (2019a) proposes an algorithm to align cognate sound segments. Others employ machine learning methods: for example, Meloni et al. (2021) build an encoder-decoder-with-attention model to predict the Latin root word common to romance language cognates. Similarly, Dekker and Zuidema (2020) investigate the use of neural networks for prediction of cognates from Slavic and Germanic subfamilies.

In the SIGTYP 2022 Shared Task, participants are requested to predict a cognate reflex form from other cognate reflex forms. The present article reports on the model I have build for the challenge. In Section 2, the dataset is described, while, in Section 3, the method employed to tackle the task is detailed. Section 4 contains the results, and Section 5 their discussion. Section 6 provides some concluding remarks.

2 Dataset

The initial dataset provided for training consisted of cognate reflexes from 10 language families (see List et al. 2022 for a description of the language database). The data for each language family in turn consists of 5 `tsv` training files containing cognate reflexes for a variable number of languages: the 5 files contain training data with different percentages of missing data, ranging from 10% to 50%.

This data structure has been designed to test model reliability on progressively sparser data, with the file containing 50% missing data being the most challenging. The 5 training files are matched

[1]The code is made available at https://github.com/sigtyp/ST2022

Proceedings of the 4th Workshop on Computational Typology and Multilingual NLP (SIGTYP 2022), pages 80 - 85
July 14, 2022 ©2022 Association for Computational Linguistics

BelejeGonfoye	Fadashi	Maiyu	Undulu
g o r a	k o r a	?	g o r a f a
n d u	n d u	n d u	?
?	b o ʃ a	b ɔ ʃ a	b o: ʃ a

Table 1: Example of entries from a test file of `bremerberta`.

predictor	language	target (Undulu)
m u l h i	Maiyu	m u l h i
m u l h i	Fadashi	m u l h i
b o ŋ o ʃ	Fadashi	b o ŋ k o ʃ
m b ə m a	BelejeGonfoye	m b u m a

Table 2: Examples of remodelling of training data of `bremerberta`

by 5 test files presenting the exact same structure as the training files plus question marks in those table cells whose values are requested to be predicted. Solutions and baseline results for each of the 5 test files are also provided. Table 1 shows a few example rows from a test file of the language family labeled as `bremerberta` (Bremer, 2016), where question marks indicate the cognate reflexes to predict.

It is important to note that the initial training data are only provided in order for the participant to familiarize with data structure: indeed, the test data, which only are required to be submitted for the challenge, contain different languages (also called 'surprise languages'), whose model parameters need to be calculated singularly and independently. The test data also consists of 10 language families. In what follows, I present my work concerning the surprise languages[2] only.

3 Method

3.1 Modeling Strategy and Data Vectorization

The surprise data comes from 10 language families. The data for each language family is organized in separate folders containing 5 training files with different percentage of missing data (from 10% to 50%). Remarkably, the training files with different percentages have overlapping data, and therefore have to be kept separate in the training phase.

Each file corresponds to a table, where columns represent languages and rows examples of cognate reflexes. The data is highly sparse, in that single rows can show more than one empty cell. Moreover, the test files, as shown in Table 1, require prediction of cognate reflexes not only for one but all languages, with some rows having a given language as their target variable and other rows other languages.

To tackle these issues, I have build as many models as the number of languages contained in each training file. The number of models created for each language family can therefore be calculated thus:

$$languages \cdot train\_files = models$$

For example, 45 models are trained for the language family labeled as `hillburmish` because it consists of 9 languages, and 5 training files with different percentages of missing data are available.

The original tabular data of each training file has been reorganized as to create new tabular structures: each language is considered as a target variable in turn, with the other languages' data being used as predictors. To address the issue of sparsity, each new data point is modeled as to only represent one single (predictor) cognate reflex plus its language label.

Table 2 shows how data are remodeled to predict, for example, cognate reflexes of the Undulu language. The rows contain cognate reflexes that may be on one single row in the original data (this holds true for the first two rows). Each cognate reflex is considered—with regard to the target variable—separately. The language column refers to the languages of the cognate reflexes used as predictors. It is to be noted that this modeling strategy allows ignoring the missing data in the original files: if a cognate reflex for a given language is missing, it is simply ignored.

Cognate reflexes have been vectorized as character embeddings, while one hot encoding has been employed for language labels. The term 'character' is here used to refer to all space-separated values provided in the original data (most of which, but not all, correspond to one Unicode character).

3.2 A Transformer Architecture

Transformers have increasingly become popular to solve a variety of NLP tasks, especially through fine-tuning of a pretrained model (e.g, see Wolf et al., 2020).

Transformers are characterized by an encoder-decoder architecture with attention mechanism

[2]This data coincides with that in the `data-surprise` folder at `https://github.com/sigtyp/ST2022`.

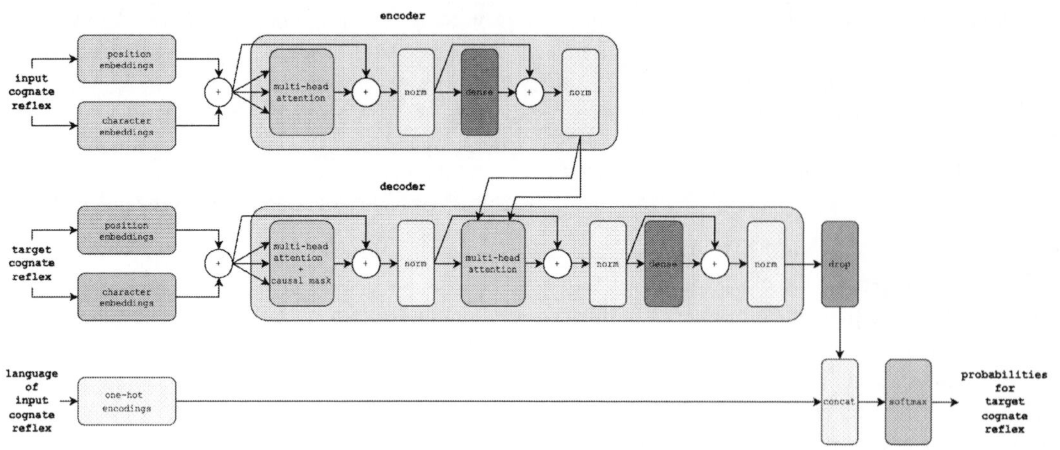

Figure 1: The transformer architecture

(Vaswani et al., 2017). In the present task, the encoder is meant to transform an input sequence of characters into a new context-aware sequence via a multi-head attention layer. The decoder can then predict each character of a target sequence relying on the entire context-aware input sequence and all the target sequence steps *preceding* the (target) sequence step to predict: this is possible because the target sequence used as an input is made context-aware via a multi-head attention layer with masking, which prevents the use of sequence steps from the future.[3]

In the implementation proposed (see Figure 1)[4], the input to the encoder is represented by character embeddings added to character position embeddings: these latter are meant to vectorize the position of each character within the character sequence (indeed, no recurrent neural network will be used to keep track of character order).

The heart of the encoder coincides with a multi-head attention layer outputting a context-aware representation of the input embeddings that accounts for how strongly each character is associated with the others within the character sequence. Remarkably, attention mechanism is character order independent. Since `query`, `key`, and `value` of the encoder's multi-head attention layer are all input character embeddings, the layer instantiates self-attention.

The decoder component has a more complex architecture, which consists of two main layers:

- A multi-head attention layer whose input is a target sequence masked as to avoid that prediction of a target sequence step takes advantage from future steps

- A multi-head attention layer aimed to merge the encoder output, used as `key` and `value`, with the output of the masked multi-head attention layer used as `query`.

The output of the decoder is passed to a dropout layer, and the output of it is then concatenated with the one-hot encoding computed for the language of the input character sequence. Finally, a `softmax` function is meant to output the probabilities for each target character.

The new remodeling of data described in Section 3.1 also requires a strategy to deal with multiple cognate reflexes 'at once' at inference time: since test files contain more than one cognate reflex for a given target cognate reflex (i.e., there are many cognate reflexes as predictors on a single row), the probabilities returned for each predictor cognate reflex are summed and then averaged (by the number of predictor cognate reflexes) to produce one single target tensor of probabilities (see Figure 2). At inference time, the string for the target cognate reflex used as an input first consists only of a dollar sign, which conventionally represents the beginning of a target character sequence: recursively, after a character is predicted, it is added to the target character

[3]At training time, the target character sequence and the target character sequence used as input differ in that the former is offset by one step.

[4]The architecture is the one implemented at `https://github.com/keras-team/keras-io/blob/master/examples/nlp/neural_machine_translation_with_transformer.py`, adapted for the present SIGTYP 2022 Shared Task to account for the presence of language labels as predictors. The code is available at `https://github.com/sigtyp/ST2022/tree/main/systems/PRECOR_transformer`.

sequence used as an input, so that it can also be used for prediction of the following character, until a hash sign, which conventionally signals the end of a cognate reflex, is reached.

4 Results

Results are shown in Table 3. The scores given for each language family are averages over all the scores for each language within a given language family. They have been calculated using the function `compare_words` made available by the SIGTYP 2022 Shared Task organizers. Three main metrics have been employed: the Levenshtein distance (Levenshtein, 1965), the B-Cubed F-scores (List, 2019b), and the BLEU scores (Papineni et al., 2002). In Table 3, each score of the transformer is provided together with the corresponding one of the baseline rule-based system (this latter being in parentheses). Highlighted are the best scores for each language family. More details on the metrics of the SIGTYP 2022 Shared Task and the baseline scores are given in List et al. (2022).

5 Discussion

The presence of 5 different training sets for each language family and the need of building a model for each language within a language family (see Section 3) resulted in the training of as high a number of models as 495. Since training of different algorithms and, especially, hyperparameter optimization for each model would have required a high computation load, I focused on a transformer architecture with fixed hyperparameters for all languages.[5]

The Levenshtein distance shows that the transformer always performs better than the rule-based system relative to the language family `kesslersignificance`. The transformer's performances for `beidazihui` and `bremerberta` are better relative to the datasets with proportions 0.1, 0.2, and 0.3 and the datasets with proportions 0.1 and 0.5, respectively.

The major challenge posed by the SIGTYP 2022 Shared Task seems to be data scarsity and sparsity, which affects data representativeness. The transformer's model tended to overfit the training data. A dropout layer and early stopping were employed, but more regularization and hyperparameter tuning would probably lead to better results. Due to the high variance, I consider the results of the transformer and the baseline model very similar.

[5]Details can be found at `https://github.com/sigtyp/ST2022/tree/main/systems/PRECOR_transformer`.

Proportion 0.1			
Language family	**ED**	**B-Cubed FS**	**BLEU**
bantubvd	1.37 (1.13)	0.67 (0.78)	0.52 (0.61)
beidazihui	1.04 (1.10)	0.67 (0.73)	0.59 (0.58)
birchallchapacuran	2.42 (1.63)	0.51 (0.65)	0.36 (0.53)
bodtkhobwa	0.56 (0.49)	0.73 (0.76)	0.69 (0.72)
bremerberta	1.39 (1.72)	0.71 (0.72)	0.63 (0.50)
deepadungpalaung	1.26 (1.07)	0.74 (0.76)	0.39 (0.44)
hillburmish	1.66 (1.21)	0.53 (0.65)	0.42 (0.56)
kesslersignificance	2.49 (2.77)	0.45 (0.49)	0.15 (0.16)
luangthongkumkaren	0.87 (0.38)	0.76 (0.91)	0.65 (0.84)
wangbai	0.81 (0.62)	0.73 (0.80)	0.65 (0.73)
Proportion 0.2			
Language family	**ED**	**B-Cubed FS**	**BLEU**
bantubvd	1.70 (1.38)	0.58 (0.69)	0.45 (0.53)
beidazihui	1.03 (1.14)	0.64 (0.68)	0.59 (0.57)
birchallchapacuran	2.90 (2.02)	0.44 (0.58)	0.29 (0.45)
bodtkhobwa	0.62 (0.45)	0.67 (0.75)	0.66 (0.75)
bremerberta	1.68 (1.68)	0.61 (0.67)	0.53 (0.51)
deepadungpalaung	1.51 (1.30)	0.58 (0.67)	0.33 (0.39)
hillburmish	1.76 (1.23)	0.49 (0.63)	0.39 (0.55)
kesslersignificance	2.56 (2.93)	0.38 (0.40)	0.14 (0.14)
luangthongkumkaren	1.01 (0.47)	0.68 (0.87)	0.59 (0.80)
wangbai	1.00 (0.76)	0.64 (0.75)	0.60 (0.68)
Proportion 0.3			
Language family	**ED**	**B-Cubed FS**	**BLEU**
bantubvd	2.18 (1.55)	0.47 (0.66)	0.34 (0.51)
beidazihui	1.09 (1.12)	0.60 (0.67)	0.56 (0.57)
birchallchapacuran	3.19 (2.36)	0.39 (0.54)	0.26 (0.41)
bodtkhobwa	0.67 (0.48)	0.64 (0.73)	0.63 (0.72)
bremerberta	1.97 (1.84)	0.55 (0.63)	0.46 (0.49)
deepadungpalaung	1.63 (1.35)	0.50 (0.60)	0.30 (0.38)
hillburmish	2.00 (1.40)	0.44 (0.58)	0.33 (0.49)
kesslersignificance	2.78 (3.10)	0.33 (0.35)	0.13 (0.11)
luangthongkumkaren	1.13 (0.45)	0.66 (0.87)	0.56 (0.81)
wangbai	1.10 (0.81)	0.60 (0.72)	0.56 (0.66)
Proportion 0.4			
Language family	**ED**	**B-Cubed FS**	**BLEU**
bantubvd	2.16 (1.64)	0.45 (0.63)	0.34 (0.49)
beidazihui	1.12 (1.11)	0.59 (0.67)	0.55 (0.57)
birchallchapacuran	3.51 (2.82)	0.37 (0.50)	0.24 (0.36)
bodtkhobwa	0.71 (0.59)	0.62 (0.69)	0.60 (0.66)
bremerberta	2.32 (2.32)	0.48 (0.57)	0.40 (0.39)
deepadungpalaung	1.84 (1.51)	0.43 (0.54)	0.24 (0.32)
hillburmish	2.17 (1.58)	0.41 (0.54)	0.30 (0.45)
kesslersignificance	2.89 (3.91)	0.28 (0.30)	0.13 (0.05)
luangthongkumkaren	1.23 (0.53)	0.61 (0.85)	0.53 (0.78)
wangbai	1.29 (0.90)	0.55 (0.70)	0.49 (0.62)
Proportion 0.5			
Language family	**ED**	**B-Cubed FS**	**BLEU**
bantubvd	2.36 (2.00)	0.41 (0.57)	0.29 (0.39)
beidazihui	1.18 (1.15)	0.56 (0.66)	0.53 (0.56)
birchallchapacuran	3.72 (3.17)	0.34 (0.47)	0.21 (0.31)
bodtkhobwa	0.81 (0.62)	0.58 (0.66)	0.55 (0.65)
bremerberta	2.50 (2.53)	0.44 (0.53)	0.36 (0.34)
deepadungpalaung	2.04 (1.62)	0.36 (0.49)	0.19 (0.30)
hillburmish	2.42 (2.13)	0.37 (0.46)	0.25 (0.33)
kesslersignificance	3.00 (4.06)	0.27 (0.28)	0.11 (0.05)
luangthongkumkaren	1.47 (0.66)	0.55 (0.81)	0.46 (0.73)
wangbai	1.54 (1.02)	0.49 (0.66)	0.42 (0.58)

Table 3: Results for the transformer and the baseline rule-based system (in parentheses).

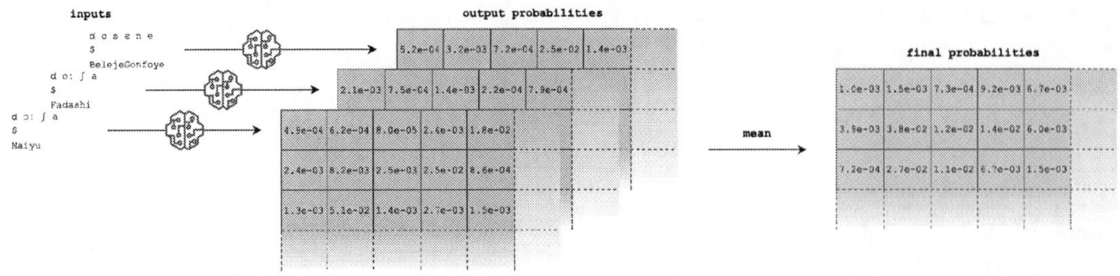

Figure 2: Example of calculation of final probabilities at inference time (fictitious numbers). The inputs are represented by cognate reflexes of one single row in the file `test-0.10.tsv` of `bremerberta`.

6 Conclusions

The paper presented the transformer model built for the SIGTYP 2022 Shared Task. Despite the transformer's complex architecture, which can model input characters in context and even rely on past target sequence steps, its performance was not overall superior to that of the baseline rule-based system. This may be due to data scarsity and sparsity. For this reason and in light of the considerable computational overhead that may be required at inference time, in that target sequence decoding may involve thousands of dictionary lookups—which can only be executed on CPU—one might prefer to test simpler model architectures.

Supplementary Material

The code described in this paper has been archived at `https://github.com/sigtyp/ST2022/releases/tag/v1.4` and `https://doi.org/10.5281/zenodo.6586772`.

Acknowledgements

This work has been supported by the German Research Foundation (DFG project number 408121292).

References

Nate D. Bremer. 2016. *A sociolinguistic survey of six Berta speech varieties in Ethiopia*. SIL International, Addis Ababa.

Peter Dekker and Willem Zuidema. 2020. Word prediction in computational historical linguistics. *Journal of Language Modelling*, 8:295–336.

Liviu P. Dinu and Alina Maria Ciobanu. 2014. Building a dataset of multilingual cognates for the Romanian lexicon. In *Proceedings of the Ninth International Conference on Language Resources and Evaluation (LREC'14)*, pages 1038–1043.

Winfred Philipp Lehmann. 1952. *Proto-Indo-European Phonology*. University of Texas Press.

Vladimir. I. Levenshtein. 1965. Dvoičnye kody s ispravleniem vypadenij, vstavok i zameščenij simvolov. *Doklady Akademij Nauk SSSR*, 163(4):845–848.

Johann-Mattis List. 2019a. Automatic inference of sound correspondence patterns across multiple languages. *Computational Linguistics*, 45(1):137–161.

Johann-Mattis List. 2019b. Beyond Edit Distances: Comparing linguistic reconstruction systems. *Theoretical Linguistics*, 45(3-4):1–10.

Johann-Mattis List, Ekaterina Vylomova, Robert Forkel, Nathan W. Hill, and Ryan Cotterell. 2022. The SIGTYP 2022 shared task on the prediction of cognate reflexes. In *The Fourth Workshop on Computational Typology and Multilingual NLP*, Online. Association for Computational Linguistics.

Carlo Meloni, Shauli Ravfogel, and Yoav Goldberg. 2021. Ab antiquo: Neural proto-language reconstruction. In *Proceedings of the 2021 Conference of the North American Chapter of the Association for Computational Linguistics: Human Language Technologies*, pages 4460–4473.

Kishore Papineni, Salim Roukos, Todd Ward, and Wei-Jing Zhu. 2002. Bleu: a method for automatic evaluation of machine translation. In *Proceedings of the 40th Annual Meeting of the Association for Computational Linguistics*, pages 311–318, Philadelphia, Pennsylvania, USA. Association for Computational Linguistics.

Andrew L. Sihler. 1995. *New Comparative Grammar of Greek and Latin*. Oxford University Press.

Ashish Vaswani, Noam Shazeer, Niki Parmar, Jakob Uszkoreit, Llion Jones, Aidan N Gomez, Łukasz Kaiser, and Illia Polosukhin. 2017. Attention is all you need. *Advances in Neural Information Processing Systems*, 30.

Thomas Wolf, Lysandre Debut, Victor Sanh, Julien Chaumond, Clement Delangue, Anthony Moi, Pierric Cistac, Tim Rault, Remi Louf, Morgan Funtowicz, Joe Davison, Sam Shleifer, Patrick von Platen, Clara Ma, Yacine Jernite, Julien Plu, Canwen Xu,

Teven Le Scao, Sylvain Gugger, Mariama Drame, Quentin Lhoest, and Alexander Rush. 2020. Transformers: State-of-the-art natural language processing. In *Proceedings of the 2020 Conference on Empirical Methods in Natural Language Processing: System Demonstrations*, pages 38–45, Online. Association for Computational Linguistics.

Approaching Reflex Predictions as a Classification Problem Using Extended Phonological Alignments

Tiago Tresoldi
Department of Linguistics and Philology
University of Uppsala
Uppsala
tiago.tresoldi@lingfil.uu.se

Abstract

This work describes an implementation of the "extended alignment" model for cognate reflex prediction submitted to the "SIGTYP 2022 Shared Task on the Prediction of Cognate Reflexes". Similarly to List et al. (2022a), the technique involves an automatic extension of sequence alignments with multilayered vectors that encode informational tiers on both site-specific traits, such as sound classes and distinctive features, as well as contextual and suprasegmental ones, conveyed by cross-site referrals and replication. The method allows to generalize the problem of cognate reflex prediction as a classification problem, with models trained using a parallel corpus of cognate sets. A model using random forests is trained and evaluated on the shared task for reflex prediction, and the experimental results are presented and discussed along with some differences to other implementations.

1 Introduction

The Special Interest Group of Linguistic Typology (SIGTYP) organized in 2022 the "SIGTYP 2022 Shared Task on the Prediction of Cognate Reflexes" (List et al., 2022b), providing the community with cognate-coded wordlists from which varying amounts of cognate sets were withheld. Participants were asked to submit models capable of predicting the missing words and morphemes from the non-withheld members. This work describes the submission named `ceot-extalign-rf`.

Reflex prediction is particularly interesting to computational historical linguistics, since most approaches to reconstruction are rooted in comparative methods operating on cognate sets (Jäger, 2019; Greenhill et al., 2020; List et al., 2018), i.e., sets of words that are assumed to derive from a common proto-word. We can therefore define a cognate as a member of a set of words (a "cognate set") that share an etymological origin via vertical descent. Such a definition highlights how the defining property of a cognate set is the regular sound correspondences between the words involved, even when they are not judged as "similarly sounding" by human evaluators. Homologies don't imply homogenies, as processes like word borrowing and chance resemblance can lead to similarities, while true cognates can be very dissimilar, as in the often cited example of English "two" and Armenian "erku", both from a reconstructed form *dwóh$_1$ (Kroonen, 2013).

The task can be seen as a form of zero-shot learning (Xian et al., 2018), where a model must learn to predict the "reflexes" of a potentially unknown ancestral word form, with no examples of the relevant cognate set provided during the training phase. When considering the landscape of machine learning methods available and the approaches so far proposed (Dinu and Ciobanu, 2014; Bodt and List, 2022; Meloni et al., 2021; Beinborn et al., 2013; Dekker and Zuidema, 2021; Fourrier et al., 2021; List et al., 2022a), including other submissions to this challenge (Jäger, 2022; Celano, 2022; Kirov et al., 2022), it is possible to identify two main strategies for the task. The first one treats the problem as one of classification, potentially refining sequence results with probabilities from a character model, while the second employs sequence transformation methods, especially those akin to *seq2seq* approaches (Sutskever et al., 2014), making the task one analogous to that of "translation". This submission is of the first kind, with results provided by random forests (Kam et al., 1995; Hastie et al., 2009), but attention should focus on the proposed method of data transformation.

The method is based on "multitiered" proposals, originally based on an idea by J.-M. List, which have been described and implemented in other works (Tresoldi et al., 2018; List, 2019b; Bodt and List, 2022; Chacon and List, 2016), including for the baseline for the shared task at hand (List et al., 2022b). It is an approach for modeling historical

Proceedings of the 4th Workshop on Computational Typology and Multilingual NLP (SIGTYP 2022), pages 86 - 93
July 14, 2022 ©2022 Association for Computational Linguistics

linguistic relationships developed to solve problems that are not addressed by pure-correspondence approaches, such as those involving cross-site generalization and the need to capture contextual and suprasegmental information. By considering how discrete representations of phonological sequences can be an unsuitable provision, as the latter are abstract representations of both discrete and continuous multidimensional phonological domains, the technique extends base alignments with multilayered vectors, encoding additional and derived features. Here, such an informational extension is knowingly and intentionally similar to the analytical frameworks of Firthian (Mitchell, 1975) and autosegmental phonology (Goldsmith, 1990), where sequence representation is given by more than a single string of segments.

This work first summarizes the extended alignment technique, with a focus on how it can be used to predict cognate reflexes. Then, it describes the experimental setting used for the submission, and how the extended alignment method can apply to the task at hand. It concludes with a discussion on the results and future work.

2 Materials and Methods

2.1 Materials

Data for the experiment comprised 20 standardized datasets derived from the Lexibank project (List et al., forthcoming), each encompassing a single linguistic family and providing good geographic and typological variation. The datasets were split into five partitions each, with different ratios of words kept for training and evaluation, and were provided by the task's organizers. They provided a more comprehensive description of the data and the way they prepared it in List et al. (2022b).

The submission also extensively uses the phonological information provided by the *mipa* and *tresoldi* models of the `maniphono` library (Tresoldi, 2021), which were incorporated into the code in order to simplify installation requirements. The information provided by these models is adapted from the data of CLTS (Anderson et al., 2018; List et al., 2021), with additional mappings and structures partly described in Tresoldi (2020).

2.2 Methods

2.2.1 Multitiered Extension

It is important to distinguish between the method for representing phonological data and the actual model for reflex prediction. The first, building upon the theoretical discussions also shown in List et al. (2022a), is the most promising element because of its innovative treatment of alignment sites: instead of just being linear components of a sequence under an alignment set, they are treated as independent records in a database. Such a database is turned into a two-dimensional matrix, from which observed and predicted features are extracted and used by common classification models. The method thus facilitates the usage of established algorithms for machine learning, allowing to reframe tasks from historical linguistics as more common tasks of classification, regression, or transformation by using conventional methods and well-researched implementations.

Let's consider the example given in the challenge's call, reproduced in Table 1, with three cognate sets, identified by comparable concepts, involving German, English, and Dutch.

Cognate Set	German	English	Dutch
ASH	a ʃ ɛ	æʃ	ɑ s
BITE	b ai s ə n	b ai t	b ɛi t ə
BELLY	b au x	?	b œi k

Table 1: Exemplary cognate reflexes in German, English, and Dutch. Adapted from List et al. (2022b).

The first step in producing an alignment enriched with new tiers is to perform multiple sequence alignment (List, 2012), which in this case yields three independent alignment sets, as shown in Tables 2, 3, and 4. This is a step common to most classification methods for reflex prediction.

Language	#1	#2	#3
German	a	ʃ	ɛ
English	æ	ʃ	-
Dutch	ɑ	s	-

Table 2: Alignment for cognate set ASH for German, English, and Dutch reflexes.

Language	#1	#2	#3	#4	#5
German	b	ai	s	ə	n
English	b	ai	t	-	-
Dutch	b	ɛi	t	ə	-

Table 3: Alignment for cognate set BITE for German, English, and Dutch reflexes.

Language	#1	#2	#3
German	b	au	x
English	?	?	?
Dutch	b	œi	k

Table 4: Alignment for cognate set BELLY for German, English, and Dutch reflexes.

Even without extensions, by considering each alignment site an independent observation it is possible to combine multiple sets into a single data frame. The operation "transposes" the alignments, joining them into a single frame as shown in Table 5, following the common steps of this framework (List, 2019a; Tresoldi et al., 2018; Bodt and List, 2022; List et al., 2022a).

ID	Source	German segment	English segment	Dutch segment
1	ASH.1	a	æ	ɑ
2	ASH.2	ʃ	ʃ	s
3	ASH.3	ɛ	-	-
4	BITE.1	b	b	b
5	BITE.2	ai	ai	ɛi
6	BITE.3	s	t	t
7	BITE.4	ə	-	ə
8	BITE.5	n	-	-
9	BELLY.1	b	?	b
10	BELLY.2	au	?	œi
11	BELLY.3	x	?	k

Table 5: Extended data frame, without any contextual extension, from the aligned German, English, and Dutch reflexes for the cognate sets ASH, BITE, and BELLY. Note that "Source" is only provided here for ease of exposition, and is not part of actual implementation.

Such an organization of the data is already appropriate for training statistical methods, as each observation is independent, making it possible to identify correspondences and fill gaps by imputing values. For instance, the partial match between the sites of index 4 and 9 in Table 5 strongly suggests that we should impute the missing information for the English segment as /b/, or that site 11 should be a dorsal consonant. Despite disappointing performance in most cases given by the lack of information for a proper zero-shot classification, reflex prediction would already be possible due to the comparatively high number of informative features extracted from a small set of alignments, especially if the prediction refers to phonological traits instead of atomic segments. For example, if given a hypothetical partial cognate set with a German reflex /ʃaus/ and an English /ʃout/, most statistical methods could already classify the first site in the alignment as analogous to site 2 (given the /ʃ/ to /ʃ/ correspondence between German and English), the second one to site 10 (even though English /ou/ is not attested in this example), and the third one to site 6 (given the /s/ to /t/ correspondence), yielding a hypothetical Dutch form /sœit/.

The data frame can be extended in two ways. First, it can be enriched with information specific to each alignment site, allowing machine learning methods to generalize from observed instances (for example, learning that a correspondence applies not just to one sound, but to one or more sets of sounds) and to restrict the effect of correspondences to certain word or syllable positions[1]. In Table 6, such features are added by extending sites with tiers for the "sound class" (Dolgopolsky, 1986) under the SCA model (List, 2012) and the alignment position for each segment. In an actual implementation, more site-specific information would likely be added, such as tiers derived from distinctive features (both from commonly used models, like those derived from Chomsky and Halle 1968, and from binary models designed for machine learning, like those provided by `maniphono`) and indexes related to the position in the word and in the syllable when counting either left-to-right ("index") and right-to-left ("rindex").

The second type of extensions addresses the fact that making each alignment site independent loses contextual information. In Table 7, two contextual tiers are added for each segment tier, one specifying the previous segment (the segment one position to the left, thus L1) and one carrying information on the following sound class (the SCA one position to the right, thus R1). There is no limit on the amount of contextual information with which each alignment site can be enriched, and, in fact, when using a complete system of phonological features it is possible to encode complex phonological information such as "the preceding syllable has a nasal consonant" or "the word ends with a front vowel".

Depending on the size of the context window, the

[1]Note that position of the alignment site in the word is explicitly tested by List et al. (2022a), who report no improvements in performance.

ID	Index	German segment	German SC	English segment	English SC	Dutch segment	Dutch SC
1	1	a	A	æ	E	ɑ	A
2	2	ʃ	S	ʃ	S	s	S
3	3	ɛ	E	-	-	-	-
4	1	b	P	b	P	b	P
5	2	ai	A	ai	A	ɛi	E
6	3	s	S	t	T	t	T
7	4	ə	E	-	-	ə	E
8	5	n	N	-	-	-	-
9	1	b	P	?	?	b	P
10	2	au	A	?	?	œi	U
11	3	x	G	?	?	k	K

Table 6: Multitiered representation extended with information on the alignment index and the corresponding SCA sound class, from the aligned German, English, and Dutch reflexes for sets ASH, BITE, and BELLY.

number, and the type of tiers used for extending the alignment, the shape of the data frame can increase to hold hundreds or thousand of features. While the human inspection of such data will rapidly become impractical, this property should not be considered an issue because, at this stage, the representation is intended for machine consumption. Methods for extracting information for human consumption should rely on these enlarged data frames, without reducing their size beforehand. Nonetheless, before carrying any kind of statistical analysis, it is recommended to perform common tasks of data preparation, such as dimensionality reduction and scaling of the features. Data standardization and normalization can ensure that features extracted from different tiers are placed on a common scale, and transformation processes such as Principal Component Analysis (PCA) (Tipping and Bishop, 1999) can be improve training times and performance.

The implementation presented in this work differs from the previous ones due to the greater attention to the principles of autosegmental phonology. A general advantage of the approach (outlined already in List 2019b), is that it allows to use the propagation strategy of contextual information also for suprasegmental features, such as stress and tone, to all alignment sites where it applies. With tones, for example, instead of marking the tone as a segment-like token at the end of the syllable or as a property of the nucleus alone, it is possible to expand the alignment with one or more tiers regarding the relevant tonality, which will apply to all the segments that make up the relevant syllable. Such information is not restricted to the tone itself, but can be decomposed into properties like "tone contour" or "starting pitch". With complex correspondences involving suprasegmental features, machine learning methods will not need to "look ahead" for a tone token, as one or more columns will carry the relevant information in the data frame record itself. In addition, the representation structure allows more easily composing results from different information tiers: instead of establishing models that only predict segments, as atomic units, the implementation allows to predict, contemporaneously or individually, two or more tiers. whose information can be combined for the final results. For example, especially with a binary model, it is possible to predict the manner and place of articulation of a segment independently, aggregating the results into a phoneme or sound class.

2.2.2 Cognate Prediction

Cognate prediction is performed by training classifiers on the data frames prepared by the code for extending alignments. When paying attention to issues such as scaling of features, missing data, and the encoding of multistate categorical features (usually with one- or multi-hot binary encoders), any machine learning method can be used.

The task will involve two subtasks: the first for training all the classifiers that are needed, and the second for generating output in the expected format once the classifiers have been prepared.

The steps for the first subtask are:

1. **Align raw data**. This step can be performed manually or with tools for linguistic alignments, such as LingPy (List and Forkel, 2021).

2. **Prepare extended data frames**. From the alignment sets, a single data frame is generated with all the requested additional tiers, both for in-site and contextual information.

3. **Prepare the training data for each language**. The training data comprises a data frame for input variables *X*, including all features save for those related to the language being predicted, and a vector for the output variable *y*, from the appropriate "segment" column. All

ID	Index	German segment	German SC	German segment L1	German SC R1	English segment	English SC	English segment L1	English SC R1	Dutch segment	Dutch SC	Dutch segment L1	Dutch SC R1
1	1	a	A	Ø	S	æ	E	Ø	S	ɑ	A	Ø	S
2	2	ʃ	S	a	E	ʃ	S	æ	-	s	S	ɑ	-
3	3	ɛ	E	ʃ	Ø	-	-	ʃ	Ø	-	-	s	Ø
4	1	b	P	Ø	A	b	P	Ø	A	b	P	Ø	E
5	2	ai	A	b	S	ai	A	b	T	ɛi	E	b	T
6	3	s	S	ai	E	t	T	ai	-	t	T	ɛi	E
7	4	ə	E	s	N	-	-	t	-	ə	E	t	-
8	5	n	N	ə	Ø	-	-	-	Ø	-	-	ə	Ø
9	1	b	P	Ø	A	?	?	Ø	?	b	P	Ø	U
10	2	au	A	b	G	?	?	?	?	œi	U	b	K
11	3	x	G	au	Ø	?	?	?	Ø	k	K	œi	Ø

Table 7: Data frame of alignment sites extended with information on the alignment index, the corresponding SCA sound class, the preceding segment, and the following SCA sound class, from the aligned German, English, and Dutch reflexes for the cognate sets ASH, BITE, and BELLY. Missing information, such as the segment to the left of the first site in an alignment, is marked with Ø.

other features related to the language under study are discarded.

4. **Train and save classifiers**. This will result in a collection with one classifier for each language in the dataset.

Once the classifiers are ready, it is possible to perform reflex prediction with the following steps:

1. **Align raw data**. As above.
2. **Prepare extended data frames**. As above; it is highly recommended, and depending on the machine learning method it is necessary, that the set of tiers added to the alignment is equal to or a subset of the one used in training.
3. **Prepare the *X* data frame and generate a *y* prediction**. For most classification methods, *y* will yield a probability for different segments.
4. **Prepare the output**. Build the sequences of predicted reflexes and organize them in the expected data structure for evaluation.

3 Implementation and Results

For the shared task, data and classifiers were prepared according to the workflows described in subsection 2.2.2.

Due to design decisions aiming at testing the method more than achieving the best performing model, only few additional tiers were used for extending the base alignments. These were the segments and SCA sound classes pertinent to each language, with a left and right order of 1 and 2 (i.e., L1, L2, R1, R2), thus increasing four times the number of phonological tiers. Indexing tiers related to the position in the alignment, counting both left-to-right and right-to-left, were also added. No pruning or preemptive dimensionality reduction was performed. Random forests (Breiman, 2001; Kam et al., 1995; Hastie et al., 2009) were trained using the default implementation in *scikit-learn* version 1.1.0 (Pedregosa et al., 2011). Other classification methods were explored using samples of the datasets, yielding good performance improvements in the cases of XGBoost (Chen and Guestrin, 2016), LightGBM (Ke et al., 2017), and multi-layer perceptrons (Hinton, 1990), particularly when performing hyperparameter optimization (Akiba et al., 2019). The decision to only submit the results using the random forest method was based on the time and computational constraints to perform a full training, as well as in the goal of establishing a baseline for this implementation of the method.

Comparing with both the baseline and other submitted methods, the final results suggest much room for improvement. Performance was in general between the Baseline and Baseline-SVM method, mostly due to gains in prediction offered by Support Vector Machines (Koutroumbas and Theodoridis, 2008), for the partitions with most information, degrading rapidly when the amount of withheld data was increased, as illustrated by the global results reported in List et al. (2022b).

The implementation performed particularly poorly with the datasets `bantudvd` (Greenhill and Gray, 2015) (as illustrated by the 0.7053 B-Cubes for the 10% partition, versus 0.7835 of the Baseline submission), `felekesemitic` (Feleke, 2021) (0.6661 B-Cubes for the 10% partition, versus 0.6925 of the baseline). It performed better with datasets `beidazihui` (Běijīng Dàxué, 1962) (as illustrated by the 0.8356 B-Cubes for the 10% partition, versus 0.7279 of the baseline), `bodtkhobwa` (Bodt and List, 2022) (0.7993 B-Cubes for the 10% partition, versus 0.7566 of the baseline), `bremerberta` (Bremer, 2016) (0.7915 B-Cubes for the 10% partition, versus 0.7187 of the baseline), `deepadungpalaung` (Deepadung et al., 2015) (0.8143 B-Cubes for the 10% partition, versus 0.7597 of the baseline), `wangbai` (Wang and Wang, 2004) (0.8326 B-Cubes for the 10% partition, versus 0.8048 of the baseline), `hattorijaponic` (Hattori, 1973) (0.8127 B-Cubes for the 10% partition, versus 0.7889 of the baseline), `listsamplesize` (List, 2014) (0.5325 B-Cubes for the 10% partition, versus 0.4048 of the baseline). Full results are available along with the submission, with performance for other datasets comparable to the baseline.

4 Discussion

Similarly to the implementation in List et al. 2022a, the method of extending alignments implemented here can be conceived as a learned data augmentation strategy, since it is not based on statistical properties of each dataset (that is, each collection of alignment sets), but on the contribution from specialized linguistic knowledge. Such a strategy does not exclude the use of purely statistical methods, allowing them to more easily find the correspondences between sets, especially when they convey phonological traits that are sparse and non sequential. Once mature, we believe that the strategy will be beneficial for most machine learning methods, as it should allow for increased generalization due to increased complexity of the data sets, incorporating informational tiers beyond phonological or sequence properties.

Extended alignments have proven their usefulness for tasks like supervised phonological reconstruction and cognate reflex prediction. There are, however, many other problems to which they could also be applied, either by replacing or by complementing existing methods. The probability of correspondence between certain phonemes, for example, can be used for fine-grained decisions in cases of doubts in the domain of sequence alignment, using information which is "local" to the languages under study along with default correspondence score matrices that are generally computed for global usage. Likewise, the method can credibly be used in the detection of loanwords (Miller et al., 2020), especially in cases of large exchange of words between two languages and of "learned loanwords". Finally, like the other models proposed for this challenge, the method can be used to manage linguistic data, identifying forms that are not predicted by a model trained on the data itself, which may be due to either particularly rich individual histories or different amounts data noise.

Acknowledgements

The author is supported by the Cultural Evolution of Texts project, with funding from the Riksbankens Jubileumsfond (grant agreement ID: MXM19-1087:1). Theoretical work was partly developed when the author received funding from the European Research Council (ERC) under the European Union's Horizon 2020 research and innovation programme (grant agreement No. #715618, "Computer-Assisted Language Comparison").

Supplementary Material

Code and data for reproducing the analyses is deposited at `https://doi.org/10.5281/zenodo.6586772`.

References

Takuya Akiba, Shotaro Sano, Toshihiko Yanase, Takeru Ohta, and Masanori Koyama. 2019. Optuna: A next-generation hyperparameter optimization framework. In *Proceedings of the 25th ACM SIGKDD International Conference on Knowledge Discovery & Data Mining*, KDD '19, page 2623–2631, New York, NY, USA. Association for Computing Machinery.

Cormac Anderson, Tiago Tresoldi, Thiago Costa Chacon, Anne-Maria Fehn, Mary Walworth, Robert

Forkel, and Johann-Mattis List. 2018. A Cross-Linguistic Database of Phonetic Transcription Systems. *Yearbook of the Poznań Linguistic Meeting*, 4(1):21–53.

Lisa Beinborn, Torsten Zesch, and Iryna Gurevych. 2013. Cognate production using character-based machine translation. In *Proceedings of the Sixth International Joint Conference on Natural Language Processing*, pages 883–891.

Timotheus Adrianus Bodt and Johann-Mattis List. 2022. Reflex prediction. A case study of Western Kho-Bwa. *Diachronica*, 39(1):1–38.

Leo Breiman. 2001. Random forests. *Machine learning*, 45(1):5–32.

Nate D. Bremer. 2016. *A sociolinguistic survey of six Berta speech varieties in Ethiopia*. SIL International, Addis Ababa.

Beijing University Běijīng Dàxué. 1962. *Hànyǔ fāngyīn zìhuì [Chinese dialect character pronunciation list]*. Wénzì Gǎigé, Běijīng.

Giuseppe G. A. Celano. 2022. A Transformer architecture for the prediction of cognate reflexes. In *The Fourth Workshop on Computational Typology and Multilingual NLP*, Online. Association for Computational Linguistics.

Thiago Costa Chacon and Johann-Mattis List. 2016. Improved computational models of sound change shed light on the history of the tukanoan languages. *Journal of Language Relationship*, 13(3-4):177–204.

Tianqi Chen and Carlos Guestrin. 2016. XGBoost: A scalable tree boosting system. In *Proceedings of the 22nd ACM SIGKDD International Conference on Knowledge Discovery and Data Mining*, KDD '16, pages 785–794, New York, NY, USA. ACM.

Noam Chomsky and Morris Halle. 1968. *The sound pattern of English.* ERIC.

Sujaritlak Deepadung, Supakit Buakaw, and Ampika Rattanapitak. 2015. A lexical comparison of the Palaung dialects spoken in China, Myanmar, and Thailand. *Mon-Khmer Studies*, 44:19–38.

Peter Dekker and Willem Zuidema. 2021. Word prediction in computational historical linguistics. *Journal of Language Modelling*, 8(2):295–336.

Liviu Dinu and Alina Maria Ciobanu. 2014. Building a dataset of multilingual cognates for the Romanian lexicon. In *Proceedings of the Ninth International Conference on Language Resources and Evaluation (LREC'14)*, pages 1038–1043, Reykjavik, Iceland. European Language Resources Association (ELRA).

A. B. Dolgopolsky. 1986. A probabilistic hypothesis concerning the oldest relationships among the language families of northern Eurasia. In Vitalij V. Shevoroshkin, editor, *Typology, Relationship and Time*, pages 27–50. Karoma Publisher, Ann Arbor.

Tekabe Legesse Feleke. 2021. Ethiosemitic languages: Classifications and classification determinants. *Ampersand*, page 100074.

Clémentine Fourrier, Rachel Bawden, and Benoît Sagot. 2021. Can cognate prediction be modelled as a low-resource machine translation task? In *Findings of the Association for Computational Linguistics: ACL-IJCNLP 2021*, pages 847–861, Online. Association for Computational Linguistics.

John A Goldsmith. 1990. *Autosegmental and metrical phonology*, volume 1. Basil Blackwell.

Simon J Greenhill and Russell D Gray. 2015. Bantu Basic Vocabulary Database.

Simon J Greenhill, Paul Heggarty, and Russell D Gray. 2020. Bayesian phylolinguistics. *The handbook of historical linguistics*, 2:226–253.

Trevor Hastie, Robert Tibshirani, Jerome H Friedman, and Jerome H Friedman. 2009. *The elements of statistical learning: data mining, inference, and prediction*, volume 2. Springer.

Shirō Hattori. 1973. Japanese dialects. In Henry M. Hoenigswald and Robert H. Langacre, editors, *Diachronic, areal and typological linguistics*, number 11 in Current Trends in Linguistics, pages 368–400. Mouton, The Hague and Paris.

Geoffrey E Hinton. 1990. Connectionist learning procedures. In *Machine learning*, pages 555–610. Elsevier.

Gerhard Jäger. 2019. Computational historical linguistics. *Theoretical Linguistics*, 45(3-4):151–182.

Gerhard Jäger. 2022. Bayesian phylogenetic cognate prediction. In *The Fourth Workshop on Computational Typology and Multilingual NLP*, Online. Association for Computational Linguistics.

Ho Tin Kam et al. 1995. Random decision forest. In *Proceedings of the 3rd international conference on document analysis and recognition*, volume 1416, page 278282. Montreal, Canada, August.

Guolin Ke, Qi Meng, Thomas Finley, Taifeng Wang, Wei Chen, Weidong Ma, Qiwei Ye, and Tie-Yan Liu. 2017. Lightgbm: A highly efficient gradient boosting decision tree. In *Advances in Neural Information Processing Systems*, volume 30. Curran Associates, Inc.

Christo Kirov, Richard Sproat, and Alexander Gutkin. 2022. Mockingbird at the SIGTYP 2022 Shared Task: Two types of models for the prediction of cognate reflexes. In *The Fourth Workshop on Computational Typology and Multilingual NLP*, Online. Association for Computational Linguistics.

Konstantinos Koutroumbas and Sergios Theodoridis. 2008. *Pattern recognition*. Academic Press.

Guus Kroonen. 2013. Etymological dictionary of proto-germanic. In *Etymological Dictionary of Proto-Germanic*. Brill.

Johann-Mattis List. 2012. SCA: Phonetic alignment based on sound classes. In Marija Slavkovik and Dan Lassiter, editors, *New directions in logic, language, and computation*, pages 32–51. Springer, Berlin and Heidelberg.

Johann-Mattis List. 2014. Investigating the impact of sample size on cognate detection. *Journal of Language Relationship*, 11:91–101.

Johann-Mattis List. 2019a. Automatic inference of sound correspondence patterns across multiple languages. *Computational Linguistics*, 45(1):137–161.

Johann-Mattis List. 2019b. Automatic sound law induction (Open problems in computational diversity linguistics 3). *The Genealogical World of Phylogenetic Networks*, 6(4).

Johann-Mattis List, Cormac Anderson, Tiago Tresoldi, and Robert Forkel. 2021. *Cross-Linguistic Transcription Systems [Dataset, Version 2.1.0]*. Max Planck Institute for the Science of Human History, Jena.

Johann-Mattis List and Robert Forkel. 2021. *LingPy. A Python library for quantitative tasks in historical linguistics [Software Library, Version 2.6.9]*. Max Planck Institute for Evolutionary Anthropology, Leipzig.

Johann-Mattis List, Robert Forkel, Simon J. Greenhill, Christoph Rzymski, Johannes Englisch, and Russell D. Gray. forthcoming. Lexibank, A public repository of standardized wordlists with computed phonological and lexical features. *Scientific Data*, pages 1–31.

Johann-Mattis List, Nathan W. Hill, and Robert Forkel. 2022a. A new framework for fast automated phonological reconstruction using trimmed alignments and sound correspondence patterns. In *Proceedings of the 3rd Workshop on Computational Approaches to Historical Language Change*, pages 89–96, Dublin. Association for Computational Linguistics.

Johann-Mattis List, Ekaterina Vylomova, Robert Forkel, Nathan W. Hill, and Ryan D. Cotterell. 2022b. The SIGTYP 2022 shared task on the prediction of cognate reflexes. In *The Fourth Workshop on Computational Typology and Multilingual NLP*, Online. Association for Computational Linguistics.

Johann-Mattis List, Mary Walworth, Simon J Greenhill, Tiago Tresoldi, and Robert Forkel. 2018. Sequence comparison in computational historical linguistics. *Journal of Language Evolution*, 3(2):130–144.

Carlo Meloni, Shauli Ravfogel, and Yoav Goldberg. 2021. Ab antiquo: Neural proto-language reconstruction. In *Proceedings of the 2021 Conference of the North American Chapter of the Association for Computational Linguistics: Human Language Technologies*, pages 4460–4473, Online. Association for Computational Linguistics.

John E. Miller, Tiago Tresoldi, Roberto Zariquiey, César A. Beltrán Castañón, Natalia Morozova, and Johann-Mattis List. 2020. Using lexical language models to detect borrowings in monolingual wordlists. *PLOS ONE*, 15(12):1–23.

Terence Frederick Mitchell. 1975. *Principles of Firthian Linguistics*. Longman, London.

F. Pedregosa, G. Varoquaux, A. Gramfort, V. Michel, B. Thirion, O. Grisel, M. Blondel, P. Prettenhofer, R. Weiss, V. Dubourg, J. Vanderplas, A. Passos, D. Cournapeau, M. Brucher, M. Perrot, and E. Duchesnay. 2011. Scikit-learn: Machine learning in Python. *Journal of Machine Learning Research*, 12:2825–2830.

Ilya Sutskever, Oriol Vinyals, and Quoc V Le. 2014. Sequence to sequence learning with neural networks. *Advances in neural information processing systems*, 27.

Michael E Tipping and Christopher M Bishop. 1999. Probabilistic principal component analysis. *Journal of the Royal Statistical Society: Series B (Statistical Methodology)*, 61(3):611–622.

Tiago Tresoldi. 2020. A model of distinctive features for computer-assisted language comparison. *Computer-Assisted Language Comparison in Practice*, 3(6).

Tiago Tresoldi. 2021. Maniphono, a library for the symbolic manipulation of phonological entities. version 0.3.3. `https://github.com/tresoldi/maniphono`.

Tiago Tresoldi, Cormac Anderson, and Johann-Mattis List. 2018. Modelling sound change with the help of multi-tiered sequence representations. In *Proceedings of the 48th Poznań Linguistic Meeting*, Poznań.

Feng Wang and William S.-Y. Wang. 2004. Basic words and language evolution. *Language and Linguistics*, 5(3):643–662.

Yongqin Xian, Christoph H Lampert, Bernt Schiele, and Zeynep Akata. 2018. Zero-shot learning—a comprehensive evaluation of the good, the bad and the ugly. *IEEE transactions on pattern analysis and machine intelligence*, 41(9):2251–2265.

Investigating information-theoretic properties of the typology of spatial demonstratives

Sihan Chen
MIT
sihanc@mit.edu

Richard Futrell
University of California, Irvine
rfutrell@uci.edu

Kyle Mahowald
University of Texas at Austin
mahowald@utexas.edu

Spatial deictic demonstratives (e.g., "here" and "from there") denote spatial relations between speaker(s) and referent(s) and play a crucial role in cognition and language processing (Levinson, 2006). Languages vary in the complexity of their spatial demonstrative systems, both in the granularity of their **distal levels** (e.g. English has two distal levels "here" and "there", with an optional third distal level "(over) there", whereas Kaba has four) as well as in the extent of syncretism across their possible **orientations**: PLACE, GOAL, and SOURCE. English has syncretism between the place and goal demonstratives ("I am there", "I am going there") but distinguishes the source demonstratives ("I am coming from there" is not the same as "I am coming there", see Table 1), whereas Finnish has unique words for each orientation, at each distal level (Table 2).

	GOAL	PLACE	SOURCE
D1	(to) here	here	from here
D2	(to) there	there	from there
D3	(to over) there	(over) there	from (over) there

Table 1: English spatial deictic demonstratives (words in the parenthesis are optional)

Using data from Nintemann et al. (2020), we explore the variability in complexity and informativity across spatial demonstrative systems using spatial deictic lexicons from 223 languages. We argue from an information-theoretic perspective (Shannon, 1948) that spatial deictic lexicons fall on an efficient frontier, balancing informativity and complexity. Specifically, we adopt the **Information Bottleneck** (IB) family of approaches (e.g. Tishby et al., 2000; Strouse and Schwab, 2017; Zaslavsky et al., 2018), where a world state U (distal levels and orientations for a referent) is mentally represented by the speaker as meaning M, which is encoded with words W using a language-specific encoder $q(w \mid m)$ and then decoded by a Bayesian listener. To this end, **informativity** is defined as the mutual information between words and world states, and **complexity** is defined as the mutual information between mental representations of meaning and words. An efficient lexicon optimizes a tradeoff of these two factors (Eq. 1). The relationship between meaning and world states is determined by a **cost function** (Eq. 2) that defines a penalty for confusing distal levels and orientations. Broadly, this approach lets us ask: given a prior and a cost function, if a language has n spatial adverb wordforms, how should those n wordforms be distributed across m slots in the paradigm? We predict that attested systems are more efficient than the logically possible paradigms that are rare or unattested in world languages.

	GOAL	PLACE	SOURCE
D1	tänne	täällä	täältä
D2	sinne	siellä	sieltä
D3	tuonne	tuolla	tuolta

Table 2: Finnish spatial deictic demonstratives

$$J_{IB}[q] = \underbrace{I[M:W]}_{\text{Complexity}} - \beta \cdot \underbrace{I[W:U]}_{\text{Informativity}} \quad (1)$$

$$p(u \mid m) \propto \mu^{C_{rr'}+C_{\theta\theta'}} \quad (2)$$

We make three main contributions. First, we find that among all the 21,146 theoretically possible lexicons, real lexicons lie near the efficient frontier (Fig. 1) for appropriate choice of cost function and prior "need probability" over meanings (Regier et al., 2015), thus adding deictic adverbs to the growing list of lexical semantic domains whose form can be explained in terms of information-theoretic efficiency (e.g. Zaslavsky et al., 2018, 2021; Mollica et al., 2021; Kemp and Regier, 2012; Zaslavsky et al., 2019; Denić et al., 2021). Second,

Proceedings of the 4th Workshop on Computational Typology and Multilingual NLP (SIGTYP 2022), pages 94 - 95
July 14, 2022 ©2022 Association for Computational Linguistics

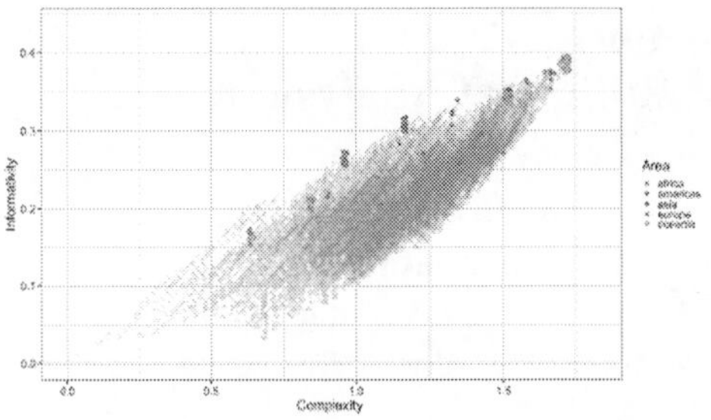

Figure 1: Each colored point represents a real lexicon, with the horizontal axis denoting the complexity and the vertical axis denoting the informativity. The gray points represent simulated lexicons. The real lexicons fall along an efficient frontier (minimizing Eq. 1 for some choice of tradeoff parameter β). The points are jittered to avoid overlap.The parameters here are as follows: μ = 0.3, C_{PS} =1.3, and C_{PG} = 0.8.

we investigate the minimal properties that the cost function and prior must have such that actual lexicons lie on the efficient frontier, finding that the key properties are (1) the cost for confusing GOAL and SOURCE is higher than that for confusing PLACE with SOURCE, which is then higher than that for confusing PLACE and GOAL, and (2) the SOURCE orientation has the least prior probability. Both of these properties are plausible for this semantic domain and consistent with prior observations in the cognitive science literature, specifically regarding asymmetries between the source and goal orientations (Papafragou, 2006, 2010; Nikitina, 2009). Third, we find that the IB approach does not fully capture the patterns in human lexicons, as there are theoretically efficient lexicons that are unattested. We then introduce the notion of **systematicity**, which means that the pattern of distinctions should be consistent across distal levels and orientations. We show that real lexicons are systematic in addition to balancing between informativity and complexity.

In addition to being explanatory for the typology of spatial demonstratives, we believe these methodological innovations could be fruitfully applied to information-theoretic analyses in other typological domains.

References

Milica Denić, Shane Steinert-Threlkeld, and Jakub Szymanik. 2021. Complexity/informativeness trade-off in the domain of indefinite pronouns. In *Semantics and linguistic theory*, volume 30, pages 166–184.

Charles Kemp and Terry Regier. 2012. Kinship categories across languages reflect general communicative principles. *Science*, 336(6084):1049–1054.

Stephen Levinson. 2006. Cognition at the heart of human interaction. *Discourse studies*, 8(1):85–93.

Francis Mollica, Geoff Bacon, Noga Zaslavsky, Yang Xu, Terry Regier, and Charles Kemp. 2021. The forms and meanings of grammatical markers support efficient communication. *Proceedings of the National Academy of Sciences*, 118(49).

Tatiana Nikitina. 2009. Subcategorization pattern and lexical meaning of motion verbs: a study of the source/goal ambiguity.

Julia Nintemann, Maja Robbers, and Nicole Hober. 2020. *Here–Hither–Hence and Related Categories: A Cross-linguistic Study*, volume 26. Walter de Gruyter.

Anna Papafragou. 2006. Spatial representations in language and thought. In *ITRW on Experimental Linguistics*.

Anna Papafragou. 2010. Source-goal asymmetries in motion representation: Implications for language production and comprehension. *Cognitive science*, 34(6):1064–1092.

Terry Regier, Charles Kemp, and Paul Kay. 2015. 11 word meanings across languages support efficient communication. *The Handbook of Language Emergence*, 87:237.

C.E. Shannon. 1948. A Mathematical Theory of Communication. *Bell System Technical Journal*, 27:623–656.

DJ Strouse and David J Schwab. 2017. The deterministic information bottleneck. *Neural computation*, 29(6):1611–1630.

Naftali Tishby, Fernando C Pereira, and William Bialek. 2000. The information bottleneck method. *arXiv preprint physics/0004057*.

Noga Zaslavsky, Charles Kemp, Terry Regier, and Naftali Tishby. 2018. Efficient compression in color naming and its evolution. *Proceedings of the National Academy of Sciences*, 115(31):7937–7942.

Noga Zaslavsky, Mora Maldonado, and Jennifer Culbertson. 2021. Let's talk (efficiently) about us: Person systems achieve near-optimal compression.

Noga Zaslavsky, Terry Regier, Naftali Tishby, and Charles Kemp. 2019. Semantic categories of artifacts and animals reflect efficient coding. In *41st Annual Meeting of the Cognitive Science Society*.

How Universal is Metonymy?
Results from a Large-Scale Multilingual Analysis

Temuulen Khishigsuren[1], **Gábor Bella**[2], **Thomas Brochhagen**[3],
Daariimaa Marav[1], **Fausto Giunchiglia**[2], **Khuyagbaatar Batsuren**[1]
[1]National University of Mongolia [2]University of Trento [3]Universitat Pompeu Fabra
kh.temulen@gmail.com; khuyagbaatar@num.edu.mn

1 Introduction

Several works from cognitive linguistics claim that systematic metonymy is universal across human languages (Barcelona et al., 2003; Brdar and Brdar-Szabó, 2003; Croft, 2002; Gibbs et al., 1994; Kövecses and Radden, 1998; Lakoff and Johnson, 2008; Panther and Radden, 1999). However, cross-linguistic surveys on the phenomenon have so far been limited to a small number of well-studied languages such as English. An important reason for this limitation is that current methodologies in cross-linguistic semantic analysis require serious involvement of language experts (Brdar-Szabó and Brdar, 2003a,b, 2012) or native speakers (Kamei and Wakao, 1992; Slabakova et al., 2013; Srinivasan and Rabagliati, 2015) or simply not suitable for metonymy studies such as the elicitation techniques (Koptjevskaja-Tamm et al., 2015).

On the other hand, the recent trend of exploiting digitally available lexical resources makes large-scale semantic studies feasible; e.g., the study of the emotion domain in 2474 languages (Jackson et al., 2019). This method is especially suitable for systematic metonymy as it is lexically encoded. Therefore, we used a lexico-semantic content of multilingual lexical databases to build a large-scale metonymy corpus that covers 26 metonymy patterns and 20 thousand metonymy instances (word pairs) in 189 languages belonging to 69 genera. Due to the broad linguistic coverage, our results considerably strengthen the stance on metonymy as a universal phenomenon. This new, freely available, online corpus of metonymy examples categorized by patterns is also reusable for future studies.

2 Methods

Among the various kinds of resources—databases, dictionaries, corpora—that were available to us, *multilingual lexical databases* were suitable to semi-automatically build a large multilingual corpus of metonymies. The explicit representation of words, their meanings, and their domains in multiple languages, as well as the presence of a cross-lingual alignment of meanings and domains enable us to extract metonymy in an efficient, partially automated manner.

Our database of choice is the Universal Knowledge Core (UKC)[1] (Giunchiglia et al., 2017), due to its wide linguistic, lexical, and conceptual coverage (120 thousand word meanings, 2 million words in 1127 languages). Metonymy patterns are straightforward to model through the three-layered *domain–concept–lexicon* architecture of the UKC. The concept layer represents *supra-lingual meanings* as a hierarchy of concepts based on the standard lexicographic broader–narrower relationship. The domain layer of the UKC provides a simple semantic categorization of concepts into domains such as *Animal*. The lexical layer, finally, consists of a separate *lexicon* for each language, each one lexicalizing the supra-lingual concept layer.

Metonymy corpus extraction process consisted of three steps. First, from the metonymy patterns mentioned in the literature, we selected a subset for which the UKC provides data. Second, through automatic extraction and expert validation, we identified metonymically related concepts. Third, based on the definitive set of metonymically related concept pairs, we automatically extracted lexicalizations for all languages in the database.

3 Results

Table 1 reports the statistics of the metonymy corpus[2] extracted semi-automatically from the database. Overall, 4,951 concept pairs were annotated as metonymically related, and the corresponding 20,095 metonymy instances were retrieved in 189 languages from the database. These 189 lan-

[1]http://ukc.datascientia.eu/

[2]The metonymy corpus is freely accessible as a stand-alone resource at https://github.com/kbatsuren/UniMet.

Proceedings of the 4th Workshop on Computational Typology and Multilingual NLP (SIGTYP 2022), pages 96 - 98
July 14, 2022 ©2022 Association for Computational Linguistics

Table 1: Metonymy corpus statistics

Metonymy pattern	Illustrative example	Met. concepts	Met. instances	Langs	Families	Genera
Substance for Artifact	He filled the *glass* with water.	390	1,775	110	24	46
Fruit for Plant	The gardener watered the *lemon*.	408	3,330	114	24	43
Instrument for Action	She *combed* her hair.	617	2,083	95	24	40
Community for Place	He traveled to the *country*.	87	735	97	22	38
Plant for Food	*Broccoli* is delicious.	318	1,539	80	19	34
Animal for Meat	The *chicken* is tasty.	156	746	85	19	33
Action for Result	My thumb has a deep *cut*.	729	1,559	77	17	32
Object for Action	They are well *dressed*.	546	1,653	79	17	31
Substance for Action	I *milked* cows by hand.	242	942	78	17	31
Emotion for Cause	You are my *joy*.	104	405	64	14	28
State for Causal agent	He was a *success*.	160	645	59	15	27
Food for Action	They had *breakfasted* so early.	51	210	55	13	27
Building for People	*Church* sang a song.	71	384	63	15	26
Possessed for Possessor	She married *power*.	190	713	60	14	26
Agent for Action	The sheep will be *butchered*.	232	655	53	14	26
Product for Content	The *book* is interesting.	46	546	60	14	25
Body part for Person	I saw many new *faces* today.	156	442	61	12	25
Action for Food	They provided a *drink* at the party.	16	90	47	14	22
Animal for Fur	She likes to wear *mink*.	51	271	35	14	20
Container for Contained	He drank half of the *bottle*.	88	461	42	10	19
Event for People	*Party* went crazy.	61	257	39	11	18
Action for Object	A *lift* fell to the bottom of its shaft.	91	153	41	12	17
Action for Agent	You may be a *help* later.	57	207	34	12	17
Time for Action	We *honeymooned* in Bali.	25	108	36	11	17
Food for Event	*Dinner* took longer than usual.	9	132	36	11	17
Action for Time	My *shift* is over this morning.	50	54	21	8	14
	Total	4,951	20,095	189	34	69

guages belong to 34 different families (phyla) and 69 genera. They are also geographically stratified (Figure 1). To the best of our knowledge, these results provide the widest linguistic coverage so far on metonymy (the broadest prior study we are aware of is by Hilpert (2007) that reported 39 phylogenetically different languages using *eye* to refer to *vision*).

Figure 1: The presence of metonymy in world's languages (the same colors indicate the same family).

Based on the number of genera, the most universal pattern is SUBSTANCE FOR ARTIFACT for which we found 110 languages from 46 genera. FRUIT FOR PLANT and INSTRUMENT FOR ACTION are also very widely attested patterns for each we found 43 and 40 genera, respectively. Nevertheless, even the least widely covered patterns are attested across phylogenetically diverse languages from around the world. For example, the least diverse pattern, ACTION FOR TIME, is still attested in 21 languages from 14 genera and eight families from Africa, East Asia, the Pacific, Europe, and the Middle East. This result suggests that diverse societies use ACTION FOR TIME metonymies.

On the conceptual level, even specific concept pairs appear to be universal: for instance, 49 languages from 22 genera use the concept 'pear' to refer to its plant name. The English examples of COMMUNITY FOR PLACE and INSTRUMENT FOR ACTION patterns in Table 1 are attested in 69 and 39 other languages from 34 and 22 genera, respectively.

4 Conclusions

Metonymy is regarded by most linguists as a universal phenomenon. However, the field data backing up claims of universality has not been large enough so far to provide conclusive evidence. We introduce a large-scale analysis of metonymy based on a lexical corpus of over 20 thousand metonymy instances from 189 languages and 69 genera. No prior study, to our knowledge, is based on linguistic coverage as broad as ours. Drawing on corpus analysis, evidence of universality is found at three levels: systematic metonymy in general, particular metonymy patterns, and specific metonymy concepts.

References

Antonio Barcelona et al. 2003. Names: A metonymic "return ticket" in five languages. *Jezikoslovlje*, 4(1):11–41.

Mario Brdar and Rita Brdar-Szabó. 2003. in english, croatian and hungarian. *Metonymy and pragmatic inferencing*, 113:241.

Rita Brdar-Szabó and Mario Brdar. 2003a. The manner for activity metonymy across domains and languages. *Jezikoslovlje*, 4(1):43–69.

Rita Brdar-Szabó and Mario Brdar. 2003b. Referential metonymy across languages: What can cognitive linguistics and contrastive li nguistics learn from each other? *International Journal of English Studies*, 3(2):85–106.

Rita Brdar-Szabó and Mario Brdar. 2012. The problem of data in the cognitive linguistic research on metonymy: a cross-linguistic perspective. *Language Sciences*, 34(6):728–745.

William Croft. 2002. The role of domains in the interpretation of metaphors and metonymies. *Metaphor and metonymy in comparison and contrast*, pages 161–205.

Raymond W Gibbs, Raymond W Gibbs, and Jr Gibbs. 1994. *The poetics of mind: Figurative thought, language, and understanding*. Cambridge University Press.

Fausto Giunchiglia, Khuyagbaatar Batsuren, and Gabor Bella. 2017. Understanding and exploiting language diversity. In *IJCAI*, pages 4009–4017.

Martin Hilpert. 2007. Chained metonymies in lexicon and grammar. *Aspects of meaning construction*, pages 77–98.

Joshua Conrad Jackson, Joseph Watts, Teague R Henry, Johann-Mattis List, Robert Forkel, Peter J Mucha, Simon J Greenhill, Russell D Gray, and Kristen A Lindquist. 2019. Emotion semantics show both cultural variation and universal structure. *Science*, 366(6472):1517–1522.

Shin-ichiro Kamei and Takahiro Wakao. 1992. Metonymy; reassessment, survey of acceptability, and its treatment in a machine translation system. In *30th Annual Meeting of the Association for Computational Linguistics*, pages 309–311.

Maria Koptjevskaja-Tamm, Ekaterina Rakhilina, and Martine Vanhove. 2015. The semantics of lexical typology. In *The Routledge handbook of semantics*, pages 450–470. Routledge.

Zoltán Kövecses and Günter Radden. 1998. Metonymy: Developing a cognitive linguistic view. *Cognitive linguistics*, 9(1):37–77.

George Lakoff and Mark Johnson. 2008. *Metaphors we live by*. University of Chicago press.

Klaus-Uwe Panther and Günter Radden. 1999. *Metonymy in language and thought*, volume 4. John Benjamins Publishing.

Roumyana Slabakova, Jennifer Cabrelli Amaro, and Sang Kyun Kang. 2013. Regular and novel metonymy in native korean, spanish, and english: Experimental evidence for various acceptability. *Metaphor and Symbol*, 28(4):275–293.

Mahesh Srinivasan and Hugh Rabagliati. 2015. How concepts and conventions structure the lexicon: Cross-linguistic evidence from polysemy. *Lingua*, 157:124–152.

PaVeDa – Pavia Verbs Database: Challenges and Perspectives

Chiara Zanchi
University of Pavia
chiara.zanchi01@unipv.it

Silvia Luraghi
University of Pavia
silvia.luraghi@unipv.it

Claudia Roberta Combei
University of Pavia
claudiaroberta.combei@unipv.it

Abstract

This paper describes an ongoing endeavor to construct Pavia Verbs Database (PaVeDa) – an open-access typological resource that builds upon previous work on verb argument structure, and in particular the Valency Patterns Leipzig (ValPaL) project (Hartmann et al., 2013). The PaVeDa database features four major innovations as compared to the ValPaL database: (i) it includes data from ancient languages enabling diachronic research; (ii) it expands the language sample to language families that are not represented in the ValPaL; (iii) it is linked to external corpora that are used as sources of usage-based examples of stored patterns; (iv) it introduces a new cross-linguistic layer of annotation for valency patterns which allows for contrastive data visualization.

1 Introduction

In this paper, we introduce a new typological resource, the Pavia Verbs Database (PaVeDa)[1] which is modeled upon the Valency Patterns Leipzig (ValPaL)[2] database by Hartmann et al. (2013), while introducing a number of innovations detailed below.

PaVeDa has been designed at the University of Pavia and is currently being constructed. The final version of the resource will allow to contrastively and simultaneously display valency patterns and alternations for ancient and modern languages.

2 State of the art and current challenges

In the last decades, researchers have observed that cross-linguistically verb classes show similar patterns as to their valency patterns and possible alternations.

This observation led scholars to study the extent of possible variation across verb classes emerging from languages of different genetic and areal affiliation in order to discover general tendencies. Additionally, typologists have striven to design and build foundational toolkits, data-sets, and other resources useful to ease and systematize research on verb classes.

The open-access ValPaL database which is the output of the 2009-2013 project "Valency classes in the languages of the world" carried out at Leipzig University represented a ground-breaking tool for the field. The rationale behind its construction is fully documented in Malchukov and Comrie (2015). The ValPaL contains data for 80 verb meanings (and occasionally additional others) from 36 languages. Data includes translational equivalents for these verb meanings together with their associated participants called "microroles" (see example (1)a), the basic valency pattern (see example (1)b) and the valency alternations (see example (1)c), all represented through "coding frames".

(1) Verb meaning: LOAD
  a. Italian equivalent: *caricare*
    1. loader
    2. loaded thing
    3. loading place
  b. Basic coding frame:
     1 > V.subj[1] > 2 (su+3)
  c. Alternations: Locative alternation:
     1 > V'.subj[1] > 3 > di+2

Examples of basic (2) and non-basic usages and alternations (3) of stored verbs are also provided.

(2) *I venditori caricano i giornali e i libri sulla loro macchina.*
  i venditor-i carica-no i giornal-i e i libr-i su-lla loro macchin-a
  ART.DEF.M.PL seller-M.PL load-PRS.PL ART.DEF.M.PL newspaper-M.PL and ART.DEF.M.PL book-M.PL on-ART.DEF.F.SG their car-F.SG
  'The sellers load the newspapers and the books into their car.'

[1] https://hodel.unipv.it/paveda
[2] https://ValPaL.info

Proceedings of the 4th Workshop on Computational Typology and Multilingual NLP (SIGTYP 2022), pages 99 - 102
July 14, 2022 ©2022 Association for Computational Linguistics

(3) *I venditori caricano la loro macchina di giornali e libri.*
i venditor-i carica-no la loro macchin-a di giornal-i e libr-i
ART.DEF.M.PL seller-M.PL load-PRS.PL ART.DEF.F.SG their car-F.SG of newspaper-M.PL and book-M.PL
'The sellers load newspapers and books onto their car.'

The ValPaL paved the way both for investigating transitivity scales and construction alternations Aldai and Wichmann (2018) while further verbal databases, such as the BivalTyp database[3] and the MultiVal lexicons[4] have also been created. In spite of these advances, the ValPaL database can be further improved, in terms of architecture, languages, and data coverage.

In the first place, (i) the language sample is unbalanced from the point of view of representability, as several language families are not included. Moreover, (ii) it does not contain data from ancient languages: this reflects a more general issues, as no systematic comparative study on diachronic developments across languages is available (see Luraghi and Roma, 2021a, Luraghi and Roma, 2021b). Additionally, (iii) the examples stored in the database are only occasionally extracted from corpora; their elicitation relies mainly on the native speakers' intuition of contributors (or elicited from speakers by contributors) or on reference handbooks and dictionaries. Finally, (iv) the current interface does not support comparative visualization of constructions and alternations, and comparison is further complicated by the use of language specific labels that make it virtually impossible to retrieve functionally similar alternations across languages.

For example, if one searches for the "locative" type among the "All alternations" variable in the database, the online query interface returns 28 entries, i.e., all alternations of all 36 languages available that contain the word "locative" in their name such as "Locative Alternation" (Standard Italian, see (1)c and (3) above), "Locative applicative o-" (Ainu), and "Locative alternation (argument rearranging)" and "Locative alternation (oblique to object)" (Balinese); however, it does not return the Russian "Prefixal Goal-Instrumental alternation". As shown in examples (4) and (5) taken from Malchukov (2015) and made available on the ValPaL database, this Russian alternation is functionally similar to the Italian "Locative alternation" in example (3), although in Russian it is coded on the verb through prefixation, whereas in Italian it is not.

(4) *Он нагрузил сено на телегу.*
On nagruzil seno na telegu.
on na-gruzil seno na teleg-u
he PFV-loaded hay.ACC on cart-ACC
'He loaded the hay onto the cart.'

(5) *Он загрузил телегу сеном.*
On zagruzil telegu senom.
on za-gruzil teleg-u sen-om
he PFV-loaded cart-ACC hay-INS
'He loaded the cart with hay.'

Instead, Ainu "Locative applicative o-" and Balinese "Locative alternation (oblique to object)" point to a valency increasing alternation usually called "applicative" (see Peterson, 2007).

Therefore, the results of this simple query seem both inhomogeneous and incomplete, which is a byproduct of the alternations being language-specific and at the same time being included in the database by separate contributors. Impossible as collecting these data would otherwise be, we find the current architecture problematic in different respects: one may not simultaneously visualize how alternations are encoded cross-linguistically (e.g., comparing Italian and Russian data) nor how similar alternations are encoded in the same language (e.g., comparing all Balinese locative alternations).

3 PaVeDa: where it stands and the road ahead

To overcome the issues discussed above, a research team based at the University of Pavia developed the PaVeDa database – the output of the PaVeDa project which received funding in 2021 from the University of Pavia[5]. Besides the local team, several international partners have agreed to take part in this project, in an attempt to build a more insightful typological resource that also allows for diachronic research.

The PaVeDa resource complies to the up-to-date standards regarding cross-linguistic data formats, as proposed by Forkel et al. (2018) in the *Cross-Linguistic Data Formats initiative (CLDF)*[6].

[3]https://www.bivaltyp.info

[4]https://typecraft.org/tc2wiki/Multilingual_Verb_Valence_Lexicon

[5]https://hodel.unipv.it/paveda

[6]https://cldf.clld.org

Particular attention has been paid to preserving compatibility with other linguistic resources and to avoiding multiplying information by referencing existing data. More specifically, we plan to enhance the database with the four main features described below.

(i) Concerning data coverage, we plan to include languages from families that are currently not represented on ValPaL (Uralic and Turkic) or are underrepresented (Afro-Asiatic).

(ii) To allow diachronic research, we also plan to add ancient Indo-European and Afro-Asiatic languages. For part of such languages the relevant data-sets have already been extracted and will soon be uploaded into the database (Early Latin, Ancient Greek, Gothic, Old Irish, Old English, and Classical Armenian, see Giuliani, 2021, Inglese and Zanchi, 2022 forthc., Zanchi and Tarsi, 2021, Roma, 2021) and they will be made available to the research community.

(iii) The work we have conducted so far on ancient languages has prompted us to redesign our methodology, as no native speakers are available for these languages they may only be studied by means of data retrieved from corpora. In order to assess which coding frames are basic, we plan to give a greater weight to the frequencies of attested patterns and to implement this type of usage-based methodology for modern languages as well, linking the data on constructional patterns to existing corpora and to other machine-readable resources. This raises further challenges: while for some modern languages reference corpora are indeed available and represent both the written and the spoken varieties (see e.g., the Russian National Corpus[7]), some of the languages already in the database or that we plan to include are low-resourced in terms of reference corpora for either oral varieties or written varieties and in same cases for both. For example, in the case of Italian, we will use CORIS[8]– the reference corpus for written Italian consisting of a balanced, representative, and up-to-date reference sample of 165 million tokens. As far as the oral variety of Italian is concerned, in the absence of a reference corpus, we will supplement the PaVeDa database with data from two spoken corpora, KIParla[9] and RadioCast-it[10]. We will adopt similar strategies of documentation for all low-resourced languages included in the PaVeDa database.

(iv) Regarding the database structure, PaVeDa makes contrastive visualizations possible and at the same time ensures interoperability with the ValPaL resource, due to a new layer of annotation that contains non-language-specific alternations. This layer enables generalizations over language-specific patterns, as it is mapped onto the current ValPaL set of alternations. This solution still allows including a language-specific level of alternations, which is crucial to account for the coding aspects and distributional restrictions of alternations.

Our proposed set of "general" alternations is conceived with the following aims in mind: avoid multiplying terminology, be as functional and conceptual as possible, and maximize language coverage. For instance, the Italian "Locative alternation", the Balinese "Locative alternation (argument rearranging)", and the Russian "Prefixal Goal-Instrumental alternation" are mapped onto the "Locative alternation (argument rearranging)", whereas Ainu "Locative applicative o-" and Balinese "Locative alternation (oblique to object)" are mapped onto "Locative alternation (oblique to object)". "Locative alternation (oblique to object)" is preferable over "Applicative", as the latter usually implies explicit encoding on the verb. In contrast, the former also accounts for marginal transitive occurrences of *abitare* 'inhabit' in Italian, shown in example (7) as compared to the basic coding frame in example (6) in which the locative microrole is indicated by the preposition *in* – both examples are retrieved from Cennamo and Fabrizio (2013).

(6) 1 > V.subj[1] > LOC 2
Mario abita in campagna.
Mario abit-a in campagn-a
Mario live-PRS.SG in countryside-F.SG
'Mario lives in the countryside.'

(7) 1 > V.subj[1] > LOC 2
La famiglia abita una villa abbandonata.
la famigli-a abit-a un-a vill-a abbandonat-a
ART.DEF.F.SG family-F.SG live-PRS.SG ART.INDF-F.SG country_house-F.SG abandoned-F.SG
'The family lives in an abandoned country house'

The database will be made freely available to the scientific community on an open-source basis through a dedicated web platform. This will promote the collaboration and reproducible research in

[7]https://ruscorpora.ru/old/en/index.html
[8]https://corpora.ficlit.unibo.it/TCORIS/
[9]http://kiparla.it/
[10]https://site.unibo.it/radiocast/it

linguistics. Last but not least, besides contributing to the scholar research on verbal constructions, the contrastive studies promoted by the PaVeDa resource will also enable applications with an impact on first language acquisition and on teaching and learning typologically diverse languages.

References

Gontzal Aldai and Søren Wichmann. 2018. Statistical observations on hierarchies of transitivity. *Folia Linguistica*, 52(2):249–281.

Michela Cennamo and Claudia Fabrizio. 2013. Italian. In Iren Hartmann, Martin Haspelmath, and Bradley Taylor, editors, *Valency Patterns Leipzig*. Max Planck Institute for Evolutionary Anthropology, Leipzig.

Robert Forkel, Johann-Mattis List, Simon J. Greenhill, Christoph Rzymski, Michael Cysouw Sebastian Bank, Harald Hammarström, Martin Haspelmath, Gereon A. Kaiping, and Russell D. Gray. 2018. Cross-linguistic data formats, advancing data sharing and re-use in comparative linguistics. *Scientific Data*, 5:1–10.

Martina Giuliani. 2021. Valency patterns in latin. Master's thesis, University of Pavia, Italy.

Iren Hartmann, Martin Haspelmath, and Bradley Taylor. 2013. *The Valency Patterns Leipzig online database*. Max Planck Institute for Evolutionary Anthropology, Leipzig.

Guglielmo Inglese and Chiara Zanchi. 2022 forthc. Ancient greek valency patterns and alternations. In *The 3rd International Colloquium on Ancient Greek Linguistics*, Universidad Autónoma de Madrid, Spain, 16-18 June 2022.

Silvia Luraghi and Elisa Roma. 2021a. Valency and transitivity over time: An introduction. In Silvia Luraghi and Elisa Roma, editors, *Valency over Time: Diachronic Perspectives on Valency Patterns and Valency Orientation*, pages 1–12. De Gruyter Mouton, Berlin.

Silvia Luraghi and Elisa Roma, editors. 2021b. *Valency over Time: Diachronic Perspectives on Valency Patterns and Valency Orientation*. De Gruyter Mouton, Berlin.

Andrej Malchukov. 2015. Valency classes and alternations: parameters of variation. In Andrej Malchukov and Bernard Comrie, editors, *Valency Classes in the World's Languages. Volume 1: Introducing the Framework, and Case Studies from Africa and Eurasia*, pages 73–130. De Gruyter Mouton, Berlin.

Andrej Malchukov and Bernard Comrie, editors. 2015. *Valency Classes in the World's Languages. Volume 1: Introducing the Framework, and Case Studies from Africa and Eurasia*. De Gruyter Mouton, Berlin.

David A. Peterson. 2007. *Applicative constructions*. Oxford University Press, Oxford.

Elisa Roma. 2021. Valency patterns of old irish verbs: finite and non-finite syntax. In Silvia Luraghi and Elisa Roma, editors, *Valency over Time: Diachronic Perspectives on Valency Patterns and Valency Orientation*, pages 89–132. De Gruyter Mouton, Berlin.

Chiara Zanchi and Matteo Tarsi. 2021. Valency patterns and alternations in gothic. In Silvia Luraghi and Elisa Roma, editors, *Valency over Time: Diachronic Perspectives on Valency Patterns and Valency Orientation*, pages 31–88. De Gruyter Mouton, Berlin.

ParaNames: A Massively Multilingual Entity Name Corpus

Jonne Sälevä and **Constantine Lignos**
Michtom School of Computer Science
Brandeis University
{jonnesaleva,lignos}@brandeis.edu

Abstract

We present ParaNames, a Wikidata-derived multilingual parallel name resource consisting of over 118 million names for 13.7 million entities, spanning over 400 languages. ParaNames is useful for multilingual language processing, both for defining name translation tasks and as supplementary data for other tasks. We demonstrate an application of ParaNames by training a multilingual model for canonical name translation to and from English.

1 Introduction and Related Work

Our goal for ParaNames is to introduce a massively multilingual entity name resource that provides names for diverse entities in the largest possible set of languages and can be kept up to date through a mostly-automated preprocessing procedure. In this extended abstract, we summarize our approach to transforming the Wikidata knowledge graph into a set of parallel entity names identified with the high-level types of person, location, and organization.

We do not claim to be the first to harvest the parallel entity names available from Wikidata or Wikipedia. There is scattered prior work in this area, with one of the earliest explorations at scale being performed by Irvine et al. (2010). Recently, Benites et al. (2020) used Wikipedia as a data source and automatically extracted potential transliteration pairs, combining their outputs with several previously published corpora into an aggregate corpus of 1.6 million names.

2 Constructing the resource

To construct our dataset, we began by extracting all entity records from Wikidata and ingesting them into a MongoDB instance. Each entity in Wikidata is associated with several types of metadata, including names for it across languages. Given that we are working with such a large-scale dataset, there are important challenges that arise.

Script usage While language codes can identify a specific script for a language, many Wikidata labels do not conform to the scripts used by each language. In many cases, this is simply a data quality issue, such as with Greek where approximately 8.9% of ORG entities are written in Latin script.

However, in other cases, the presence of several scripts can also reflect real variation in the citation forms used in the language, as many languages (e.g. Kazakh) commonly use several scripts. While we explored automated methods of identifying names in incorrect scripts, we decided that manually constructing a list of allowed scripts for each language would yield the best results. We used Wikipedia as an authoritative source to look up which scripts are used to write each language, and filtered out all names whose most common Unicode script property is not among the allowed ones.

Providing entity types Downstream tasks and analysis of performance across different entity types often require that entities have a single high-level type. Wikidata has a complex type hierarchy, but we infer simpler entity types for as many entities as possible. We identified suitable high-level Wikidata types—Q5 (human) for PER, Q82794 (geographic region) for LOC, and Q43229 (organization) for ORG—and classified each Wikidata entity that is an instance of these types as the corresponding named entity type. In total, our resource includes 8,726,033 PER entities, 3,078,428 LOC entities and 2,196,035 ORG entities.

3 Experiments

To demonstrate an application of ParaNames, we train multilingual Transformer-based models that map entity name from English to one of Arabic, Armenian, Georgian, Greek, Hebrew, Japanese, Kazakh, Korean, Latvian, Lithuanian, Persian (Farsi), Russian, Swedish, Tajik, Thai, Vietnamese, and Urdu and vice versa. We chose these languages

Proceedings of the 4th Workshop on Computational Typology and Multilingual NLP (SIGTYP 2022), pages 103 - 105
July 14, 2022 ©2022 Association for Computational Linguistics

Language	Accuracy	CER	F1
Swedish	88.25 ± .02	0.08 ± .00	97.15 ± .01
Vietnamese	80.75 ± .02	0.17 ± .00	94.08 ± .01
Latvian	67.86 ± .02	0.14 ± .00	95.19 ± .01
Kazakh	55.38 ± .04	0.16 ± .00	93.93 ± .01
Tajik	49.62 ± .05	0.20 ± .00	92.77 ± .01
Lithuanian	47.39 ± .03	0.28 ± .00	89.53 ± .01
Thai	43.94 ± .05	0.29 ± .00	89.91 ± .01
Armenian	39.92 ± .05	0.28 ± .00	90.04 ± .01
Georgian	34.44 ± .02	0.29 ± .00	89.29 ± .01
Korean	33.27 ± .05	0.32 ± .00	88.46 ± .01
Russian	32.81 ± .06	0.38 ± .00	84.80 ± .02
Urdu	31.92 ± .03	0.23 ± .00	91.48 ± .01
Japanese	29.00 ± .04	0.33 ± .00	87.79 ± .01
Persian	28.68 ± .05	0.28 ± .00	89.84 ± .02
Arabic	25.74 ± .03	0.32 ± .00	89.23 ± .01
Greek	24.70 ± .03	0.35 ± .00	86.60 ± .01
Hebrew	15.24 ± .07	0.44 ± .00	84.58 ± .02
Overall	42.88 ± .02	0.27 ± .00	90.27 ± .01

Table 1: Canonical name translation performance for the X → En task, computed on the test set using our baseline configuration with language special tokens on the source side.

Language	Accuracy	CER	F1
Swedish	85.60 ± .04	0.10 ± .00	96.11 ± .02
Vietnamese	48.86 ± .01	0.35 ± .00	82.87 ± .01
Latvian	69.28 ± .07	0.13 ± .00	95.49 ± .01
Kazakh	58.69 ± .09	0.14 ± .00	94.85 ± .02
Tajik	54.38 ± .02	0.18 ± .00	93.82 ± .02
Lithuanian	50.76 ± .09	0.23 ± .00	91.61 ± .03
Thai	14.80 ± .04	0.42 ± .00	83.01 ± .02
Armenian	50.45 ± .05	0.22 ± .00	92.41 ± .01
Georgian	51.82 ± .04	0.22 ± .00	92.56 ± .01
Korean	38.63 ± .05	0.33 ± .00	88.18 ± .01
Russian	44.59 ± .04	0.33 ± .00	89.81 ± .02
Urdu	14.14 ± .08	0.45 ± .00	80.74 ± .03
Japanese	28.70 ± .01	0.42 ± .00	84.42 ± .02
Persian	22.90 ± .05	0.41 ± .00	81.64 ± .05
Arabic	41.70 ± .02	0.28 ± .00	89.40 ± .01
Greek	29.67 ± .06	0.36 ± .00	86.88 ± .01
Hebrew	35.71 ± .03	0.34 ± .00	88.16 ± .01
Overall	43.57 ± .02	0.29 ± .00	88.94 ± .01

Table 2: Canonical name translation performance for the En → X task, computed on the test set using our baseline configuration with language special tokens on the source side.

as they cover a wide geographic distribution, as well as several different orthographic systems, language families and typological features.

To create the parallel data, we extracted all entities that had names in English and at least one of the selected languages and split them into train, dev, and test sets using an 80/10/10 split. We also added "special tokens" to the beginning of each input to provide the model with additional information, e.g. entity type (<PER>), language of non-English label (<kk>) and/or its script (<Cyrillic>).

We use a single NVIDIA RTX 3090 GPU for training and decoding, and train our model for up to 90k updates using Adam.[1] We evaluate using three metrics: accuracy, mean F1-score (Chen et al., 2018), and character error rate (CER).

As our first experiment, we trained our models with only a language special token on the source side. The results in both translation directions can be seen in Tables 1 and 2. When translating to English, our model performs best on Swedish, Vietnamese and Latvian, which is unsurprising as all use the Latin script. However, Latvian names tend to be more inflected and generally match English less often, which explains its lower ranking. Kazakh and Tajik follow next, which also makes sense as Cyrillic can be transliterated to Latin script relatively unambiguously. Model performance is consistently worst on Hebrew—most likely caused by the lack of vowels in the Hebrew names, which the model must infer when translating to English.

When translating from English, the model performs best on languages similar to when translating to English. Swedish and Latvian have the highest accuracy, followed by Kazakh, Tajik, and Georgian. For Hebrew, the model performs much better; a potential explanation for this is the lack of vowel diacritics. Interestingly, the reverse is true for Thai, where the model performs less than half as accurately as when translating into English.

We also hypothesized that incorporating other information could be helpful, and repeated the experiment using a mixture of language, type token, and script special tokens. Overall, the results within each language tended to be quite similar regardless of tokens. The best settings were to use all three special tokens when translating from English, and language and type tokens when translating to English. While small, the differences from baseline were statistically significant for almost all settings.

4 Conclusion

ParaNames supports the modeling of parallel names for millions of entities in over 400 languages. It can enable multifaceted research in names, including name translation/transliteration and further research in named entity recognition and linking, especially in lower-resourced languages.

[1]Other hyperparameter values are nearly identical to the best configuration in Moran and Lignos (2020).

References

Fernando Benites, Gilbert François Duivesteijn, Pius von Däniken, and Mark Cieliebak. 2020. TRANSLIT: A large-scale name transliteration resource. In *Proceedings of the 12th Language Resources and Evaluation Conference*, pages 3265–3271, Marseille, France. European Language Resources Association.

Nancy Chen, Xiangyu Duan, Min Zhang, Rafael E. Banchs, and Haizhou Li. 2018. NEWS 2018 whitepaper. In *Proceedings of the Seventh Named Entities Workshop*, pages 47–54, Melbourne, Australia. Association for Computational Linguistics.

Ann Irvine, Chris Callison-Burch, and Alexandre Klementiev. 2010. Transliterating from all languages. In *Proceedings of the 9th Conference of the Association for Machine Translation in the Americas: Research Papers*, Denver, Colorado, USA. Association for Machine Translation in the Americas.

Molly Moran and Constantine Lignos. 2020. Effective architectures for low resource multilingual named entity transliteration. In *Proceedings of the 3rd Workshop on Technologies for MT of Low Resource Languages*, pages 79–86, Suzhou, China. Association for Computational Linguistics.

Author Index

Batsuren, Khuyagbaatar, 96
Bella, Gábor, 96
Brochhagen, Thomas, 96

Celano, Giuseppe, 80
Chen, Sihan, 94
Combei, Claudia Roberta, 99
Cotterell, Ryan, 52

De Varda, Andrea Gregor, 1

Forkel, Robert, 52
Futrell, Richard, 94

Georges, Munir, 22
Giunchiglia, Fausto, 96
Gröttrup, Sören, 22
Guo, Qingxia, 42
Gutkin, Alexander, 70

Hartung, Kai, 22
Hill, Nathan, 52

Imel, Nathaniel, 42

Jäger, Gerhard, 22, 63

Khishigsuren, Temuulen, 96
Kirov, Christo, 70

Lau, Jey Han, 27
Lignos, Constantine, 103
List, Johann-Mattis, 52
Luraghi, Silvia, 99

Mahowald, Kyle, 94
Marav, Daariimaa, 96

Nikolaev, Dmitry, 11

Otmakhova, Yulia, 27

Pado, Sebastian, 11

Sproat, Richard, 70
Steinert-Threlkeld, Shane, 42
Sälevä, Jonne, 103

Talamo, Luigi, 36
Tresoldi, Tiago, 86

Verspoor, Karin, 27
Vylomova, Ekaterina, 52

Zamparelli, Roberto, 1
Zanchi, Chiara, 99

Association for Computational Linguistics
209 N. Eighth Street
Stroudsburg, Pennsylvania 18360

ISBN 978-1-7138-5639-9

CURRAN ASSOCIATES INC.
proceedings.com